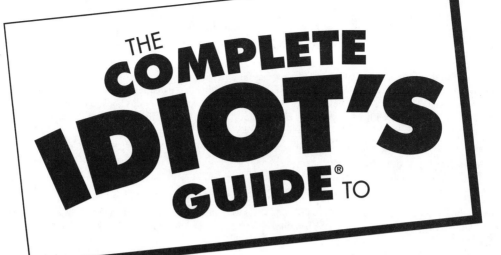

THE COMPLETE **IDIOT'S** GUIDE® TO

Music Theory

by Michael Miller

ALPHA

A member of Penguin Group (USA) Inc.

This book is dedicated to Beth Ogren, who has been a good friend for more years than I remember. She's been waiting a long time for me to write a book about a topic she's interested in—so here it is, Beth!

International Standard Book Number: 0-02-864377-1
Library of Congress Catalog Card Number: 2002106343

06   05   04   8   7   6

Interpretation of the printing code: The rightmost number of the first series of numbers is the year of the book's printing; the rightmost number of the second series of numbers is the number of the book's printing. For example, a printing code of 02-1 shows that the first printing occurred in 2002.

Printed in the United States of America

Note: This publication contains the opinions and ideas of its author. It is intended to provide helpful and informative material on the subject matter covered. It is sold with the understanding that the author and publisher are not engaged in rendering professional services in the book. If the reader requires personal assistance or advice, a competent professional should be consulted.

Publisher: *Marie Butler-Knight*
Product Manager: *Phil Kitchel*
Managing Editor: *Jennifer Chisholm*
Senior Acquisitions Editor: *Renee Wilmeth*
Development Editor: *Joan D. Paterson*
Production Editor: *Katherin Bidwell*
Copy Editor: *Rachel Lopez*
Illustrator: *Jody Schaeffer*
Cover/Book Designer: *Trina Wurst*
Indexer: *Julie Bess*
Layout/Proofreading: *John Etchison, Becky Harmon*

Contents at a Glance

Contents

Foreword

During the summer of 2001, I taught a class at the University of Indianapolis for our School for Adult Learning. The class was Introduction to Music Theory for Non-musicians. The students would be 24 years old or older and have no experience with music or performance other than their pleasure in listening. As time for the class to begin neared, I felt uneasy about how I would approach teaching and selecting a text. When the class began, I tried to cover the basics of pitch and rhythm. But I soon realized that what I really needed to do was start where the students were and with music with which they were familiar.

I also realized that everyone has music inside himself or herself. Music is in *time*. It is regular. It occurred to me that humans all walk *in time*. We all speak *in time*. Our bodies have a natural rhythm. We only need to find out how to take advantage of these abilities we all share.

We have all had the experience of playing something back on our internal tape recorder. Everyone has a memory of some piece of music. I can close my eyes and internally hear "Take Five," the song that Michael mentions in Chapter 6. I first listened to it as a youngster. I still have it locked in my head. Everyone can hear "Happy Birthday" internally. Mike will show how this trait will help you to understand the theory of music.

Music theory is part of the written language of music. It is the written word of this aural art, music. It is not something only intended for music students. We don't have to use it only to analyze a Bach fugue. It is a living part of all music. I wish Michael's book had been available for my class.

Music *is* a language. It has its own vocabulary. I teach several classes in jazz theory each year. One point I like to make to my students is that they need to have the ability to communicate with the rest of the free world. This means using the same nomenclature all musicians use. Michael has done an outstanding job of teaching you to speak music as musicians speak it. He also has used several styles of music to teach the language. This stuff is not just for academe.

I was excited to read Chapter 12, "Transcribing What You Hear." Musicians would agree that listening and practice are of equal importance. Step by step, Michael leads you through all the basics you need to realize the music inside you. It doesn't matter if you like classical, jazz, rock, or any other genre of music. This book will allow you to understand the principles by which music is organized.

This book is not just another music theory text. This is a book about the nuts and bolts of the music language. The presentation of material in "learnable" chunks allows you to understand everything about the language. He is right on with the "Least You Need To Know" section of each chapter. The exercises at the end of each chapter serve as meaningful and helpful ways to understanding by doing.

I am convinced this book will lead you to new abilities, understanding, and enjoyment of music.

Harry Miedema
Assistant Professor
Director, Jazz Studies
University of Indianapolis

Introduction

Or, Why You Need to Know a Little Theory

Back when I was in high school and college (a long time ago, I realize), a lot of my fellow students regarded music theory as only slightly more fun than listening to paint dry. I didn't share that opinion, and still don't; I think music theory is interesting and fun and an essential part of any serious music education.

Still, if all you live for is to play your instrument (or to sing) 24 hours a day, taking time out from practicing to move a bunch of notes around on paper might not be tremendously appealing. In fact, I believe introductory-level music theory classes are the second most-skipped classes in college music schools, with only music history classes being less well received. (Some enterprising soul is bound to combine the two classes into a "Theory of Music History"—or "History of Music Theory"—course, thus creating new levels of student apathy.)

I'm not sure why some budding musicians are so down on theory. Maybe it's because of the way it's presented. (Let's face it: Some instructors can be pretty dull with this type of material.) Maybe it's because of the way music theory resembles sentence diagramming and other dreary grammar-related stuff. I don't know; maybe to some people, it just seems like a lot of work.

But the fact remains: Every musician needs to know some music theory.

That's a bold statement, and one that you might take issue with. After all, you've gotten this far in your music studies without knowing theory—why do you need to start studying theory now?

Or perhaps you know of a famous musician who doesn't know the least little bit of music theory—and might not even know how to read music. If this person became rich and famous without knowing the theory behind the music, why should *you* have to learn that theory?

Music Theory Is Important

Famous musicians who don't know how to read a note of music are the exception rather than the rule. Most musicians, if they want to communicate with other musicians—to play in a band, or to teach them their songs—have to know at least the basics about how music works. These basics—notes, chords, and so on—are what we call music theory.

Notes and chords are the building blocks of the language of music. Music theory defines the many different ways you can arrange those blocks into songs and compositions. Without the theory, all you have is noise; applying music theory, you can create great works of art.

Musicians apply music theory every time they sit down to play or sing—whether they know it or not. When you read a piece of music, you're using music theory. When you write down a series of notes, you're using music theory. When you play a chord, you're using music theory. When you sing a harmony line, you're using music theory.

Even those musicians who don't have any formal training use music theory. When they put their hands on the piano, they might not know that they're playing a major ninth chord with the fourth in the bass; they *do* know that those notes fit together well, even if they can't tell you the strict chord construction.

Now, if they did have formal training, they could go beyond just playing the notes to sharing those notes with others. Instead of pointing at their fingers and saying "play this," they could actually write their notes and chords down on paper, in a format universally understood by musicians the world over. After all, it's a lot easier to tell someone to play a CM9/F chord than it is to say "put your first finger here, and your second finger here," and so on.

The knowledge of how different notes work together also helps you expand on the simple melodies you're currently playing. When you know theory, you know how to accompany a melody with chords and how to voice those chords so that they sound good to your ears. You also can learn how to turn that simple melody into a full-blown arrangement for groups of voices and instruments, and how to create your own melodies and compositions.

Without a knowledge of basic music theory, you won't be able to fully express your musical ideas; nor will you be able to share those ideas with others.

Music Theory Is Useful

Of course, it isn't just professional musicians who need to know theory. Even if you're just doing it for your own personal enjoyment, a knowledge of theory will help you better appreciate the music you play or sing.

Here's a good example: Let's say you're helping out at your daughter's school and someone, knowing that you're a musician, asks you to work up an arrangement of "Mary Had a Little Lamb" for the upcoming school pageant. There are two girls and one boy in the class who sing pretty well, and another boy who knows how to play trumpet. You'll accompany them on guitar.

This doesn't sound like a tall order, but it's one that requires a lot of theory to complete. First of all, you need to know how to read and write music—which includes the knowledge of clefs and keys and time signatures. Then you need to know about chords and chord progressions, and how to create harmonies and counterpoint. You also need to know how to arrange music for different voices and instruments, and even how to transpose music from one key to another. (That's because the trumpet reads music in a different key from everybody else.)

But here's the deal: If you don't know your theory, you won't be able to complete this rather simple assignment. It's as simple as that.

When you know the theory behind the music, playing and singing gets a lot more interesting. With a little grounding in theory, it's easier to understand why some melodies are more appealing than others, and why certain chord progressions work better with certain melodies. You'll see how harmony works, which will really help if you're singing background or accompanying someone on piano or guitar. You'll even be able to arrange music for your choir or band, or to create your own compositions.

And here's the neat part: Music theory isn't hard. Once you learn the basic notes and scales, the rest falls together fairly easily. After all, a chord is just three notes put together. That's all—just three notes. And a song is nothing more than a few chords strung together in a series, along with a melody—which is just a series of notes all in a row. Figuring out what goes where (and which notes sound good together) is what theory is all about.

Music Theory Is for Nonmusicians

Music theory isn't just for musicians, either. There are a lot of listeners out there who are curious about how music is created. Just what makes a particular song so special? Why does some music sound uplifting, and other music sound sad? And just what are your musician friends talking about when they say things like "cool changes" or "take this up a third"?

You don't have to be a music student to be interested in how music works—just as you don't have to have a literature degree to be interested in how words and sentences fit together. Basic music theory is for anyone who is interested in music; the more you know, the more you can appreciate the music that you listen to.

Music Theory and Me

There are many different ways to learn music theory. Your school might have music theory classes you can take. Your music teacher also might teach a little theory, or know a private teacher you can study with. Or you can learn theory the way I did: by yourself, from a book.

I taught myself music theory back when I was in eighth grade. My junior high school had the usual general music classes, as well as choir and band, but didn't have any theory classes. So, because I wanted to arrange some tunes for a band I was in, I had to teach myself the theory behind the arranging.

My theory education came from a lot of trial and error, and from two books: Dick Grove's *Arranging Concepts: A Guide to Writing Arrangements for Stage Band Ensembles* (1972) and David Baker's *Arranging & Composing for the Small Ensemble* (1970). Both of these books are still in print today, and still as valuable as they were back then. I recommend you check them out.

Now, if you look at the titles of those books, you'll see that they really don't have anything to do with basic music theory. There's theory in the books, of course, but you really have to read between the lines (so to speak) to pull it out. I would have given my right arm back then for a book that focused on beginning-level theory, written at a level that I could comprehend.

Well, 30 years later, I've written that book.

It's interesting. I was a fairly serious musician throughout my junior high and high school years, and went on to attend the prestigious Indiana University School of Music, in its even more prestigious jazz studies program. But something shifted along the way, and I ended up graduating IU with a business degree, and found myself some years later working in the book publishing industry. After serving my time in the corporate world, I became a full-time author, writing books about all manner of topics, from computers to business plans to home theater systems.

Then, about two years ago, I wrote a music book—*The Complete Idiot's Guide to Playing Drums* (available at a bookstore near you). Things had finally come full circle, and I was writing about the music that I loved, and lived, so many years ago.

Now, with the book you hold in your hands, I have the opportunity to introduce a new audience to the joys of music—in, I hope, a manner that is easy to follow, reasonably comprehensive, and somewhat practical. You'll let me know, of course, how well I succeed.

The Complete Idiot's Guide to Music Theory is designed to be a self-teaching tool for anyone wishing to learn music theory. The book starts with basic notes and rhythms; advances through scales, melodies, chords, and harmony; and ends with valuable information about accompanying, arranging, and conducting your music. In short, it presents pretty much everything you'll need to know about music theory—for musicians of any level.

Of course, I always recommend studying with a good teacher. Even if you're reading this book, you can learn even more by supplementing the material in these pages with the hands-on instruction you can get from a real human being. To me, that's really the best of both worlds; self-paced study accompanied by interaction with a good music theory instructor.

What You'll Find in This Book

However you decide to learn, I hope you find the information in this book useful. I've arranged the material in such a way that even if you know *nothing* about music or music theory, you can start on page one and progress through the book, moving from the basics to more advanced concepts. If you do know *some* theory, you can skip those chapters that you already know and go right to the new material you want to learn. And, once you've learned what you need to know, you can still use this book as a reference, to look up those scales or chords that you never can seem to remember.

The Complete Idiot's Guide to Music Theory is composed of 20 chapters, each of which presents a different aspect of music theory. The chapters are organized into six general parts, as follows:

Part 1, "Tones," gets you started with reading music. You'll learn about the notes on a piano, the intervals between different notes, and how those notes combine into different scales. You'll also learn about clefs and keys—both major and minor.

Part 2, "Rhythms," shows you how to arrange your notes sequentially in space. You'll learn how to count and how to notate your music, using whole notes, half notes, quarter notes, and more. You'll also learn about different time signatures, and about tempo, dynamics, accents, and other musical effects.

Part 3, "Tunes," helps you combine tones and rhythms to create your own melodies. You'll learn how melodies and chords are constructed; you'll also learn about chord progressions and different song forms.

Part 4, "Accompanying," shows you how to make more out of your basic melodies. You'll learn how to write down the songs you hear on the radio, how to accompany simple melodies on piano or guitar, and how to add harmony and counterpoint to your songs.

Part 5, "Embellishing," goes beyond basic theory to present advanced music notation and show you how to transpose music to other keys. You'll also learn how to spice up your music by substituting more sophisticated chords in your arrangements.

Part 6, "Arranging," presents real-world advice for taking your music public. You'll learn how to create lead sheets and scores, use music notation software to create sophisticated arrangements, arrange for groups of instruments and voices, and get your music performed. You'll even learn the right way to wave the baton when you conduct a choir or orchestra!

What You Need to Use This Book

Any practicing or aspiring musician can learn basic music theory from *The Complete Idiot's Guide to Music Theory*. You don't need any initial knowledge to get started; you can use this book even if you don't know how to read music or play an instrument.

However, it will help if you have access to some sort of keyboard instrument. That can be a piano or organ, or some sort of inexpensive synthesizer or consumer-grade music keyboard. It doesn't have to be a great keyboard or a big one; you'll use it mainly to perform some of the examples and exercises in the book. (You can use this book without having a keyboard, but then you'll have to envision some of the examples in your head.)

Most of the examples and exercises can be performed on any instrument—piano, guitar, trumpet, or whatever. If you don't play an instrument, you can sing most of the exercises. If you can't play or sing, I suggest you go the cheap keyboard route, so that you have some way of hearing the theory presented.

It will also help if you have some blank music paper at your disposal. If you don't have any handy, there are a few pages of blank staves in the back of this book; you can photocopy these pages to make your own instant music paper.

How to Get the Most out of This Book

To get the most out of this book, you should know how it is designed. I've tried to put things together in such a way to make learning music theory both rewarding and fun.

Each chapter presents a basic concept of music theory, and progresses through that concept using a combination of text and musical examples. In some chapters you'll find pages of reference material—scale listings, chord charts, and the like—that you can turn back to whenever necessary.

At the end of each chapter are exercises based on the theory presented in that chapter. Work through these exercises to test your newfound knowledge—and find out what areas you need to work on a little more!

(In case you're wondering, the answers to these exercises are in the back of the book, in Appendix C.)

Throughout the entire book you'll see a number of little boxes (what we in the publishing profession call *margin notes*) that present additional advice and information. These elements enhance your knowledge or point out important pitfalls to avoid. Here are the types of boxes you'll see scattered throughout the book:

 Definition

These boxes contain definitions of words or terms pertaining to a specific aspect of music theory.

 Note

These boxes contain additional information about the topic at hand.

Tip

These boxes contain advice about how best to use the theory presented in the main text.

Warning

These boxes contain warnings and cautions about what to avoid when you're reading and writing music.

Let Me Know What You Think

I always love to hear from my readers—especially when the readers are fellow musicians! If you want to contact me, feel free to e-mail me at theory@molehillgroup.com. I can't promise that I'll answer every e-mail, but I will promise that I'll read each one!

If you want to learn more about me and any new books I've written, check out my personal website at www.molehillgroup.com. Who knows—you might find some other books there that you'd like to read.

It's Time to Start—in Theory, at Least!

I hope I've convinced you of the many benefits of learning music theory. Now it's time to stop talking and start doing—so turn the page and get ready to learn!

Acknowledgments

I had assistance from dozens of individuals in the creation of this book and would like to thank the following for their help:

Thanks to the usual suspects at Alpha Books, including but not limited to Marie Butler-Knight, Renee Wilmeth, Kathy Bidwell, and Joan Paterson, for helping to turn my manuscript into a printed book.

Thanks to my junior high school music teacher and lifelong friend, Phyllis Fulford, for suggesting some important changes to the book's outline, and for encouraging my talents way back when.

Thanks, as well, to another old friend, Orson Mason, who helped me arrange contact with Harry Miedema, and who also deserves many thanks for turning me on to a lot of good jazz at the Jazz Kitchen—and great jambalaya at the Cajun joint next door!

Thanks also to Harry Miedema for agreeing to write the foreword for this book. Harry's a great educator and a very vocal proponent of the jazz community; his kind words mean a lot.

Special thanks go to Allen Winold, professor emeritus in the Department of Music Theory at Indiana University, for graciously taking time out of his busy schedule (and his vacation!) to review this book's manuscript. Allen jumped into this project with a very welcome enthusiasm, and his comments and suggestions helped to make this a better book than it otherwise would have been.

Trademarks

All terms mentioned in this book that are known to be trademarks or service marks are listed below. In addition, terms suspected of being trademarks or service marks have been appropriately capitalized. Alpha Books and Penguin Group (USA) Inc. cannot attest to the accuracy of this information.

Part 1

Tones

Discover the building blocks of all music: the pitches you play or sing. You'll learn about the notes of a scale, the different types of clefs and staves, the intervals between notes, major and minor scales, and all sorts of different keys and key signatures. (That's a lot for just four chapters!)

Pitches and Clefs

In This Chapter

♦ Understanding musical tones

♦ Assigning names to specific pitches

♦ Putting notes on a staff

♦ Using the treble, bass, and other clefs

As you can tell from the title, this is a book about music theory. But what exactly *is* music theory? And, even more basic than that, what is *music*?

There are lots of different definitions of the word "music," some more poetic than practical. For example, William Shakespeare called music the "food of love," George Bernard Shaw called music the "brandy of the damned," and Gottfried Wilhelm Leibnitz called music "sounding mathematics."

Interesting definitions all, but not really what we're looking for here.

Let's try another definition:

> Music is the art, the craft, and the science of organizing sound and silence in the framework of time.

Now that's a little more helpful, but it's still fairly broad. This definition could describe a tremendous range of activities—a mother singing a lullaby to her child, an orchestra playing a Mozart symphony, a rock group performing their latest hit, a group of Native Americans playing ceremonial drum beats, Louis Armstrong playing trumpet in a jazz quartet, a group of sailors chanting "yo heave ho," or a nightingale warbling a serenade. You probably didn't buy this book to learn about *all* these things, although all of them have been called "music," at one time or another.

So we'll use a slightly different definition of music in this book. This definition is a lot more specific:

> Music is a succession of tones arranged in a specific rhythm.

Better? This definition doesn't cover *everything* that's ever been called "music," but it probably covers those types of music that you're familiar with—primarily, twentieth-century popular music, from ragtime to reggae to rock, and everything in between.

Now to the word "theory." In scientific circles, this word is used as the formulation of a hypothesis, such as Einstein's theory of relativity. While academic music theorists sometimes do formulate hypotheses in this scientific fashion, that's not what this book is about.

In our context, we'll use the word "theory" to mean a study of the rudiments of music—the basic things that performers and listeners need to know to produce and enjoy this marvelous art. This goes back to the root meaning of the word, which means "a way of looking." If we broaden this definition to include not just looking, but also listening and performing, then we're set.

Now that we've defined our terms, it's time to get started—and learn the theory behind the music. To do this, we have to go back to our definition of music, which says that music is a succession of tones, arranged in a specific rhythm. To study music, then, we have to learn about notes, and about arranging them.

We'll get to the "arranging in a specific rhythm" bit starting with Chapter 5. That lets us focus our attention, for the time being, on tones.

Understanding Musical Tones

So what's a tone? The definition is simple; a tone is a sound that is played or sung at a specific *pitch*.

When you hum (go ahead …), you're humming a tone. When you whistle, you're whistling a tone. When you go "aaaahhhh," you're sounding a tone. If you put two or more hums, whistles, or "aaaahhhhs" together, you have music.

You can hum lots of different tones, high or low. The higher tones are referred to as *higher pitched;* lower tones are called *lower pitched.*

Here's an exercise: Hum a tone. Now hum a tone higher than the first tone.

Definition

Pitch describes the specific frequency or tuning of a tone. (Frequency is a measurement of how fast air molecules are vibrating.)

Note

Some instruments produce tones that aren't at specific pitches. These instruments—such as drums and cymbals—are called unpitched or nonpitched instruments. The tones they produce can be high or low, but typically don't correspond to specific note pitches.

What you've just hummed are two separate tones, at two separate pitches. The second tone was higher pitched than the first tone.

Different voices, and different instruments, produce different ranges of tones. For example, women tend to have higher voices than men; the tones most women sing are higher-pitched than the tones most men sing. (There are exceptions to this rule, of course; listen to some of the doo-wop singers of the 1950s and you'll hear some fairly high male voices!)

In the world of musical instruments, bigger instruments tend to produce lower-pitched tones, whereas smaller instruments tend to produce higher-pitched tones. This is why a flute produces higher notes than a tuba, and why the thin strings on a guitar are higher-pitched than the thick strings.

Some instruments produce a broader range of tones than other instruments. In particular, the piano has a very broad range. From the lowest tone (the key on the far left of the keyboard) to the highest (the key on the far right), the piano reproduces more tones than just about any other instrument—and certainly a lot more than the human voice!

Time for another exercise: Hum the lowest tone you can hum; then gradually raise the pitch until you're humming the highest tone you can hum. You just hummed a whole lot of different tones. How, then, do you describe a specific tone so that someone else can hum the same tone?

> **Note**
>
> You'll find lots of musical terms in this book, but you need to know that musicians tend to use a lot of these terms interchangeably. A conductor who says "That *note* was wrong," might mean that the *pitch* was wrong, or that the *note value* (rhythm) was wrong. That's because the word "note" can be used in place of either more specific definition.
>
> Don't get hung up on the differences between "tones" and "pitches" and "notes." While there are specific definitions for each word, it's acceptable to be a little loose on the usage. I might even substitute one word for another in this book. You'll understand what I mean from the context.

Tones Have Value

When it comes to describing a tone, it helps to know that every tone you can sing or play has a specific value. You can measure that value scientifically, and use that value to describe the tone—or, more precisely, it's pitch. If that's too complicated, you also can assign an arbitrary name to each tone. (Go ahead: Hum a note called "Bob.")

What's the Frequency, Kenneth?

If you plug a microphone into an oscilloscope, and then hum a tone into the microphone, the oscilloscope will measure the *frequency* of the tone. This is actually a measurement of how fast the molecules of air are vibrating; the faster the vibrations, the higher the pitch.

These vibrations are measured in *cycles per second*, and there are a lot of them. (Cycles per second are often called *hertz*; abbreviated Hz.) If you hum the pitch we call middle C (the white key in the exact center of a piano keyboard, or the third fret on the A string of a guitar), the oscilloscope will measure 256Hz—that is, the air is cycling back and forth 256 times per second.

So one way to identify specific pitches is by their frequency. Unfortunately, writing out even a simple melody in terms of frequency gets a tad unwieldy.

For example, here's the first half of "Mary Had a Little Lamb" ("Mary had a little lamb, little lamb, little lamb") notated by frequency:

```
659Hz, 587Hz, 523Hz, 587Hz, 659Hz, 659Hz, 659Hz,
587Hz, 587Hz, 587Hz,
659Hz, 783Hz, 783Hz
```

The specific frequencies of "Mary Had a Little Lamb."

Not easy to read, is it?

Which is why we don't use the frequency method to write music.

> **Note**
>
> Actually, the "standard" pitch today is the A above middle C, which equals 440Hz; all the other notes are pitched in relation to this note. In earlier times and cultures, this note had other values—as low as 376Hz in early eighteenth-century France, and as high as 560Hz in early seventeenth-century Germany (referred to as *North German church pitch*).

Note

One good way to determine a specific pitch is with a *tuning fork,* which is a fork-shaped piece of metal that resonates at a specific frequency when struck. Most tuning forks resonate at 440Hz, which is the pitch A. Some people have what is called *perfect pitch,* in that they can hear absolute pitches in their heads. However, most people need the guidance of a tuning fork, pitch pipe, piano, or other musical instrument to fix a specific pitch.

Play by Numbers

An easier way to designate tones is to number each individual pitch. But before we start numbering, it helps to know a little bit about how different pitches relate to each other.

Because you can slide a hum from lower to higher, you might think that there are an infinite number of pitches available. (You can certainly see this when you look at frequencies; you have one tone at 256Hz, another at 257Hz, another at 258Hz, and so on.)

Although that might be true in theory, in practice some pitches are too close together to clearly distinguish them. For example, if you hum a 256Hz tone and a 257Hz tone, they sound almost identical in pitch because there isn't a big enough *interval* between the tones.

We need to place a reasonable interval between tones, and then assign values to those main pitches that result: You end up with a series of pitches called a *scale.* (You'll learn more about scales in Chapter 2.) Each scale starts on a specific tone, and ends on a higher-pitched version of that same tone.

In the Western world, we divide our scales into seven main notes—eight if you count the first note, which is repeated at the end of the scale. Because there are seven notes, it's easy to number them—one through seven. Using this numbering system, here's what the first half of "Mary Had a Little Lamb" looks like:

```
3 2 1 2 3 3 3
2 2 2
3 5 5
```

"Mary Had a Little Lamb" by the numbers.

If you're reading ahead and want to see how the numbering system applies to traditional music notation, here's what the C Major scale looks like, by the numbers:

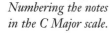
Numbering the notes in the C Major scale.

Now, not to be confusing here, but there are actually notes *between* some of these main notes—enough of them that we really have *twelve* pitches before they start repeating. These in-between pitches are equally spaced in what we call *half steps,* where the major pitches (A, B, C, etc.) have either one or two half steps between them, depending on the note. (I know, it's getting confusing already …)

For the time being, we're going to focus on the seven main notes of a scale, since that's easiest to understand. We'll leave the half steps for Chapter 2. Feel free to read ahead if you're interested.

Do Re Mi

Another way to remember each tone is by assigning a simple syllable to each tone. Remember the song from *The Sound of Music* that goes "Do, a deer, a female deer"? That's what we're talking about here.

In this particular method, called *Solfège* (or Solfeggio), each of the seven notes of a scale has its own name. The following table shows the words to use.

Tip _____

Solfège (pronounced sol-fezh) is a method of naming musical tones using a set of syllables—do, re, mi, and so on. These syllables come from the initial syllables of the first six words to the Hymn to St. John; the seventh syllable (Ti) is derived from the name St. John, in Latin.

The Solfège Method

Tone	Solfège name	Pronunciation
1	Do	Doh
2	Re	Ray
3	Mi	Mee
4	Fa	Fah
5	So (Sol)	So
6	La	Lah
7	Ti	Tee
8	Do	Doh

Here's what the first half of "Mary Had a Little Lamb" looks like using the Solfège method:

```
Mi Re Do Re Mi Mi Mi
Re Re Re
Mi So So
```

"Mary Had a Little Lamb" in Solfège.

If you're reading ahead and want to know how the Solfège names apply to traditional music notation, here's what the C Major scale looks like:

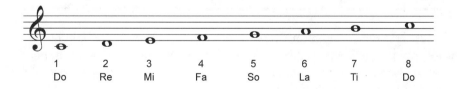

The Do Re Mis of the C Major scale.

Tones Have Names

It's important to know that both the numbering and the Solfège methods are *relative* ways of naming musical tones. That is, the first note in a scale is always number one, and is always called Do. The second tone is always number two, and is always called Re. It doesn't matter what actual tone you start with, these names always apply.

The problem with using relative naming is that it doesn't tell you what precise pitch to start with. You might start your Do Re Mi on a low pitch, and your neighbor might start hers on a higher pitch, and your duet will end up sounding like two water buffaloes in heat.

And that's not good. (Unless you're a water buffalo, of course.)

No, what we need is a way to designate specific pitches—without resorting to the cumbersome frequency method.

Learning the ABCs

The accepted way of naming musical specific pitches uses the first seven letters of the alphabet—A, B, C, D, E, F, and G. While the numbering method is relative (the number 1 can be assigned to any pitch), the letter method is absolute. This means that A always refers to a specific frequency. When you tell someone to sing or play an A, they'll always sing or play the same pitch.

The only problem with this method is that you can sing or play more than one A.

Try this exercise: Sing A B C D E F G A (think "Do Re Mi Fa So La Ti Do"). The first A and the second A should be the same tone, with the second A an *octave* higher than the first A. (You'll learn about octaves a little later in this chapter—suffice to say it's a way of presenting a lower or higher version of the same note.)

You can play an A with a low pitch, and an A with a higher pitch—and other As both below and above those. Now, all the As will have the same tone; they're just higher or lower versions of the basic pitch.

How, then, do you tell which A to play or sing?

Notes on a Piano Keyboard

A good way to visualize the seven basic notes (A through G) is to look at a piano keyboard. Each white key on the keyboard corresponds to one of these seven main notes, as shown in the following figure. (And ignore the black keys, for the time being.)

The white keys on a piano keyboard.

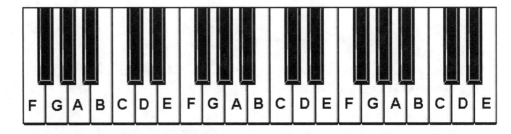

As you can see, the black and white keys on a piano form a certain pattern. If you start in the right place, you'll see that the black keys are arranged in groups of threes and twos. The first white key to the left of a group of *three* black notes is always assigned to the tone of F. The first white key to the left of a group of *two* black notes is always assigned to C. Once you know where F and C are, you can figure out the location of the other tones.

To figure out which A (or F or C) to play, know that the C located in the very middle of the piano keyboard—directly underneath the manufacturer's logo or pull-down door handle—is called *middle C*. (It's the C in the middle of the keyboard—easy to remember.) All other notes can be described relative to middle C—as in "the F above middle C" or "the D below middle C."

Notes on a Staff

Now that you know the seven basic notes and where they lay on a piano keyboard, how do you go about communicating those notes to others? You could just spell out a song; if you used this method, the first half of "Mary Had a Little Lamb" would look like this:

```
E D C D E E E
D D D
E G G
```

The notes of "Mary Had a Little Lamb."

Now, that's more specific than using numbers or Solfège, but it's still somewhat difficult to read. A better way to notate pitches is to do so *visually*, using a graphic that in some ways resembles a basic piano keyboard. This graphic is called a *staff*.

The basic music staff is composed of lines and spaces, like this:

A blank staff.

Tip

Some musicians identify the specific pitch by placing a number after the note name. Using this method (which is sometimes called *scientific pitch notation*), the lowest C on a grand piano is notated C1. The next C up from that is C2; then C3, C4, and so on—and the same for all the other notes. (In this notation, middle C is C4.)

As you can see, the staff has precisely five lines and four spaces. Each line or space represents a specific pitch. The pitches are determined by the *clef* at the beginning of the staff; the staff we're looking at here uses what is called the treble clef. (There are several different types of clefs, which we'll discuss later in this chapter.)

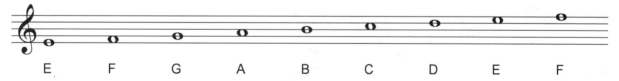

| E | F | G | A | B | C | D | E | F |

The notes of a staff (treble clef).

This treble clef staff pictures the notes in the exact middle of a piano keyboard—just above middle C. (The bottom line of the staff represents the E above middle C.) The following figure shows how the notes of the staff relate to specific piano keys.

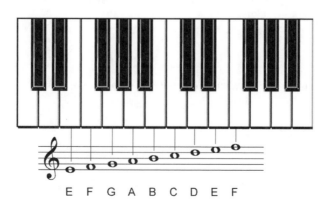

The notes on a staff and where they appear on a piano keyboard.

Back to "Mary Had a Little Lamb"; here's what the first part of that song looks like on a music staff:

The notes of "Mary
Had a Little Lamb"
on a music staff.

Above—and Below—the Staff

The basic staff describes nine basic notes. What about all those notes either above or below these nine notes? (Like that last note in "Mary Had a Little Lamb"?)

Notes higher than the F at the top of the staff are written in the lines and spaces *above* the staff. For example, the first space above the staff is the first note after F: G. The first line above the staff is the first note after G: A. You can keep adding spaces and lines above the staff to describe higher and higher notes, as shown in the following figure.

Notes above the staff.

               G   A   B   C

Definition

The lines you add above or below a staff are called **ledger lines**.

Just as you can add lines and spaces above the staff, you can also add lines and spaces below the staff to describe lower notes. For example, the first space below the staff is the first note before E: D. The first line below the staff is the first note before D: C. The following figure shows the first few notes below the standard staff. By the way, the first line below the staff is middle C.

Notes below the staff.

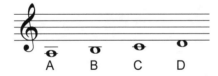

             A   B   C   D

Different Clefs

Up till now, we've been looking at a staff that represents the notes just above middle C on the piano keyboard. The notes of this staff are determined by the type of *clef* that appears at the beginning of the staff—and there are several different types of clefs.

The Treble Clef

The clef we've been working with so far is called the *treble clef;* it looks like this:

The treble clef.

As you've already learned, in real-world terms the treble clef is positioned just above middle C. The bottom line of the treble clef staff is an E; the top line is an F.

The treble clef, like all clefs, fixes the position of a single pitch—from which you can figure out where all the rest of the notes go. In the case of the treble clef, the pitch it fixes is G, which is the second line on the staff. (If you look closely at the treble clef itself, you see that the big round part of the clef circles around the second line of the staff.) For this reason, the treble clef is sometimes called the G clef—and the clef itself looks a little like a capital G.

If you ever have trouble remembering which note goes with which line or space on a staff, here's an easy way to remember them. The lines of the treble clef staff are assigned, bottom to top, to the notes E, G, B, D, and F. You can remember the lines by recalling the first letters in the phrase "Every Good Boy Does Fine." The spaces of the treble clef staff are assigned, bottom to top, to the notes F, A, C, and E. You can remember the spaces by remembering the word "FACE."

Most higher-pitched instruments and voices use the treble clef. This includes trumpets, flutes, clarinets, and guitars, as well as singers singing the soprano, alto, and tenor parts.

The Bass Clef

When you need to write music below the treble clef, you can use a different clef, called the _bass_ clef. The bass clef is positioned just _below_ middle C, and is sometimes called the F clef. (That's because the two dots on the clef surround the fourth line, which is F.)

Here's what the bass clef looks like, with the notes of a bass clef staff:

G   A   B   C   D   E   F   G   A

The bass clef.

Most lower-pitched instruments and voices use the bass clef. This includes trombones, tubas, bass guitars, and singers singing the bass part.

An easy way to remember the lines of the bass clef is with the phrase "Good Boys Do Fine Always." (The first letter of each word describes each line of the staff, from bottom to top.) To remember the spaces of the bass clef, remember the first letters in the phrase "All Cows Eat Grass."

The Grand Staff

If you play or write for piano, there's another staff you need to know. This staff, called the _grand staff_, links together a treble clef staff and a bass clef staff. (That's because you play the piano with two hands; each staff roughly corresponds to each hand.)

The grand staff looks like this:

The grand staff.

When you use a grand staff, it's important to note that the two staffs neatly flow into each other. The A at the top of the bass clef extends above that staff to a B and a C. The C is then linked to the treble clef, goes on up to a D, and then the E on the bottom line of the treble clef.

The neat thing is that the C—which just happens to be middle C—is halfway between each staff. So when you write a middle C on a grand staff, it might extend down from the treble clef staff or extend up from the bass clef staff, depending on where the surrounding notes are placed.

Specialty Clefs

There are a handful of specialty clefs you must learn, although you probably won't use them much. These clefs are designed for instruments whose range doesn't fit comfortably within the traditional treble or bass clefs.

One of the most common specialty clefs is the *alto clef*, shown here:

The alto clef.

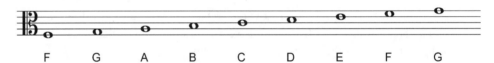

F   G   A   B   C   D   E   F   G

The alto clef is used primarily by the viola, which is a slightly bigger version of a violin. The pointer on this clef points at middle C.

The tenor clef looks a lot like the alto clef, except the pointer points at a different line. (It still points to middle C, but middle C is positioned at a different point on the staff.) The tenor clef looks like this, and is sometimes used by bassoons, bass violins, and tenor trombones.

The tenor clef.

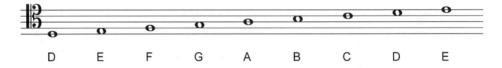

D   E   F   G   A   B   C   D   E

Although there are several other specialty clefs (including the baritone, subbass, and French violin clefs), you probably won't run into them too often; they're not widely used. However, you might run into what is called an *octave clef*, which looks like a normal treble or bass clef with the number 8 either above or below the clef. When you see this type of clef, you're supposed to transpose the normal treble clef notes either up (if the 8 is above the clef) or down (if the 8 is below the clef) an octave.

Octave clefs.

The Percussion Clef

There's one more clef you should know, and it's really the easiest of them all. This clef is used when you're writing for drums and other percussion instruments—those that don't play a fixed pitch. It's called either the *percussion clef* or the *indefinite pitch clef*, and it looks like this:

The percussion clef.

The neat thing about this clef is that the lines and spaces don't correspond to any specific pitches. Instead, you assign different instruments to different parts of the staff.

For example, if you're writing for drum set, you might assign the bass drum to the bottom space, the snare drum to the third space, and two tom-toms to the second and fourth spaces; you can put the ride cymbal on the top line of the staff.

Tip

There really aren't any rules for how to assign instruments to a percussion clef, so you're pretty much on your own. It's probably a good idea to consult a few drummers or look at a few percussion parts to get a better idea of how to use the percussion clef.

The Least You Need to Know

◆ Music is a succession of tones arranged in a specific pattern; a tone is a sound that is played or sung at a specific pitch.

◆ There are many different ways to describe a specific pitch. You can describe a pitch by its vibration frequency, by where it lies numerically compared to other pitches, or by using the Do Re Mi (Solfège) method.

◆ Established music notation assigns letters to the seven basic pitches, A through G. The letters repeat as you generate higher pitches.

◆ Pitches are assigned to specific keys on a piano keyboard, and to specific lines and spaces on a musical staff.

◆ The clef placed at the start of a staff determines which notes appear where on the staff. The most-used clef is the treble clef; the bass clef is used for lower-pitched instruments and voices.

Exercises

Exercise 1-1

Write the name of each note below the note.

F

Exercise 1-2

Write the name of each note below the note.

C

Exercise 1-3

Write each note on the staff.

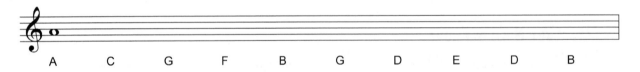

A   C   G   F   B   G   D   E   D   B

Exercise 1-4

Write each note on the staff.

E   F   D   G   C   A   B   G   A   C

Exercise 1-5

Draw the indicated clefs on the staff.

Bass   Treble   Alto   Tenor   Treble (octave above)

Exercise 1-6

Write the following notes above the staff.

G   B   A   D   C   B   D   C   E   F

Exercise 1-7

Write the following notes below the staff.

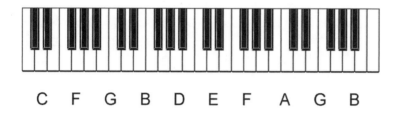

C D B A G F E C D B

Exercise 1-8

Identify the following notes on the piano keyboard.

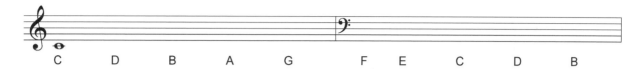

C F G B D E F A G B

Chapter 2

Intervals

In This Chapter

◆ Changing pitches with sharps and flats

◆ Understanding half steps and whole steps

◆ Counting the intervals between notes

◆ Using major, minor, perfect, diminished, and augmented intervals

In the last chapter you learned all about musical pitches: how they're named and how they're presented on a staff. In this chapter we'll go beyond that by looking at how pitches can be raised and lowered, and how you can describe the differences between pitches in terms of *intervals*.

To make things as simple as possible, we'll discuss these pitches and intervals in terms of the C Major scale—that is, the notes between one C on the piano keyboard and the next C above that. The basic concepts can be applied to *any* scale, as you'll see; it's just that sticking to a single scale makes it all a little easier to grasp. (And, at least on the piano, the C Major scale is the easiest scale to work with—it's all white keys!)

Be Sharp—or Be Flat

As you learned in Chapter 1, the lines and spaces on a music staff correspond exactly to the white keys on a piano. But what about those black keys? Where are they on the staff?

When we say there are 7 main pitches in a Western musical scale (A through G), that's a bit of an oversimplification: There actually are 12 possible notes in an octave, with some of them falling between the 7 main pitches.

Just count the keys between middle C and next C on the piano—including the black keys, but without counting the second C. If you counted correctly, you counted 12 keys, which represent 12 pitches; each pitch/key is the same interval away from the previous pitch/key.

Definition

An **interval** is the space between two pitches. The smallest interval in Western music is a half step; intervals are typically measured in the number of half steps between the two notes.

Definition

Two notes that sound the same but can be spelled differently are called **enharmonic** notes.

These black keys are called *sharps* and *flats*. Sharps and flats are halfway between the pitches represented by the white keys on a piano; a sharp is above a specific key and a flat is below a specific key.

Put another way, a sharp raises the natural note; a flat lowers the note.

Take the black key above the middle C key, for example. You can refer to this key as *C-sharp*, because it raises the pitch of C. It also can be called *D-flat*, because it lowers the next white key up, D. (Whenever you have two notes that describe the same pitch—C-sharp being the same as D-flat—the notes are *enharmonic*.)

Here are the dual names you can use for a piano's black keys:

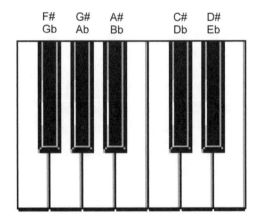

The black keys on a piano keyboard.

On a music staff, sharps and flats are designated by special characters placed *before* the affected note. These characters, called *accidentals*, look like this:

A sharp, a flat, and a natural sign.

♯ ♭ ♮

That third character is called a *natural*. When you see a natural sign on a piece of music, it means to return the specific note to its natural state, without any sharps or flats.

It's important to know that you can add sharps and flats to any note—even those keys on a piano that don't have black notes between them. So, for example, if you add a flat to the C note, you lower it to the next note on the keyboard—which happens to be B natural. (This means B natural is the same pitch as C-flat.)

Definition

Any modification to a natural note is called an **accidental**. Sharps and flats are accidentals; the natural sign (used to return a sharped or flatted note to its natural state) is also an accidental.

Steppin' Out ...

The smallest interval in Western music is the *half step*. On the piano keyboard, half steps appear between the white keys B and C and between E and F. In all other cases they appear between a white key and a black key—for example, D to D-sharp, or F-sharp to G.

Two half steps equal one *whole step*. The interval between F and G is a whole step; the interval between B and C-sharp is also a whole step.

Now that you know about steps, it's a little easier to understand how sharps and flats work. When you sharpen a note, you move the pitch up a half step. When you flatten a note, you move the pitch down a half step.

Take the note C, for example: When you add a flat to C, you take it down a half step. Because the first key (white or black) to the left of C is the white key B, this means C-flat equals B. When you add a sharp to C, you take it up a half step. The first key to the right of C is the black key we call C-sharp. (This black key is also the first key to the left of D, which means C-sharp is the same as D-flat.)

You can use the step method to describe the intervals between two notes—although once you get more than a few steps away, the counting becomes a tad difficult. When you're trying to figure out which note is seven half steps above middle C (it's G, in case you're counting), it's time to utilize another method to describe your intervals.

Tip

While the half step is the smallest interval in Western music, music from other parts of the world often contains intervals smaller than a half step. Some Indian music, for example, divides an octave into 22 steps, each about half as large as a Western half step.

Definition

In some musical circles, a **half step** is called a *semitone*, and a **whole step** is called a *tone*.

Note

On a guitar, a half step is the distance of a single fret. A whole step is the distance of two frets.

A Matter of Degrees

A more accepted way of describing intervals is to go back to the seven main notes of a scale—and revisit the relative numbering method. You can use the numbers of the scale to denote the basic intervals between notes, and thus apply this numbering to any scale.

First Things First

As you learned in the previous chapter, you can use numbers to describe the seven main notes in any scale. The first note is numbered one, the second note is numbered two, and so on. This method of numbering actually describes the seven *degrees* of a musical scale.

There also are fancy musical names you can use in place of the numbers, which you might run into in some more formal situations. The following table presents these formal degree names.

Degrees of the Scale

Degree	Name
First (Root)	Tonic
Second	Supertonic
Third	Mediant
Fourth	Subdominant
Fifth	Dominant
Sixth	Submediant
Seventh	Leading Note
Eighth (Octave)	Tonic

There are a few more terms you need to know before we proceed. When two notes of the exact same pitch are played by two different instruments or voices, they're played in *unison*. Two identical notes with the same name, played eight degrees apart, form an *octave*. (The word octave comes from the Latin word *octo*, for eight—because an octave is eight notes above the beginning note.)

Note

All this dominant and subdominant stuff will become more important when you learn about chord progressions in Chapter 10.

Definition

The lowest note of an interval, chord, or scale, is called the **root**.

For example, if you go from middle C to the next C up the keyboard, that's an octave; F to F is another octave … and so on.

These musical degrees come in handy when you're describing intervals between notes. Instead of counting half steps and whole steps, you can simply describe an interval by using these relative numbers.

For example, let's say you want to describe the interval between C and D. If you count C as number one (the first degree), D is number two and the interval between them is called a *second*. The interval between C and E (the first and third degrees) is a *third*; the interval between C and F (the first and fourth degrees) is a *fourth* … and so on.

Pretty easy, once you get used to it!

The following figure shows the basic intervals, starting with a unison and ending with an octave, with C as the *root*.

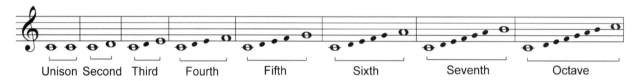

The basic intervals, starting on C.

Note

Interestingly, when you examine the frequencies of two notes, as discussed in the previous chapter, you find that the second note in an octave is an exact multiple of the first note. For example, the A above middle C has a frequency of 440Hz; the A an octave above that has a frequency twice that, 880Hz. For this reason two notes with the same name have the same sound, even if they're pitched an octave or more higher or lower.

Major and Minor Intervals

When you describe intervals by degree, you still have to deal with those pitches that fall above or below the basic notes—the sharps and flats, or the black keys on a keyboard.

When measuring by degrees, the second, third, sixth, and seventh notes can be flattened. When you flatten one of these notes, you create what is called a *minor* interval. The natural state of these intervals (in a major scale) is called a *major* interval.

Here's what these four intervals look like, with C as the root, in both major and minor forms.

Major and minor intervals, starting on C.

Perfect Intervals

Certain intervals can't be flattened or sharpened; they exist in one form only, called a *perfect* interval. Specifically, fourths, fifths, and octaves all are perfect intervals. You can't flatten these intervals to make them minor; there's no such thing as a minor fifth or a minor octave.

Here are the three perfect intervals, with C as the root.

Perfect   4th   Perfect   5th   Octave

Three perfect intervals, starting on C.

Augmented and Diminished Intervals

Okay, now you know that perfect intervals can't be major or minor. That doesn't mean that they can't be altered, however. You *can* raise and lower fourths and fifths—however, the result is not called major or minor. When you raise a perfect interval, you create an *augmented* interval. When you lower a perfect interval, you create a *diminished* interval.

For example, if you use C as the root, F is a perfect fourth away from the root. If you sharpen the F, the resulting note (F-sharp) is an augmented fourth above the root.

Along the same lines, G is a perfect fifth above C. When you flatten the G, the resulting note (G-flat) is a diminished fifth above the root.

Here are the key augmented and diminished intervals, with C as the root.

Diminished   4th   Augmented   4th   Diminished   5th   Augmented   5th

Augmented and diminished intervals, starting on C.

There's another type of augmented interval, one that results from raising a major interval by another half step. For example, F to A is a major third; if you sharpen the A (to A-sharp), the resulting interval is an augmented third.

Beyond the Octave

You don't have to stop counting intervals when you get to the octave. Above the octave are even more intervals—ninths, tenths, elevenths, and so on.

Tip

You can also create a diminished interval by lowering a minor interval by another half step. For example, F to D-flat is a minor sixth; if you flatten the D-flat (yes, there's such a thing as a double flat), the resulting interval is called a diminished sixth.

Intervals that span more than an octave are called *compound intervals* because they combine an octave with a smaller interval to create the larger interval. For example, a ninth is nothing more than an octave and a second; an eleventh is an octave and a fourth … and so on.

The following table describes the first six intervals above the octave.

Compound Intervals

Interval	Combines
Ninth	Octave plus second
Tenth	Octave plus third
Eleventh	Octave plus fourth
Twelfth	Octave plus fifth
Thirteenth	Octave plus sixth
Fourteenth	Octave plus seventh

Compound intervals can have all the qualities of smaller intervals, which means a compound interval can be (depending on the interval) major, minor, perfect, augmented, or diminished.

Intervals and Half Steps

It might be easier for you to think of all these intervals in terms of half steps. To that end, the following table shows how many half steps are between these major and minor intervals.

Half Steps Between Intervals

Interval	Number of Half Steps
Perfect unison	0
Minor second	1
Major second	2
Minor third	3
Major third	4
Perfect fourth	5
Augmented fourth	6
Diminished fifth	6
Perfect fifth	7
Minor sixth	8
Major sixth	9
Minor seventh	10
Major seventh	11
Octave	12
Minor ninth	13
Major ninth	14
Minor tenth	15

continues

Half Steps Between Intervals   (continued)

Interval	Number of Half Steps
Major tenth	16
Perfect eleventh	17
Augmented eleventh	18
Diminished twelfth	18
Perfect twelfth	19
Minor thirteenth	20
Major thirteenth	21
Minor fourteenth	22
Major fourteenth	23

The Mod-12 System

Some educators today use what is called the *Mod-12* system to teach notes and intervals. In this system, the intervals between the 12 half steps in an octave are numbered, from 0 to 11. (That adds up to 12 intervals.)

For example, the interval we call unison has zero half steps between notes, and is called "interval 0." The interval we call a minor third has three half steps, and is called "interval 3."

The nice thing about using this system is that you don't have to worry about enharmonics. A diminished fifth and an augmented fourth both have six half steps, and are both called "interval 6."

You can also use the Mod-12 system to describe individual notes—based on their interval from tonic. Tonic, of course, is note 0. The minor second degree is note 1, and the major second degree is note 2. If you wanted to describe the tonic, the major third degree, and the perfect fifth degree, you'd use the numbers 0, 4, and 7.

While many people like to use the Mod-12 system to teach intervals, I prefer the old-fashioned method presented here in this chapter—for the sole reason that this is what you'll run into in the real world. When you're playing in a concert band or a jazz trio, you won't hear other musicians say "play 4, 7, 11." You *will* hear them say "play the major third, fifth, and minor seventh."

Still, if Mod-12 works for you, use it. It's a perfectly acceptable way to learn the 12 tones we use in Western music—and it makes it a lot easier to deal with enharmonic notes.

The Least You Need to Know

◆ The smallest interval between any two notes is called a half step. Two half steps equal one whole step.

◆ A sharp raises the value of a note by a half step. A flat lowers the value of a note by a half step.

◆ The intervals between any two notes are described in terms of degree. For example, the interval between the first and third notes is called a third.

◆ In a major scale, seconds, thirds, sixths, and sevenths are called major intervals. You can create a minor interval by flattening these notes.

◆ In a major scale, fourths, fifths, and octaves are called perfect intervals. When you flatten a perfect interval, you create a diminished interval; when you sharpen a perfect interval, you create an augmented interval.

Exercises

Exercise 2-1

Add sharps before each of these notes.

Exercise 2-2

Add flats before each of these notes.

Exercise 2-3

Enter a new note an octave above each of the following notes.

Exercise 2-4

Enter a new note a specified number of half steps from the previous note.

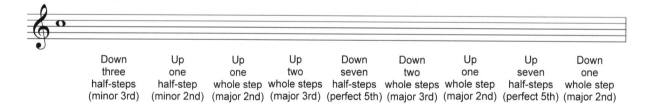

Exercise 2-5

Name each of the following intervals.

Exercise 2-6

Using the first note as the root, enter a second note to create the specified interval.

Exercise 2-7

Using sharps, flats, and naturals, change the following major intervals to minor.

Exercise 2-8

Using sharps, flats, and naturals, change the following minor intervals to major.

Chapter 3

Scales

In This Chapter

- ◆ Putting eight notes together to form a scale
- ◆ Creating major and minor scales
- ◆ Discovering the different modes within a major scale

In the first two chapters we discussed the seven key notes (A through G), and how they relate to each other. We also tossed around the word "scale" to describe all seven of those notes together.

In this chapter we further examine the concept of the musical scale, which (no surprise) is seven notes all in a row, in alphabetical order. (Actually, it's eight notes—the first note, or tonic, is repeated an octave higher at the top end of the scale.)

What might be surprising is that there are so many different types of scales. You can have a major scale, a minor scale (three different types of minor scales, actually), or any number of different *modes* within a scale. It sounds confusing, but it's really fairly simple once you understand how scales are constructed, using different intervals between the various notes.

(What's a mode, you ask? You'll have to read this entire chapter to find out!)

Scales are important because you use them to create melodies, which you'll learn about in Chapter 8. In fact, you can create a nice-sounding melody just by picking notes from a single major scale. For example, use the C Major scale (the white notes on a piano) and pick and choose notes that sound good when played together. Make sure you start and end your melody on the C note itself, and you've just written a simple song.

Eight Notes Equal One Scale

A scale is, quite simply, eight successive pitches within a one-octave range. All scales start on one note and end on that same note one octave higher.

For example, every C scale starts on C and ends on C; an F scale starts on F and ends on F; and they all have six more notes in between.

The eight notes of a scale;
C Major, in this instance.

The first note of a scale is called the tonic, or first degree, of the scale. Not surprisingly, the second note is called the second degree, the third note is called the third degree, and so on—until you get to the eighth note, which is the tonic again.

The major exception to the eight-note scale rule is the scale that includes *all* the notes within an octave, including all the sharps and flats. This type of scale is called a *chromatic scale*, and (when you start with C) looks something like this:

The C chromatic scale; the
top staff shows the scale
using sharps, the bottom staff
shows the scale using flats.

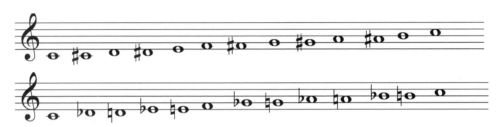

Now, any given scale has specific relationships between the different degrees of the scale. That's how you can describe different types of scales: A major scale has different intervals between specific notes from those you'll find in a similar minor scale. These different intervals give each type of scale its unique sound.

CAUTION

Warning

Most musicians don't capitalize the word "minor," or any of its abbreviations. Major chord notation is (almost) always capitalized, and minor chord notation is (almost) always lower-case.

The most common scale is called the *major* scale. Major scales are happy scales; they have pleasant and expected intervals at every turn. (Just sing "Do Re Mi Fa So La Ti Do" and you'll hear this pleasant quality.)

The mirror image of the major scale is the *minor* scale. Minor scales are sad scales; the intervals between the notes sound a little depressing.

Both major and minor scales can start on any note—from A-flat to G-sharp. No matter which note you start with, each scale has its own specific combination of intervals between notes.

The following sections go into more detail about both major and minor scales.

Major Scales

What makes a major scale major are the specific intervals between the notes of the scale. Every major scale uses the same intervals, as shown in the following table.

The Intervals of the Major Scale

Note	Half Steps to Next Note
Tonic	2
Second	2
Third	1
Fourth	2
Fifth	2
Sixth	2
Seventh	1

Put another way, the intervals in a major scale go like this: whole, whole, half, whole, whole, whole, half.

If you start your major scale on C (the C Major scale), you end up playing all white keys on the piano. C Major is the only major scale that uses only the white keys; all the other scales have black keys in them.

To make things easier for you, the following table shows all the notes in the 15 major scales:

The 15 Major Scales

Scale	Notes
C Major	
C-sharp Major	
D-flat Major	
D Major	
E-flat Major	
E Major	
F Major	
F-sharp Major	
G-flat Major	
G Major	
A-flat Major	
A Major	
B-flat Major	

continues

The 15 Major Scales   (continued)

Scale	Notes
B Major	
C-flat Major	

Note that three of these scales are enharmonic. (Remember that word from Chapter 1? It means two notes that are identical, but spelled differently.) So C-sharp Major and D-flat Major are just different ways of describing the same notes, as are F-sharp Major and G-flat Major, and B Major and C-flat Major.

> **Tip**
>
> When you're playing a piece of music, you typically stay within the notes of the designated scale. Any notes you play outside the scale are called *chromatic* notes; notes within the scale are said to be *diatonic*. For example, in the C Major scale, the note C is diatonic; the note C-sharp would be chromatic.
>
> Even though chromatic notes might sound "different" than the normal scale notes, they can add color to a piece of music. (That's where the term comes from, by the way; *chroma* means "color.")

Minor Scales

Minor scales sound a little less "up" than major scales. This is partly because the third note of the minor scale is a minor interval, whereas the third note of the major scale is a major interval. That little half step between a minor third and a major third makes all the difference in the world!

Not to confuse you; however, whereas there was a single type of major scale, there actually are three types of minor scales: natural, harmonic, and melodic. We'll look at each scale separately.

Natural Minor

> **Note**
>
> If you start your natural minor scale on A (the A minor scale), you will play all white keys on the piano. The A natural minor scale is the only minor scale that uses only the white keys; all the other scales have black keys in them.

The easiest minor scale to construct is the *natural minor* scale. You can think of the natural minor in terms of its corresponding major scale. When you start and end a major scale on the sixth note, instead of the tonic, you get a natural minor scale.

Here's an example: Play a C Major scale (C D E F G A B C). Now move up to the sixth note—or just move down two notes. (It's the same thing—up six or down two—both put you on the A.) Now play an eight-note scale, but using the notes in C Major. What you get—A B C D E F G A— is the A minor (natural) scale.

As you can see, each natural minor scale shares the same tones as a specific major scale. The following table shows you which minor scales match up with which major scales.

Relative Major and Minor Scales

Major Scale	Related Natural Minor Scale
C Major	A minor
C-sharp Major	A-sharp minor
D-flat Major	B-flat minor
D Major	B minor
E-flat Major	C minor
E Major	D-flat (C-sharp) minor
F Major	D minor
F-sharp Major	D-sharp minor
G-flat Major	E-flat minor
G Major	E minor
A-flat Major	F minor
A Major	F-sharp (G-flat) minor
B-flat Major	G minor
B Major	G-sharp minor
C-flat Major	A-flat minor

Every natural minor scale uses the same intervals, as shown in the following table.

The Intervals of the Natural Minor Scale

Note	Half Steps to Next Note
Tonic	2
Second	1
Third	2
Fourth	2
Fifth	1
Sixth	2
Seventh	2

Put another way, the intervals in a natural minor scale go like this: whole, half, whole, whole, half, whole, whole.

To make things easier for you, the following table shows all the notes in the 15 natural minor scales.

The 15 Natural Minor Scales

Scale	Notes
C minor	
C-sharp minor	

continues

The 15 Natural Minor Scales   (continued)

Scale	Notes
D minor	
D-sharp minor	
E-flat minor	
E minor	
F minor	
F-sharp minor	
G minor	
G-sharp minor	
A-flat minor	
A minor	
A-sharp minor	
B-flat minor	
B minor	

Harmonic Minor

The *harmonic minor* scale is similar to the natural minor scale, except the seventh note is raised a half step. Some musicians prefer this type of minor scale because the seventh note better leads up to the tonic of the scale.

The following table details the intervals between the notes in the harmonic minor scale.

The Intervals of the Harmonic Minor Scale

Note	Half Steps to Next Note
Tonic	2
Second	1
Third	2
Fourth	2
Fifth	1
Sixth	3
Seventh	1

Put another way, the intervals in a harmonic minor scale go like this: whole, half, whole, whole, half, whole and a half, half.

To make things easier for you, the following table shows all the notes in the 15 harmonic minor scales.

> **Note**
>
> The seventh note of any scale is sometimes called the **leading note** because it leads up to the tonic of the scale.

The 15 Harmonic Minor Scales

Scale	Notes
C minor	
C-sharp minor	
D minor	
D-sharp minor	
E-flat minor	
E minor	
F minor	
F-sharp minor	

continues

The 15 Harmonic Minor Scales (continued)

Scale	Notes
G minor	
G-sharp minor	
A-flat minor	
A minor	
A-sharp minor	
B-flat minor	
B minor	

Note: The "x" you see before several of the notes in the previous table is a *double sharp*. It means you raise the base note *two* half steps.

Melodic Minor

The only problem with the harmonic minor scale is that the interval between the sixth and seventh notes is three half steps—and you seldom have an interval in a scale wider than two half steps. (It's just too awkward to sing.) So the *melodic minor* scale raises both the sixth and seventh notes of the natural minor scale by a half step each, resulting in the following intervals:

The Intervals of the Melodic Minor Scale

Note	Half Steps to Next Note
Tonic	2
Second	1
Third	2
Fourth	2
Fifth	2
Sixth	2
Seventh	1

Put another way, the intervals in the melodic minor scale go like this: whole, half, whole, whole, whole, whole, half.

To make things easier for you, the following table shows all the notes in the 15 melodic minor scales.

The 15 Melodic Minor Scales

Scale	Notes
C minor	
C-sharp minor	
D minor	
D-sharp minor	
E-flat minor	
E minor	
F minor	
F-sharp minor	
G minor	
G-sharp minor	
A-flat minor	
A minor	
A-sharp minor	

continues

The 15 Melodic Minor Scales (continued)

Scale	Notes
B-flat minor	
B minor	

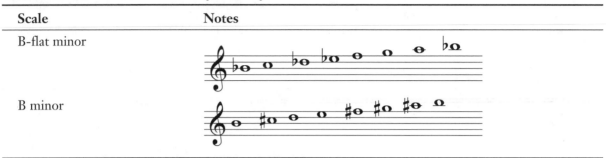

As if three minor scales weren't enough to deal with, some music theorists believe that this melodic minor scale is only used when you're going "up" the scale. (They call this the *ascending melodic minor* scale.) Going back down (the *descending melodic minor* scale), they use the notes in the natural minor scale. So the sixth and the seventh degrees are raised on the way up, but not on the way down. Theorists are split on this issue, however; some use the melodic minor scale both ascending and descending, and others use the two different scales. It's okay to use a single scale, as presented here, as long as you're aware of the alternate way of doing things.

In the Mode

If a scale is a combination of eight successive notes (in alphabetical order, of course), do any eight notes make a scale?

Not necessarily.

Once you get past the major and minor scales, all the other eight-note combinations aren't technically called scales; they're called *modes*.

Note

Modes date back to the medieval church and Gregorian chant, and were first called *church modes*. The name of each mode is based on the final note of the mode. Originally, there were only four modes: Dorian, Phrygian, Lydian, and Mixolydian. About a hundred years after the introduction of these four modes, the Aeolian and Ionian modes were conceived. The final mode, Locrian, is actually a theoretical mode; it was never used in the same context as the other church modes.

Chronologically, modes were around long before scales. The major and minor scales we use today came after the introduction of the various church modes, and were, in fact, based on the Ionian and Aeolian modes, respectively.

Note

While it's convenient to think of modes in relation to a specific major scale, modes are arrangements of intervals in and of themselves. In practice, any mode can start on any note.

There are seven essential modes, each of which can be thought of as starting on a different degree of the major scale. You stay within the relative major scale; you just start on different notes.

For example, the Dorian mode starts on the second degree of the major scale. In relation to the C Major scale, the Dorian mode starts on D, and continues upward (D, E, F, G, A, B, C, D). The same holds true for the Phrygian mode, which starts on the third degree of the related major scale—in C Major: E, F, G, A, B, C, D, E.

Modes are important when you're constructing melodies. When you create a melody based on a specific mode, you get to create a different sound or feel while staying within the notes of a traditional major scale. You just start and stop in different places. (Melodies based around specific modes are called *modal* melodies.)

Ionian

If you're a musician, you play the Ionian mode all the time without really knowing it. That's because the Ionian mode starts on the tonic of the related major scale—and contains the exact same notes as the major scale.

The following table details the half steps between the notes of the Ionian mode.

The Intervals of the Ionian

Note	Half Steps to Next Note
Tonic	2
Second	2
Third	1
Fourth	2
Fifth	2
Sixth	2
Seventh	1

The C Ionian mode consists of the following notes:

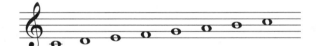

The C Ionian mode—just like the C Major scale.

Dorian

The Dorian mode can be thought of as starting on the second note of a major scale. It sounds a little like a natural minor scale, but with a raised sixth. (To get an idea what Dorian mode sounds like, listen to the Simon & Garfunkel song "Scarborough Fair"; it's composed entirely in Dorian mode.)

The intervals between notes in the Dorian mode are as follows.

The Intervals of Dorian Mode

Note	Half Steps to Next Note
Tonic	2
Second	1
Third	2
Fourth	2
Fifth	2
Sixth	1
Seventh	2

D Dorian is relative to the key of C, and consists of the following notes:

D Dorian mode, relative to the key of C.

Phrygian

The Phrygian mode can be thought of as starting on the third note of the related major scale. Like the Dorian mode, it sounds like a natural minor scale—but with a lowered second degree.

The intervals between notes in the Phrygian mode are as follows.

The Intervals of the Phrygian Mode

Note	Half Steps to Next Note
Tonic	1
Second	2
Third	2
Fourth	2
Fifth	1
Sixth	2
Seventh	2

E Phrygian is relative to the key of C, and consists of the following notes:

E Phrygian mode, relative to the key of C.

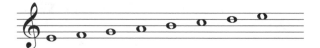

Lydian

The Lydian mode can be thought of as starting on the fourth note of a major scale. It's an almost-major scale, but with a raised fourth.

The intervals between notes in the Lydian mode are as follows.

The Intervals of the Lydian Mode

Note	Half Steps to Next Note
Tonic	2
Second	2
Third	2
Fourth	1
Fifth	2
Sixth	2
Seventh	1

F Lydian mode is relative to the key of C, and consists of the following notes:

F Lydian mode, relative to the key of C.

Mixolydian

The Mixolydian mode can be thought of as starting on the fifth note of the related major scale. Like the Lydian mode, it's sort of major sounding, but in this case with a lowered seventh.

The intervals between notes in the Mixolydian mode are as shown in the following table.

The Intervals of the Mixolydian

Note	Half Steps to Next Note
Tonic	2
Second	2
Third	1
Fourth	2
Fifth	2
Sixth	1
Seventh	2

In the key of C, the Mixolydian mode consists of the following notes:

The Mixolydian mode in the key of C.

Aeolian

The Aeolian mode contains the exact same notes as the natural minor scale. It can be thought of as starting on the sixth note of the related major scale.

The intervals between notes in the Aeolian mode are as follows.

The Intervals of the Aeolian Mode

Note	Half Steps to Next Note
Tonic	2
Second	1
Third	2
Fourth	2
Fifth	1
Sixth	2
Seventh	1

You use the Aeolian mode a lot when you play blues and jazz tunes. A Aeolian is relative to the key of C, and consists of the following notes:

A Aeolian mode, relative to the key of C.

Locrian

The Locrian mode can be thought of as starting on the seventh note of the related major scale. It's probably the weirdest sounding of all the modes, because all the leading notes are in all the wrong places.

Back in olden times, Locrian was a mode that existed in theory only; it wasn't used in actual music. Today, however, the Locrian mode is used in some jazz music, and in some new music compositions.

The intervals between notes in the Locrian mode are as follows.

The Intervals of the Locrian Mode

Note	Half Steps to Next Note
Tonic	1
Second	2
Third	2
Fourth	1
Fifth	2
Sixth	2
Seventh	2

B Locrian is relative to the key of C, and consists of the following notes:

B Locrian mode, relative to the key of C.

The Least You Need to Know

◆ A scale consists of eight notes whose letter names are in successive alphabetical order.

◆ Scales can be either major or minor. (And there are three different types of minor scales!)

◆ All major scales have the same intervals between different notes, no matter what note they start on.

◆ A mode, like a scale, consists of eight notes in a row—but aren't limited to just major and minor. Modes are derived from ancient church music, and can be thought of as starting on different degrees of the related major scale.

Exercises

Exercise 3-1

Name the following major scales.

Exercise 3-2

Name the following minor scales.

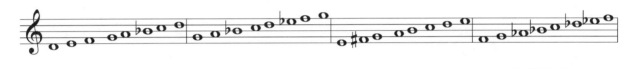

Exercise 3-3

Enter the notes for the following major scales.

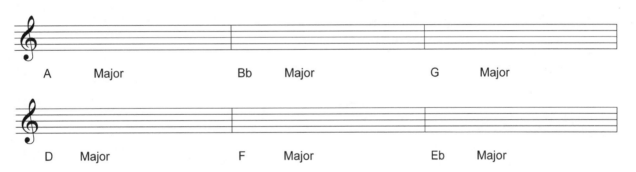

A   Major   Bb   Major   G   Major

D   Major   F   Major   Eb   Major

Exercise 3-4

Enter the notes for the following minor scales.

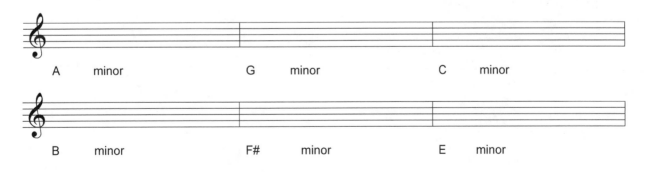

A   minor   G   minor   C   minor

B   minor   F#   minor   E   minor

Exercise 3-5

Name the natural minor scales related to the following major scales, and enter the notes for those scales.

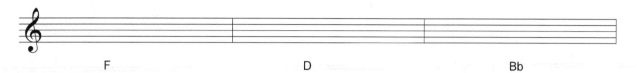

F   D   Bb

Exercise 3-6

Enter the notes for the following modes, within the C Major scale.

Lydian   Aeolian   Dorian

Chapter 4

Major and Minor Keys

In This Chapter

- ◆ Understanding major and minor keys
- ◆ Determining key by using key signatures
- ◆ Using the circle of fifths
- ◆ Applying accidentals and changing keys

If you're writing music within the C Major scale, you have it easy. All the notes fall in the lines and spaces of the treble and bass clefs; no sharps or flats are necessary.

However, if you're writing music using another scale you have to use accidentals to raise and lower notes beyond the white keys on the piano keyboard. For example, if you're using the F Major scale, you have a pesky B-flat to deal with.

Now, you could put a flat sign in front of every B-flat in your music. However, you'll end up writing a lot of flats—which is a major pain in the butt.

Fortunately, there's an easy way to designate consistent flats and sharps throughout an entire piece of music, without noting each and every instance. This approach requires the knowledge of musical *keys*—which just happen to correspond to the musical scales we discussed in previous chapter.

Keys to Success

When a piece of music is based on a particular musical scale, we say that music is in the "key" of that scale. For example, a song based around the C Major scale is in the key of C Major. A song based around the B-flat Major scale is in the key of B-flat Major.

When you assign a key to a piece of music (or to a section within a larger piece), it's assumed that most of the notes in that music will stay within the corresponding scale. So if a piece is written in A Major, most of the notes in the melody and chords should be within the A Major scale. (There are exceptions to this, of course; they're called *accidentals*; they're discussed later in this chapter.)

Using Key Signatures

One of the convenient things about assigning a particular key to a piece of music is that it enables you to designate the appropriate sharps and flats up front, without having to repeat them every time they occur in the music.

Here's how it works.

You designate a key by inserting a *key signature* at the very start of the music, next to the first clef on the first staff. This key signature indicates the sharps and flats used in that particular key. Then, when you play through the entire piece, you automatically sharpen and flatten the appropriate notes.

For example, let's say you write a song around the F Major scale. The F Major scale, if you recall, has one flatted note: B-flat. So next to the first clef on the first staff, you put a flat sign on the B line. Now, when you play that song, every time you see a B, you actually play B-flat.

The key signature for the key of F—note the flat sign on the B line, indicating the automatic B-flat.

The same would apply if you were playing in the key of G, which has one sharp: F-sharp. You put a sharp sign on the top F line on the first staff; then every time you see an F, you play an F-sharp.

Major Keys

Just as there are 15 major scales (including three enharmonics), there are 15 major keys; each with its own key signature. The following table shows what each key of these key signatures looks like, along with its corresponding scale.

The 15 Major Keys

Key	Key Signature and Scale
C Major	
C-sharp Major	
D-flat Major	
D Major	
E-flat Major	
E Major	

continues

The 15 Major Keys   (continued)

Key	Key Signature and Scale
F Major	
F-sharp Major	
G-flat Major	
G Major	
A-flat Major	
A Major	
B-flat Major	
B Major	
C-flat Major	

Minor Keys

The key signatures used to indicate major keys also can represent natural minor keys. As you remember from Chapter 3, a natural minor scale is based on the same notes as a major scale, but starts on the sixth note of the scale. This same method applies to keys, so that (for example) the key of A minor uses the same notes—and the same key signature—as C major.

The following table shows the 15 minor keys, with their corresponding key signatures and scales.

The 15 Minor Keys

Scale	Notes	Same as This Major Key
A minor		C Major

continues

The 15 Minor Keys   (continued)

Scale	Notes	Same as This Major Key
A-sharp minor		C-sharp Major
B-flat minor		D-flat Major
B minor		D Major
C minor		E-flat Major
C-sharp minor		E Major
D minor		F Major
D-sharp minor		F-sharp Major
E-flat minor		G-flat Major
E minor		G Major
F minor		A-flat Major
F-sharp minor		A Major
G minor		B-flat Major
G-sharp minor		B Major
A-flat minor		C-flat Major

The Circle of Fifths

There's a quick way to remember how many sharps or flats to include with each key signature. This method is called the *circle of fifths*; it works like this.

Starting with the key of C, for every perfect fifth you move up, you add a sharp. So the key of G (a perfect fifth up from C) has one sharp. The key of D (a perfect fifth up from G) has two sharps … and so on.

The circle of fifths works in the other direction for flats. For every perfect fifth you move down from C, you add a flat. So the key of F (a perfect fifth down from C) has one flat. The key of B-flat (a perfect fifth down from F) has two flats … and so on.

The following drawing shows how all the major keys relate in the circle of fifths. When you move clockwise around the circle, you're moving up through the fifths (and the sharp keys); when you move counterclockwise, you're moving down through the fifths (and the flat keys).

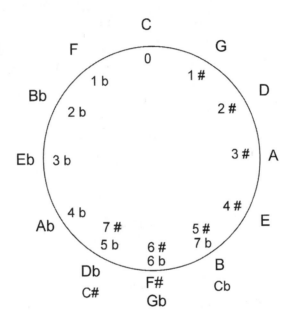

All the major keys are a fifth apart in the circle of fifths.

The next figure shows the circle of fifths for the 15 *minor* keys. It works just the same as the major-key circle; move clockwise for the sharp keys, and counterclockwise for the flat keys.

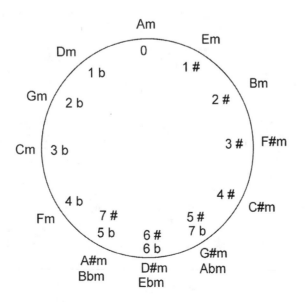

The circle of fifths works for minor keys, too.

Accidents Will Happen

When you assign a key signature to a piece of music, it's assumed that all the following notes will correspond to that particular key. How, then, do you indicate notes that fall outside that key?

> **Note**
>
> Jazz and blues music often add flatted thirds and sevenths within the designated major key, which give these styles their unique sound.

First, it should be noted that you *can* play outside a key. For example, it's okay to play the occasional B natural when you're in the key of F, which normally has a B-flat. No one will arrest you for it—in fact, certain types of music regularly employ nonscale notes.

When you decide to write a note that isn't within the current key, you have to manually indicate the change in the music—by using sharp, flat, or natural signs. When musicians see the inserted sharp, flat, or natural, they know to play the note as written, rather than as indicated by the music's key signature.

These "outside the key" notes are called *accidentals*; they're quite common.

For example, let's say a piece of music is in the key of F, which has only one flat (B-flat). You want your melody to include an E-flat, which isn't in the key. So when you get to that note, you insert a flat sign before the E to indicate an E-flat. It's as simple as that.

Use accidentals to indicate notes outside the current key signature.

> ⚠ **Warning**
>
> An accidental applies only from that point in the measure to the end of the measure. It doesn't affect those notes in the measure before the accidental appears.

The same theory would apply if you want to include a B natural in the same piece, instead of the expected B-flat. If you simply insert a natural sign before the B, you've accomplished your mission.

When you change a note with an accidental, that accidental applies until the end of the current measure. At the start of the next measure, it's assumed that all notes revert to what they should be, given the current key. So if you flat an E in measure one of an F Major melody, the first E you write in measure two will be assumed to be natural; not flatted.

The one exception to this rule occurs when you tie a note from the end of one measure to the beginning of the next. The accidental carries over—thanks to the tie—to that first note in the second measure, as you can see in the following example. (Ties are explained in Chapter 5.) Note that the accidental doesn't apply to any subsequent notes in the second measure; it applies only to the tied note.

Accidentals apply to all notes tied over a measure.

If you think other musicians might be confused about whether a note has reverted back to normal, it's okay to use a *courtesy* sharp, flat, or natural sign. (This is a sign placed within parentheses.) This reminds the reader that the note has reverted back to its normal state. You don't have to use courtesy signs like this, but when the music is complicated, it can be quite helpful.

A courtesy accidental reminds musicians that a changed note has reverted back to normal.

Changing Keys

Some long pieces of music don't always use the same key throughout the entire piece. In fact, some short pop songs change keys midway through. It's allowed.

When you change keys in the middle of a song, it's called *modulating* to another key. You can modulate to any key, although the most common modulations are up a half step (from E Major to F Major, for example), or up a fourth or fifth (from E Major to either A Major or B Major, for example).

Tip

The half-step modulation is most common in twentieth-century popular music, and can add a "lift" to the end of a pop song. The fourth or fifth modulation is more common in classical music of the seventeenth through the nineteenth centuries.

When you want to change keys, you indicate this by inserting a new key signature in the first measure of the new key. It's as simple as that, as you can see in the following figure. (Note that some composers and arrangers also insert a double bar whenever there's a key change.)

To change keys, insert a new key signature.

Tip

If you want, you can alert musicians to a key change by placing the appropriate sharps and flats at the very end of the last staff of the old key—as well as with a new key signature in the following measure. This approach is entirely optional; it's perfectly acceptable to signal the key change with a single key signature in the first measure of the new key.

The only complicated key change is when you're changing to the key of C—which has no sharps or flats. You indicate this by using natural signs to cancel out the previous sharps or flats, like this:

How to change to the key of C.

The Least You Need to Know

♦ You use key signatures to indicate what scale your music is based on.

♦ The sharps and flats in a key signature are automatically applied throughout the entire song.

♦ To indicate notes outside the current key, use accidentals—sharps, flats, and natural signs.

♦ To change the key in the middle of a piece of music, insert a new key signature.

Exercises

Exercise 4-1

Label the following major key signatures.

Exercise 4-2

Label the following minor key signatures.

Exercise 4-3

Create the indicated major key signatures.

Exercise 4-4

Create the indicated minor key signatures.

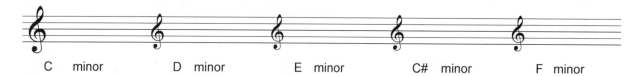

Exercise 4-5

Using the initial key signature as a guide, label each note in the following example.

Exercise 4-6

Determine what key signature you could use to write this melody without accidentals, and enter that key signature at the beginning of the staff.

Exercise 4-7

Determine what key signature you could use to write this melody without accidentals, and enter that key signature at the beginning of the staff.

Exercise 4-8

Following the circle of fifths, add the appropriate number of flats to each successive major key signature, and then label each key signature.

C   F   ____   ____   ____   ____

Part 2

Rhythms

You don't have to be a drummer to feel the beat. This section shows you how to notate any type of rhythm, from simple whole notes to sixteenth note syncopations. You'll also learn all about time signatures, tempo, and dynamics—as well as how to navigate your way through a piece of music.

Chapter 5

Note Values and Basic Notation

In This Chapter

- ◆ Grouping beats into measures
- ◆ Understanding whole, half, quarter, eighth, and sixteenth notes and rests
- ◆ Using dotted notes and ties
- ◆ Dividing beats into triplets

Part 1 of this book covered how to work with pitch—but that's only half of the music theory that you need to know. In this chapter we'll deal with the other half of the equation, which is how you work with *time*—which, in music, is called *rhythm*.

Rhythm is what drives the music forward and gives it its beat. To learn rhythm, you have to learn about note values. This type of music notation isn't that hard, really. All you need to learn is a little basic math and how to count—up to four.

Before we start, however, let's lay down some ground rules for this chapter. While a lot of songs are written with four beats to a measure—one, two, three, four—that isn't a universal. Some very popular songs only have three beats to a measure. (Think "My Favorite Things," from *The Sound of Music*.) And other tunes, especially in the jazz and classical genres, have *more* than four beats per measure.

To make it easier to learn the basics, in this chapter, we're only going to address four-beat measures—what we call *4/4 time*. All the other types of beats—three, five, seven, whatever—will be covered in Chapter 6.

And *that's* why I said you only have to know how to count to four!

Taking the Measure of Things

Rhythm is about counting. Listen to your favorite pop song, and feel the beat. (Go ahead, tap your foot—it's okay!) You'll likely feel the beats fall into groups of four—one, two, three, four; one, two, three, four …. It's easy to hear because it's very natural.

Let's use a specific example—"Mary Had a Little Lamb." The notes of the song fall into groups of four; just replace the words "Ma-ry had a" with "one two three four" and you see how it works.

In this song, and other songs based around groups of four, each group of four beats is called a *measure*, a container that holds a specific number of beats. In standard 4/4 time, a measure holds the equivalent of four quarter notes. The beginning and end of a measure are signified by bar lines, like this:

A group of measures on a staff; each measure is separated by left and right bar lines.

The first beat in a measure is counted as one. The second beat is counted as two. The third beat is counted as three, and the last beat is counted as four. There is no five; if you count out five you've counted too far! Whenever you hit four, the next beat is always one.

Every time four beats go by—one, two, three, four—another measure is completed. If you put enough measures together—one, two, three, four; one, two, three, four—you have a song.

Taking Note–of Notes

Every time you sing or play a tone, you're also singing or playing a note value. There are different types of note values, with each note value signifying a specific length of time—as measured by parts of a measure.

To better explain, we have to get into a little math. (Don't worry—there won't be any story problems!) You see, each note value lasts a specific duration, and each duration reflects a ratio to duration. As you can see from the following figure, each shorter note is precisely half the duration of the previous note. So, if you can divide and multiply by two, this should be fairly easy for you.

The most common rhythmic notes—each smaller note is exactly half the previous note.

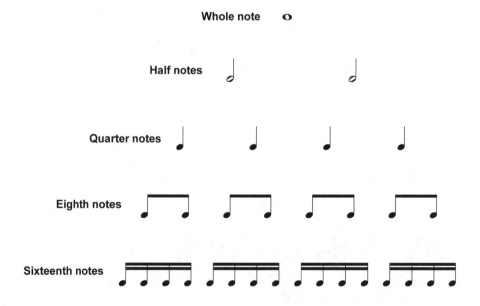

Whole Notes

The most basic note is called the *whole note*, which is called a whole note because, in 4/4 time (we'll get to this soon—I promise!), it lasts a whole measure. Because 4/4 time has four beats in a measure, this means a whole note lasts four beats. A whole note looks like a big empty oval, nice and whole.

Whole notes, at different places on the staff.

When you put a whole note in a measure of 4/4 time, that's the only note that goes in that measure; no other notes will fit. When you play a whole note, you play your instrument once at the very beginning of the measure (on beat one), and then you hold that tone through the entire measure. In other words, one whole note should last a whole measure.

Half Notes

Because the whole note is the largest note, let's go down one size and look at the next smallest note. Remember that I said each shorter note is exactly half the previous note? Let's apply a little math and divide a whole note by two to see what we get.

The next smallest note is called a *half note*. (It's half of a whole note—pretty simple, eh?) Because a whole note lasts a whole measure (in 4/4, anyway), a half note lasts a half measure. This means a half note lasts *two beats*, which is half of the four-beat duration of a whole note. Put another way, you can put two half notes in a measure, because two half notes equal one whole note.

A half note looks like a whole note with a line next to it. The line is called a *stem*; it can point up or down, depending on the pitch of the note.

Two half notes—one with the stem pointing up; the other with the stem pointing down.

Tip

If the *notehead* (the part of the note that isn't the stem) is above the third (middle) line of the staff, then the stem should point down from the notehead. If the notehead is below the third line of the staff, then the stem should point up from the notehead. If the notehead is on the middle line, then the stem can point either direction, as appropriate.

When you play a half note, make sure the tone lasts a full two beats. If you let up after the first beat, you're playing only half a half note—which is what we'll discuss next.

Quarter Notes

Let's keep going. If a half note is half a whole note, what is half a half note? Well, do your math, and when you divide $\frac{1}{2}$ by 2, you get $\frac{1}{4}$. This means half a half note is a *quarter note*.

Because a half note lasts two beats, a quarter note—which is half that duration—lasts one beat. Put another way, you can fit four quarter notes in a measure; one to a beat.

When you tap your foot to the beat of most popular songs, your foot is tapping quarter notes. One, two, three, four—each of those counts is a quarter note.

Definition

A **notehead** is the big, oval part of a note. The stem is always attached to the notehead.

A quarter note looks like a half note with the *notehead* filled in, as shown here:

Two different quarter notes, pointing in both directions.

Eighth Notes

Just like the scientists in *Fantastic Voyage* or Ray Palmer, the Atom, in DC Comics, notes just keep getting smaller. Again, we're operating on a 2-to-1 ratio, so let's take a quarter note and divide it in half. Doing the math, $\frac{1}{4} \div$ by $2 = \frac{1}{8}$—so the next-smallest note is the *eighth note*.

Just as there are four quarter notes in a measure of 4/4 time ($4 \times \frac{1}{4} = 1$), each measure holds eight eighth notes ($8 \times \frac{1}{8} = 1$). Put another way, there are two eighth notes for every quarter note ($2 \times \frac{1}{8} = \frac{1}{4}$)—or two eighth notes for every beat.

An eighth note looks like a quarter note with a *flag* on it. If you have two or more eighth notes in a row, the flags can be replaced with horizontal stems at the end of the normal horizontal stems. (The flags don't have to be joined together; sometimes it's just easier to read that way.)

A variety of different eighth notes.

Sixteenth Notes

Okay, you know where this is going. Half an eighth note is (do the math!) a *sixteenth note* ($\frac{1}{8} \div 2 = \frac{1}{16}$). There are 16 sixteenth notes in a measure ($16 \times \frac{1}{16} = 1$), or 4 sixteenth notes per one quarter-note beat ($4 \times \frac{1}{16} = \frac{1}{4}$).

A sixteenth note looks like a quarter note with *two* flags on it. As with the eighth note, if 2 or more sixteenth notes are next to each other, the flags may (or may not) be joined together.

A variety of different sixteenth notes.

Note
Although we'll end this discussion with sixteenth notes, there are lots of notes even smaller than that. Each successive note is half the value of the previous note and is indicated by an additional flag on the stem.   For example, the thirty-second note is the next-smallest note after the sixteenth note; it has three flags on its stem. After that is the sixty-fourth note, with four flags. In actuality, you won't run into too many notes smaller than the sixteenth note.

Taking Count

It's fairly easy to write down a series of notes—but how do you communicate notes and values to other musicians verbally? Do you go all mathematical and say things such as "the fourteenth sixteenth note" or "the eighth note after the two sixteenth notes on beat four"—or is there an easier way to describe your rhythms?

Just as you describe absolute pitches by using letters (A through G), you describe absolute rhythms by using numbers—and you need only to be able to count to four.

It starts fairly simple, in that each beat in a measure is counted as either one, two, three, or four. So if you're counting off four quarter notes, you count them as one, two, three, four. If you want to talk about the fourth quarter note in a measure, you call it "four," as in "in the last measure, make sure you play a B-flat on four."

If the beat is always one, two, three, or four, what about the eighth notes that lay between the beats? It's simple: count them as "and." As is "one-and, two-and, three-and, four-and," all very even. You'd talk about an eighth note like this: "Make sure you play a C-sharp on the *and* after three."

This is pretty easy—but what about sixteenth notes? This gets a little tricky, but it'll seem natural once you get into it. Use the nonsense syllables "e" and "ah" to represent the sixteenth notes between eighth notes. So if you're counting a group of straight sixteenth notes, you'd count "one-e-and-ah, two-e-and-ah, three-e-and-ah, four-e-and-ah," all nice and even. Still not sure about this?

Examine the following figure, which shows how to count various groupings of notes.

One Two Three Four   One and Two and Three and Four and   One e and a Two e and a Three e and a Four e and a

How to count various types of notes.

Taking a Rest

If a note represents the duration of a pitch, what do you call it when you're not playing or singing? In music, when you're not playing, you're resting—so any note you don't play is called a *rest*.

When you see four quarter notes, you play or sing four tones—one per beat. When you see four quarter note rests, you don't play four tones; you rest over four beats.

Each type of note—whole note, half note, and so on—has a corresponding rest of the same duration. So you have a whole rest that lasts a whole measure, a half rest that lasts a half measure, and so on. Rests are used to indicate the spaces in between the notes and are just as important as the notes you play.

The following table shows all the notes you've just learned and their corresponding rests.

Notes and Rests

Duration	Note	Rest
Whole note	𝅝	▬
Half note	𝅗𝅥	▬
Quarter note	𝅘𝅥	𝄽
Eighth note	𝅘𝅥𝅮	𝄾
Sixteenth note	𝅘𝅥𝅯	𝄿

Taking a Note—and Dotting It

Sooner or later you'll run into something a little different: a note or a rest with a dot after it. When you run into one of these *dotted notes*, that note should have a longer duration than the normal version of that note—one and a half times longer, to be precise.

Here's where your math skills come back into play. Let's take a dotted quarter note as an example. A regular quarter note is worth a single beat. If you multiply 1 × 1½, you get 1½ beats—so a dotted quarter note is worth 1½ beats. You also could go about it by saying a quarter note equals four sixteenth notes, and 4 × 1½ = 6, and 6 sixteenth notes equal 1½ quarter notes. However you do the math, it comes out the same.

So when you see a dotted note, hold that note 50 percent longer than you would do normally, as shown in the following table.

Dotted Note Values

This Dotted Note ...	Equals This
𝅗𝅥.	𝅗𝅥 + 𝅘𝅥
𝅘𝅥.	𝅘𝅥 + 𝅘𝅥𝅮
𝅘𝅥𝅮.	𝅘𝅥𝅮 + 𝅘𝅥𝅯

You can also have dotted rests, which work the same as dotted notes. When you see a dot after a rest, that rest should last one and half times the value of the main rest.

Taking Two Notes—and Tying Them Together

Another way to make a note longer is to tie it to another note. A tie is a little rounded connector placed between two notes; it essentially tells you to add the second note to the first note.

A tie makes one note out of two.

When you see two or more notes tied together, you play them as if they're a single note; for example, two quarter notes tied together equal one half note.

What do you do if the tied notes are on different pitches? Well, this may *look* like a tie, but it isn't really a tie—it's a *slur*. A slur is a way of indicating that two (or more) notes are to be played in a smoothly connected fashion, rather than as distinctly separate notes.

This isn't really a tie; it's a slur.

Taking the Beat and Dividing by Three

There's another little oddity in rhythmic notation—and this one is very important. Everything we've done up to now has divided notes and beats by two. What happens, then, if you divide by something other than two?

The most common division other than two is dividing by three; this is called a *triplet*. When you see the number three over a group of three notes (or three rests—or any combination of three equal notes and rests), you know that those three notes have to fit into a space that would normally hold just two notes.

The three notes of a triplet fit in the space of two regular notes.

Triplets have more of a rolling feel than straight notes and are counted as "trip-ah-let." You can have triplets of any note value, although quarter-note triplets (where three of them are spaced over two beats), eighth-note triplets (three on a single quarter-note beat), and sixteenth-note triplets (three in the space of a single eighth note) are the most common.

Note

Triplets are the most common uneven rhythmic division, but not the only one. You can divide a beat any way you like, which can lead to groups of five or seven or any prime number. (If you divide a beat by a nonprime number, you're actually dividing by two or more groups of a prime number. For example, if you divide a beat into six, you're really dividing into two groups of three—or two triplets.)

The Least You Need to Know

◆ Note values are named according to their duration. Whole notes last a whole measure (in 4/4 time), half notes last a half measure, and so on.

◆ Each smaller note lasts half as long as the previous note. A quarter note, for example, is half as long as a half note.

◆ Each note value has a corresponding rest of the same duration—which indicates not to play or sing.

◆ A dot after a note or rest extends the value of that note by 50 percent.

◆ When you fit three notes into a space that normally holds only two, those notes are called triplets.

Exercises

Exercise 5-1

Name the following notes and rests.

Exercise 5-2

Write the count ("one-e-and-ah") below each of the notes in the following measures.

Exercise 5-3

Fill in the balance of these measures with eighth notes.

Exercise 5-4

Write the corresponding rests for the following notes.

Exercise 5-5

Fill in the balance of these measures with eighth-note triplets.

Exercise 5-6

Tie each group of two notes (but not the rests!) together.

Exercise 5-7

Enter four whole notes, followed by four half notes, followed by four quarter notes, followed by four eighth notes, followed by four sixteenth notes.

Exercise 5-8

Draw stems and flags on these notes to make them eighth notes; make sure to point the stems in the correct direction.

Chapter 6

Time Signatures

In This Chapter

◆ Understanding how time signatures determine meter
◆ Learning both usual and odd time signatures
◆ Changing time signatures
◆ Subdividing odd time signatures

In the previous chapter you learned about measures, those containers that hold the beats of a piece of music. The start and end points of a measure are marked by vertical bar lines, and multiple measures combine to create a complete song.

To simplify things, in Chapter 5 we limited our discussion to measures with four beats apiece, with each of those beats equaling a quarter note. That covers a lot of different songs, especially in popular music. Whatever type of music you listen to—rock-and-roll, soul, jazz, country, hip hop, or even reggae—most of the songs you hear are likely to adhere to this four-beat form.

However, not all music has four beats per measure, and not every beat is equal to a quarter note. To understand all the different numbers and types of beats per measure, you need only to apply a little math—in the form of fractions.

Measuring the Beats

Written music uses something called a *time signature* to signify how many beats are in a measure and what kind of note is used for the basic beat. A time signature looks kind of like a fraction, with one number sitting on top of another number. The top number indicates how many beats are in a measure; the bottom number indicates the note value of the basic beat.

Time signatures show how beats are organized in a particular piece of music. This organization is called *meter*, and time signatures are sometimes called *meter signatures*.

Note

Classical musicians tend to refer to the organization of beats as "meter," while jazz and pop musicians tend to refer to it as "time."

Let's take the four-quarter-notes-to-a-measure form we used in the previous chapter. Because we have four beats in a measure, the top number in the time signature is a four. Because the basic beat is a quarter note, the bottom number is a four (as in the 4 in 1/4). So the standard form we've been using is called "four four" time (because of the 4 on top of the 4), and looks like this:

The time signature for 4/4 meter.

Other time signatures follow this same form. For example, if our measures have three beats instead of four, and still use a quarter note for the beat, we have a 3/4 time signature. If you have three beats per measure but the basic beat is an eighth note instead of a quarter note, that time signature is "three eight," or 3/8.

Read on to learn more about the different types of time signatures you're likely to encounter in the world of music.

Quarter-Note Time

The most common types of time signatures use a quarter note for the base beat. However, you're not limited to just four beats (quarter notes) per measure; quarter-note time signatures can have as few as one beat per measure, or as many as … well, as many as you like!

Note

In most rock and pop music, the second and fourth beats of a measure are accented, typically by the drummer, like this: one TWO three FOUR, one TWO three FOUR. (When you clap your hands to a song, you're probably clapping on two and four.) This "backbeat" is what gives rock-and-roll its rolling rhythm; it is so common that it's noticeable when it is absent.

Although 4/4 is the most common quarter-note time signature, you'll almost definitely run into its close cousin, 3/4. In 3/4 time, you have three quarter notes per measure; the measures are counted "one two three, one two three." If you've ever heard a waltz, you've heard 3/4 time.

Another common quarter-note time signature is 2/4 time. This time signature is common in marches and other fast music, and is very easy to play. After all, two measures of 2/4 add up to one measure of 4/4!

Less common are quarter-note time signatures with more than four beats per measure. For example, 5/4 time feels a little awkward, especially if you're used to feeling the "backbeat" in a 4/4 pop song. But jazz musicians play a lot of 5/4—just listen to the Dave Brubeck Quartet's recording of "Take Five" if you want to hear a great example of playing in five.

The following table shows some of the more common quarter-note time signatures.

Quarter-Note Time Signatures

Time Signature	Beats per Measure	
𝄴 4/4	♩ 1	
2/4	♩ 1	♩ 2

continues

Quarter-Note Time Signatures   (continued)

Time Signature	Beats per Measure
$\frac{3}{4}$	♩ ♩ ♩ 1 2 3
$\frac{4}{4}$	♩ ♩ ♩ ♩ 1 2 3 4
$\frac{5}{4}$	♩ ♩ ♩ ♩ ♩ 1 2 3 4 5
$\frac{6}{4}$	♩ ♩ ♩ ♩ ♩ ♩ 1 2 3 4 5 6
$\frac{7}{4}$	♩ ♩ ♩ ♩ ♩ ♩ ♩ 1 2 3 4 5 6 7
$\frac{8}{4}$	♩ ♩ ♩ ♩ ♩ ♩ ♩ ♩ 1 2 3 4 5 6 7 8
$\frac{9}{4}$	♩ ♩ ♩ ♩ ♩ ♩ ♩ ♩ ♩ 1 2 3 4 5 6 7 8 9

By the way, 4/4 time is sometimes called *common time*, and indicated by a large "C" for the time signature, like this:

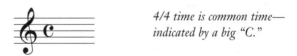

4/4 time is common time—indicated by a big "C."

Eighth-Note Time

Not all music uses a quarter note for the beat. A lot of music—especially classical music—is based on an eighth-note beat.

When you have an eighth-note time signature, such as 3/8 or 6/8, every time you tap your foot you're tapping an eighth note; not a quarter note. So for a measure of 3/8, you'd tap three eighth notes; for a measure of 6/8, you'd tap six eighth notes.

When the eighth note is the beat, half a beat (the "and" after the beat, if you're counting) will be a quarter note. Also, if you see a quarter note in an eighth-note time signature, that note takes up two beats.

It's all about math, basically. When you play in an eighth-note time signature, all your normal note values take up half as much space as they do in a quarter-note time signature. It's simple division.

The most common eighth-note time signatures are those divisible by three: 3/8, 6/8, 9/8, and so on. In fact, when you're playing one of these time signatures and you're playing really fast, you might end up tapping your foot just once every three beats, like this: ONE two three FOUR five six, ONE two three FOUR five six. These time signatures sound a lot like 3/4, the waltz time signature. The following table details the most common eighth-note time signatures.

Eighth-Note Time Signatures

Time Signature	Beats per Measure
$\frac{1}{8}$	♪ 1
$\frac{2}{8}$	♪ ♪ 1 2
$\frac{3}{8}$	♪ ♪ ♪ 1 2 3
$\frac{4}{8}$	♪ ♪ ♪ ♪ 1 2 3 4
$\frac{5}{8}$	♪ ♪ ♪ ♪ ♪ 1 2 3 4 5
$\frac{6}{8}$	♪ ♪ ♪ ♪ ♪ ♪ 1 2 3 4 5 6
$\frac{7}{8}$	♪ ♪ ♪ ♪ ♪ ♪ ♪ 1 2 3 4 5 6 7
$\frac{8}{8}$	♪ ♪ ♪ ♪ ♪ ♪ ♪ ♪ 1 2 3 4 5 6 7 8
$\frac{9}{8}$	♪ ♪ ♪ ♪ ♪ ♪ ♪ ♪ ♪ 1 2 3 4 5 6 7 8 9

Warning

Don't assume that an eighth-note time signature is automatically twice as fast as a quarter-note time signature. Although this might be true (and almost always is true when time signatures change in the middle of a song), the speed of the beat (what musicians call *tempo*) is independent of the time signature. Thus, a song in 3/8 time actually could be played slower than a song in 3/4. (Learn more about tempo in Chapter 7.)

Half Time

If you move the other direction from the basic quarter-note time signature, you get into time signatures based on a half-note beat. In a half-note time signature, each half note gets one beat; quarter notes get half a beat, and eighth notes get a quarter of a beat. Whole notes, on the other hand, get just two beats. (It's not really that confusing; it's just more math to deal with.)

Half-note beats—2/2, 3/2, and the like—are typically used in classical music for slower, more sweeping passages.

The following table presents the most common half-note beats.

Half-Note Time Signatures

Time Signature	Beats per Measure			
$\frac{2}{2}$	♩ 1	♩ 2		
$\frac{3}{2}$	♩ 1	♩ 2	♩ 3	
$\frac{4}{2}$	♩ 1	♩ 2	♩ 3	♩ 4

Just as 4/4 is sometimes called common time, 2/2 is sometimes called *cut time*. You can indicate 2/2 by either the normal time signature, or by a large C with a line through it, like this:

2/2 time is cut-time—thus you cut a "C" in half.

Changing the Time

You always indicate the time signature at the very beginning of a piece of music. However, you don't have to keep the same time signature through the entire song; you can change time anywhere you want in a piece of music; even for just a measure or two!

If the meter changes in the middle of a song, you insert a new time signature at the point of change. This new time signature remains in effect through the rest of the song, or until another new time signature is introduced.

Tip

In most music notation, the time signature is shown only on the first line of music (or when there's a time change)—unlike the key signature, which is typically shown at the start of each line.

Here's what a time change looks like in the middle of a piece of music:

Changing time signatures in the middle of a song.

Grouping the Beats

If you see a piece of music in 9/8 and despair about counting that high (nine's a lot higher than four), there's a way around the problem. You can do as many musicians do: Chop up each measure into smaller groupings.

When you're playing in odd time signatures—especially those with more than four beats per measure—it's common to subdivide the beats within a measure into an easier-to-grasp pattern. Using smaller groupings not only makes each measure easier to count; it also makes the music flow better. When you subdivide measures in this fashion, you create sub-rhythms behind the basic beat, which makes the music easier to listen to.

For example, if you're playing in 6/8 time, you could count all the beats evenly (one, two, three, four, five, six)—or you could subdivide the beat. The most common subdivision of 6/8 divides the measure into two equal parts; each containing three beats, like this:

Subdividing a 6/8 measure into two groups of three.

So you count the measure "one two three; one two three," or "one lah lay, two lah lay." Easier, isn't it?

Of course, you could also divide 6/8 into three groups of two, or one group of four and one group of two, or one group of one and one group of five, but the two groups of three is the most common way to play this particular time signature.

For another example, let's look at 5/4 time. In 5/4, measures are typically subdivided into one group of three and one group of two, like this:

Subdividing 5/4 time into one group of three and one group of two.

You count each measure "one, two, three; one, two."

Of course, you could also reverse the groupings, and end up with two beats in the first group and three beats in the second—"one, two; one, two, three." It depends on the feel and the flow of the music.

The more beats you have in a measure, the more possible groupings you can come up with. To demonstrate, the following example shows three possible groupings of 7/4 time—4+3, 3+4, and 2+3+2.

Three different ways to group 7/4 time.

Just for fun, count all the way up to eleven, and see how many groupings you can come up with for a measure of 11/4!

The Least You Need to Know

◆ You have to place a time signature at the beginning of a piece of music—or anywhere you change the basic meter or time.

◆ The top number in a time signature indicates the number of beats per measure.

◆ The bottom number in a time signature indicates what note is used for the basic beat.

◆ Odd time signatures are sometimes broken up into smaller groupings, to make each measure easier to count.

Exercises

Exercise 6-1

Write the following time signatures on the staff.

3/4	7/8	2/2	5/4	9/8

Exercise 6-2

Enter the appropriate number of quarter notes per measure for each time signature.

$\frac{3}{4}$ $\frac{5}{4}$ $\frac{2}{4}$ $\frac{4}{4}$ $\frac{7}{4}$

Exercise 6-3

Enter the appropriate number of eighth notes for each time signature.

$\frac{7}{8}$ $\frac{3}{8}$ $\frac{9}{8}$ $\frac{6}{8}$ $\frac{2}{8}$

Exercise 6-4

Enter the equivalent eighth-note time signature for each quarter-note time signature.

$\frac{4}{4}$ = $\frac{2}{4}$ = $\frac{8}{4}$ = $\frac{3}{4}$ = $\frac{5}{4}$ =

Exercise 6-5

Enter the equivalent quarter-note time signature for each half-note time signature.

$\frac{2}{2}$ = $\frac{1}{2}$ = $\frac{3}{2}$ = $\frac{5}{2}$ = $\frac{4}{2}$ =

Exercise 6-6

Enter bar lines to divide the following piece of music into four measures of 3/4 time.

Exercise 6-7

Enter bar lines to divide the following piece of music into four measures of 7/8 time.

Exercise 6-8

Group the beats in the following measures three different ways each.

Chapter 7

Tempo, Dynamics, and Navigation

In This Chapter

◆ Determining how fast to play

◆ Changing tempo

◆ Determining how loud to play

◆ Changing dynamics and accenting notes

◆ Repeating parts of a song

You might not have noticed, but the first six chapters of this book taught you how to read and write music. That's right—all those bits about staves, clefs, notes, and rests comprise what we call the standard music notation, which is the common language of all musicians.

Think of it this way: The staff, clef, and key signature determine where a note is in terms of pitch. The time signature and note value determine where a note is in terms of time, or rhythm. By placing a note in this two-dimensional space, you tell a musician everything he or she needs to know to play that note—and all the notes that follow.

The only thing you haven't learned about music notation is how to signify the speed (tempo) and loudness (dynamics) of a piece of music. That's what we'll cover in this chapter, along with some simple navigational aids to help you get from one point to another within a song.

Taking the Pulse

In Chapter 6 you learned how to figure out how many beats there are in a measure. The question remains, however, how fast those beats should be played.

The speed of a piece of music—how fast the beat goes by—is called the *tempo*. A faster tempo means a faster beat; a slower tempo makes for a slower song.

You can indicate tempo in one of two ways: by indicating the precise number of beats per minute or by using traditional Italian terms. We'll discuss both methods next.

Beats per Minute

The most accurate way to indicate tempo is by specifying a certain number of *beats per minute*, or *bpm*. This gives you a very precise speed for your song, especially when you use a *metronome*. You set your metronome to a specific bpm number, and it tick-tocks back and forth at the proper speed. When you play along to the metronome, you're playing at exactly the right tempo.

Setting the tempo—120 quarter-note beats per minute.

= 120

Italian Tempo Terms

The second way to indicate tempo, typically found in orchestral music, is through the use of traditional Italian musical terms. These terms correspond to general tempo ranges, as indicated in the following table, which is arranged from the very slowest to the very fastest tempo.

Italian Tempo Terms

Tempo	Means ...
Slow Tempos (40–75 bpm)	
grave	Very slow; solemn
largo	Slow and dignified
larghetto	A little faster than largo
lento	Slow
adagio	Moderately slow
adagietto	A little faster than adagio

continues

Italian Tempo Terms   (continued)

Tempo	Means ...
Moderate Tempos (70–115 bpm)	
andante	A "walking" tempo
andantino	A little faster than andante
moderato	Moderate pace
allegretto	Not quite as fast as allegro
Fast Tempos (110–220 bpm)	
allegro	Fast, cheerful
vivace	Lively
presto	Very fast
prestissimo	Very very fast

These tempo markings are very approximate, and even the order is not 100 percent observed. The important thing the Italian terms try to get across is the "spirit" of the music. For example, the word *allegro* in Italian really means "cheerful." When these markings are used, the precise tempo is always left to the discretion of the orchestra's conductor.

So when you see a piece of music marked "Allegro," such as Bach's *Brandenburg Concerto No. 6*, you know that it should be played fairly fast. If you see a piece marked "Largo," like the second movement of Dvořák's *New World Symphony*, you know that the tempo should be fairly slow. This method isn't terribly precise, but it will get you in the ballpark.

Tip

Sometimes you'll see these tempo terms accompanied by the word *molto*, which means "very." So if you see *molto vivace*, you know that the music should be played "very lively."

Allegro

Specifying tempo using traditional Italian terms.

Speeding Up—and Slowing Down

Some pieces of music retain the same tempo throughout the entire song (think most popular music here). Other pieces of music speed up and slow down at times; often for dramatic effect.

If a tempo change is immediate—that is, you go directly from one tempo to another, with no gradual transition—you indicate the change by inserting a new tempo marking of your choice. For example, if you've been playing at 120 bpm and want to switch to a faster tempo—160 bpm, let's say—all you have to do is insert a new 160 bpm tempo mark. If you're using Italian tempo markings, just insert the new marking where you want the tempo to change.

If you'd rather gradually speed up or slow down the tempo, it's time to learn a new set of Italian markings. There are several you can use, but the most common are *ritardando* (to gradually slow down the tempo) and *accelerando* (to gradually speed up the tempo). The following table presents all the tempo-changing markings you're likely to encounter:

Indicating Tempo Changes

Indicator	Means ...
ritardando (rit., retard.)	Gradually slow down
rallentando (rall.)	Gradually slow down
ritenuto (riten.)	Hold back the tempo
accelerando (accel.)	Gradually speed up
doppio movimento	Twice as fast
a tempo	Return to the previous tempo
tempo primo	Return to the tempo at the beginning of the piece

Decreasing the tempo using a ritardando marking.

Hold That Note!

Sometimes you don't just want to slow down, you actually want to stop. When you want to ignore the beat and hold a specific note, you use what's called a *fermata*, which looks like a little bird's eye placed on top of a note (or a rest) and indicates a pause in the music. This means you hold that note (or rest) indefinitely or until the conductor cuts you off; then you start up with the next note after the fermata, at normal tempo.

When you see a fermata, hold the note.

Getting Loud—and Getting Soft

You now know how to indicate how fast or how slow a song should be played. How do you indicate how loud or how soft you should play it?

Dynamic Markings

A song's *dynamics* indicate how loud or soft you should play. In the world of music notation, there is a set range of volume levels, from very soft to very loud, that you use to indicate the dynamic level of a piece of music. These dynamic markings are shown in the following table:

Dynamic Markings

Marking	Dynamic	Means ...
ppp	pianississimo	Very, very soft
pp	pianissimo	Very soft
p	piano	Soft
mp	mezzo piano	Medium soft

continues

Dynamic Markings   (continued)

Marking	Dynamic	Means ...
mf	mezzo forte	Medium loud
f	forte	Loud
ff	fortissimo	Very loud
fff	fortississimo	Very, very loud

The dynamic marking, just like the tempo marking, typically appears at the beginning of the song. If you don't see a dynamic marking, that means the song should be played at a medium volume.

Use dynamic markings to indicate how loud a song should be played.

Changing Dynamics

Dynamics can—and do—change throughout the course of a piece of music.

To abruptly change the volume level at a specific point, insert a new dynamic marking. It's okay to indicate dramatic changes in volume; you can go from pp in one measure to ff in the next, if you want.

To gradually change the volume of a song, you have to use what we call *crescendo* and *decrescendo* marks. The crescendo mark (which looks like a giant hairpin, closed at the left and widening to the right) indicates that you gradually increase the volume from your current level to the new level indicated at the end of the crescendo. The decrescendo mark (which looks like a hairpin open at the left and closed at the right) indicates that you gradually decrease the volume from your current level to the new level indicated at the end of the decrescendo.

Crescendos and decrescendos indicate gradual increases or decreases in volume.

Crescendos and decrescendos can be relatively short (just a beat or two) or extend over multiple measures. Obviously, the longer the crescendo or decrescendo, the more gradual is the change in volume.

Tip

The way you can remember whether the marking means to get louder or softer is that the wider the "mouth" of the hairpin, the louder the music. When the mouth is at the left and then narrows, that means you start loud and get softer. When the mouth is at the right, that means you start soft and get louder.

Play It Harder

If you want a specific note to be played louder than the other notes around it, you'll want to place an *accent* mark (>) over that note. When a note is accented, you simply play it louder than a normal note.

To indicate that a note is to be played very loud (or hit very hard, if you're writing a percussion part), you place a *marcato* (^) over the note. This means you play or hit that extra hard—with a good solid punch!

You can use three other markings to indicate a sudden accent. These markings, like all Italian notation, are placed under the note in question, as detailed in the following table.

Italian Accent Markings

Marking	Means ...
fz	Sudden accent (forzando)
sf	Forced (sforzanto)
sfz	Even more forced (sforzando)

Two accent marks and a marcato.

More Dynamics

There are even more musical markings you can use to indicate how loud or soft a piece of music is to be played, although these are less frequently used than those already presented. These additional markings are listed in the following table.

Additional Dynamic Markings

Marking	Means ...
calando	Decreasing tone and speed
con sordino (sordini)	Muted (for horn instruments: use a mute)
diminuendo (dim.)	Gradually become less powerful; diminish in intensity
dolcissimo (dolciss.)	Very gently; sweetly
incalzando	Increasing tone and speed
leggiero	Light, delicate
mancando	Dying away
marcato (marc.)	Marked or emphasized
martellato	Hammered out
mezza voce	In an undertone—literally, "half voice"
morendo	Dying away

continues

Additional Dynamic Markings (continued)

Marking	Means ...
perdendosi	Dying away
senza sordini	Without mutes
smorzando	Dying away
sotto voce	In an undertone
strepitoso	Boisterous
tacet	Silent
tutta forza	As loud as possible
una corda	For pianists: use the soft pedal

Finding Your Way

Reading a long piece of music is a little like reading a roadmap. You'll see various indications in a *score* that provide direction, to repeat a section or to jump to another section within the song.

When you're playing a long piece of music, various parts of the song might be indicated by numbers or by letters. For example, you might see the letter A at the beginning of the first verse, and the letter B at the beginning of the second verse, and the letter C at the start of the chorus. This way other musicians can tell you to start at a specific point in the song by saying "Start at letter B."

Alternatively, the measures of a song might be numbered. If this is the case, you can say "Start at measure 16"; everyone will know what you mean.

In any case, you need some way to determine just where you are in a piece of music; otherwise you'll always have to start at the beginning—even if all you need to practice is the very end!

Definition

A long piece of music (especially in the orchestral environment) is often called a **score**. More precisely, the score is the piece of music the conductor uses, which contains all the parts for all the instruments and voices. The music for each individual instrument is not technically a score, although sometimes people refer to it as such.

Note

Learn more about the various sections of a song in Chapter 11.

Repeating Sections

There are various shorthand methods you can use when writing or arranging a piece of music. Especially useful are various ways to indicate repeating sections, which saves you the trouble of writing out the exact same music two (or more) times.

When you have a section of music that should be repeated, you border that section by a pair of *repeat marks*. One repeat mark indicates the start of the section to be repeated; the other one indicates the end of that section. Unless noted otherwise, you repeat a section only once (that is, you play it twice), and then you move on to the next section.

Use repeat marks to indicate a range of measures to play twice.

Sometimes you'll need to repeat a section but play a slightly different ending the second time through. When you see this in the score—called a *first ending* and a *second ending*—you play the first ending the first time through, and then when you repeat the section you skip the first ending and play the second ending.

Use first and second endings to end a repeated section two different ways.

Definition

"D.S." is short for *Dal Segno*, which means "from the Segno" (or, in English, "from the sign"). "D.C." is short for *Dal Capo*, which means "from the head" or "from the start." (*Capo* is Italian for "head"—literally, the top of the chart.)

You also can repeat a section of a song by returning to a section designated with a sign (called a *Segno* sign). For example, when you see the notation "D.S. al Fine," you jump back to the Segno sign and play through to the end of the song.

Another navigation technique uses a separate section of music called the *Coda*. When you insert a *Coda sign* in your music, that indicates that you should jump to the section marked Coda. A common navigation technique is notated "D.C. al Coda" or "D.C. al Fine," where you jump to the beginning of the song and then follow through to the Coda or the end (Fine). The following table details these and other common Italian navigation markings.

Italian Navigation Markings

Marking	Means ...
D.C. al Fine	Go back to the beginning and play through to the end.
D.C. al Coda	Go back to the beginning and play to the Coda sign; then skip to the Coda section.
D.S. al Fine	Go back to the Segno sign and play through to the end.
D.S. al Coda	Go back to the Segno sign and play to the Coda sign; then skip to the Coda section.

Use the Segno and Coda signs to navigate a piece of music.

Repeating Measures

If you have only a single measure to repeat, you can use a *measure repeat* sign. Just insert this sign between the bar lines *after* the measure you want to repeat; musicians will know to repeat the previous measure.

Use the measure repeat sign to repeat the contents of the previous measure.

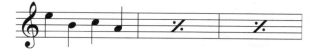

You can use the measure repeat sign in multiple measures. For example, if you have three measures worth of repeat signs, you play the original measure four times (the original time plus three repeats).

Repeating Notes

If you're really lazy, you'll like the fact that you don't always have to write each individual note in a piece of music. If you're repeating notes of the same rhythmic value and pitch, you can use *note repeat* notation to spare yourself the trouble of writing down all those eighth or sixteenth notes in a row.

Note repeats are indicated by drawing slash notes through the main note. One slash mark means play two notes in a row; each equal to half the value of the original note. For example, if you draw a single slash through a quarter note, you play two eighth notes; a single slash through an eighth note means you play two sixteenth notes.

Two slash marks means you play *four* notes in a row; each equal to one quarter the value of the original note. For example, if you draw a double slash through a quarter note, you play four sixteenth notes; a double slash through an eighth note means you play four thirty-second notes. The following table indicates some common note repeat values.

Tip _____

You can also use note repeats on dotted notes. When you put a single slash on a dotted note, you play three notes of the next-higher value; when you put a double slash on a dotted note, you play *six* notes of the second-higher value.

Note Repeat Markings

Marking	Equals ...

Repeating Rests

There's one last bit of repeat notation you need to know—and it concerns resting; not playing. In much orchestral music, each individual instrument spends a lot of time not playing. While the composer could indicate all this inactivity by writing lots of individual measures full of whole rests, it is more common (and a lot easier) to indicate the total number of measures the instrument will rest. This is done by using a multiple-measure rest sign in a single measure, with a number written above the rest. The number indicates how many measures of rest there are. For example, a multiple-measure rest with the number 6 written above indicates that that instrument is supposed to rest for six measures.

Use a multiple-measure rest sign to indicate multiple measures of rest; in this example, six measures.

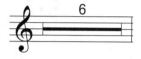

The Least You Need to Know

- The tempo of a piece of music can be indicated by traditional Italian markings or by a specific "beats per minute" instruction.

- You indicate changes in tempo by using Italian markings such as ritardano (slow down) and accelerando (speed up).

- The volume level of a piece of music is typically indicated by the use of traditional Italian dynamic markings, from pianissimo (*pp*) to fortissimo (*ff*).

- You indicate changes in dynamics by using crescendo (get louder) and decrescendo (get softer) markings.

- When you want a single note played louder than normal, use an accent mark.

- You navigate an entire piece of music using repeat signs and various Italian markings. (For example, D.C. al Coda means to go back to the beginning, play to the Coda sign; then jump to the Coda section.)

Exercises

Exercise 7-1

Play the following piece of music, paying strict attention to the tempo markings.

Exercise 7-2

Play the following piece of music, paying strict attention to the dynamic markings.

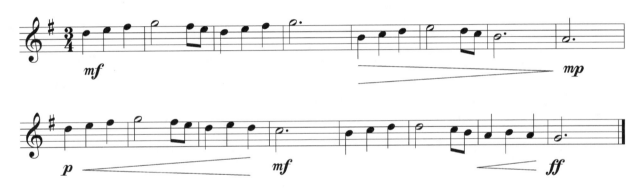

Exercise 7-3

Play the following piece of music, paying strict attention to the repeat signs and navigation markings.

Part 3

Tunes

Discover how to put tones and rhythms together to create a melody; then learn how to add chords to your tunes. You'll also find out all about chord progressions and song forms—everything you need to know to create your own songs and pieces of music.

Chapter 8

Melodies

In This Chapter

- Creating a melody from tones and rhythms
- Analyzing existing melodies
- Composing your first melody
- Discovering what makes a melody memorable

In the first part of this book (Chapters 1 through 4), you learned all about notes and pitches. In the second part (Chapters 5 through 7), you learned all about note values and rhythms. By themselves, pitches and rhythms don't amount to much. But when you combine them, they create something wonderful—a *melody*.

Melody is defined as a logical progression of tones and rhythms—a tune set to a beat. But pay close attention to that word "logical." A melody isn't a random conglomeration of notes; the notes have to relate to and follow from each other. In other words, a melody has to make sense, or else it's just a bunch of noise.

That textbook definition of melody, however precise, doesn't go far enough for my tastes. To me, a melody is the most memorable part of a piece of music. It's the song you sing, the notes you hum, the musical line that stays in your mind long after the record is over or the band has stopped playing. The best melodies pack an emotional punch; they make us jump with joy or weep with sadness. When done right, melodies can tell a story without words, or reinforce the meaning of a song's lyrics.

If you want to compose or arrange music—or even improvise to an existing song—you have to know how to create a memorable melody. That's where this chapter comes in—it's all about the art of melody.

Combining Tones and Rhythms

If you think back to Chapter 1, you'll remember how we discussed various ways to describe the tones in the song "Mary Had a Little Lamb." We finally settled on the traditional labeling of tones using the letters A through G. Each tone in the song is assigned a letter corresponding to its precise pitch; anyone reading the letters knows which tone to sing or play.

Assigning tones, of course, is only half the story. When you sing "Mary Had a Little Lamb," you give each tone a specific rhythmic value; each tone takes up a specific place in time. The rhythm of the song is described by using different note values, the half notes and quarter notes that we call music notation.

By combining the pitch values with the rhythmic values, we can now notate the entire melody of "Mary Had a Little Lamb." The notes on the staff tell us what pitches to sing; the note values tell us how long to sing each pitch.

The result looks like this:

The complete melody for "Mary Had a Little Lamb."

All melodies are described using similar notation. You set the key signature and the time signature up front, and then fill in the notes of the melody from there. Naturally, you have to arrange the notes within measures, with each measure holding the appropriate number of beats. When you're done writing down the notes, you've written your melody.

Common Melodic Techniques

Every song—every piece of music—has a melody. Some longer pieces (such as much orchestral music) have multiple melodies. Some melodies consist of multiple parts, with different parts repeated in different parts of the song. However the music is constructed, the melody is the heart of the song—the part you should be able to sing or hum or whistle all by itself, with no other instruments needed.

To get a feel for how melodies are constructed, let's take a look at some melodies from well-known pieces of music. You'll see that although they all have their distinct sound and feel, these melodies also have a lot of factors in common.

Dvořák's *New World Symphony*

We'll start with a tune from Antonin Dvořák's *Symphony #9 in E minor* ("From the New World")—more popularly known as the *New World Symphony*. This is a popular piece of orchestral music, and consists of several different sections; the melody we'll look at is just one of many used throughout the work, and it goes like this:

One of the main melodies in Dvořák's New World Symphony.

Let's first get a feel for the mechanics of the melody. As you can see, the time signature for this melody is 4/4, so there are four quarter-note beats in each measure. The key signature is D♭, with five flats. When you listen to it, the melody has a happy sound, which means it's in a major key—D♭ Major, to be precise. The piece of the melody we're looking at is four measures long.

If you look at (or listen to) this melody carefully, you'll see that it breaks into two two-measure phrases. The first two measures end on a note (E♭) that doesn't feel like an ending note (it's the second note in the scale); this sets up a kind of tension that you want to hear resolved. The second two measures resolve the tension by effectively repeating the first two measures, but ending on a more satisfying tone—D♭, the tonic of the scale.

This is a common technique, setting up some sort of tension in the first part of the melody that is then resolved in the second part. This helps to make a melody interesting; if you think about it, it's also a very logical, symmetrical, almost mathematical construction. (If you look at it like a mathematical formula, the first half of the melody "equals" the second half.)

Another technique used in this melody is the repetition of specific rhythms. Look at the rhythmic pattern used throughout—dotted eighth note, sixteenth note, and quarter note. This "dum de duh" pattern is played twice in the first measure, and twice again in the third measure, establishing a kind of rhythmic signature for the entire piece. This rhythmic repetition helps to establish a familiarity for the listener; you hear the rhythm once, then you hear it again, and it feels familiar; almost comfortable. In fact, a listener *expects* to hear some repetition; if every measure of a melody is completely different from all the preceding measures, the melody will be difficult to remember.

Bach's *Minuet in G*

Our next example is Johann Sebastian Bach's *Minuet in G*—although you might be familiar with it as the melody of the pop song "A Lover's Concerto," performed by the Toys back in the mid-1960s.

(I confess to stealing this example from the movie *Mr. Holland's Opus*, where music teacher Glenn Holland—played by Richard Dreyfuss—uses this tune to show his students the relevancy of classical music to the pop music they listen to on the radio.)

The melody for Bach's Minuet in G—*also appropriated for the pop song "A Lover's Concerto."*

This melody differs from Dvořák's melody in a number of ways. First, it's in 3/4 time; not 4/4. Second, it's in the key of G, and is based on the G Major scale.

Beyond those differences, there are a lot of similar techniques in use. Note the rhythmic repetition between measures 1-2 and 3-4, and the continued repetition of the first measure in measures 5 through 7. Also note the very slight tension created in measure 4 (the end of the first half of the melody—it sounds like there's more coming), which is then resolved in the second half of the melody.

There's something else interesting about this particular melody. The first half of the melody has an insistent upward motion; the second half uses a downward motion to deposit you pretty much where you started. Even though not all the notes go up (or down), the general flow of the melody moves in those directions, and thus propels the melody forward.

You need to have some sort of motion in a melody, or you'll put the listener to sleep. That motion can be in the tune, or in the rhythm, but it needs to be there, to help the melody get from point a to point b.

Michael, Row the Boat Ashore

Next up is the traditional folk song "Michael, Row the Boat Ashore." The words to this tune, simple as they are, can actually help us see the melodic form. When you read the words, you can clearly see that the song consists of two near-identical halves—rhythmically, anyway.

The melody for the folk song "Michael, Row the Boat Ashore."

> **Note**
>
> The two quarter notes before measure one are called *pickup notes;* that little half measure is called a *pickup measure.* You use pickup notes and measures when the melody actually starts up before the first beat of the first measure.

The first time Michael rows his boat ashore (hallelujah!), the melody has a slight upward motion, and ends with a slight bit of tension on the fifth note of the scale (A). The second time Michael goes boating, the melody sways downward slightly, and resolves itself by ending on the tonic of the key (D).

Symmetry, repetition, tension, and release—these techniques are used over and over to create memorable melodies.

Pachelbel's *Canon in D*

Our final melody is a bit different from the ones we've examined so far. It's different because rhythmically, it's very simple—nothing but half notes.

You've probably heard this melody before—it's Johann Pachelbel's *Canon in D* (sometimes just called "Pachelbel's Canon"—like he only wrote this one!) and it's been used in a number of different movies and television shows. You might have even heard it in the background of a commercial for GE light bulbs back in the 1990s. (They bring good things to light.) In any case, it's a compelling melody, despite its rhythmic simplicity.

The very simple melody for Pachelbel's Canon in D.

This melody also is different in that it doesn't use a lot of symmetry or repetition. (Except for the repeated half notes, of course!) It's actually the stepwise intervals between the notes that propel this melody forward; each pitch leaning forward to the next, one after another, almost in a giant spinning circle of tones. And then the last note, C#, is the leading tone of the scale (D Major); you jump back to F# (the third of the scale) and start all over again.

The point of examining this particular melody is that you don't need fancy rhythms to create a memorable melody. Pure tones, played slowly and simply, can be quite lyrical—if you pick the right ones!

Composing Your First Melody

Now that you know some of the techniques you can use to create a melody, let's put those techniques to work.

As you learned with Pachelbel's *Canon*, a melody doesn't have to include complex rhythms. The right notes on the right pitches are what you need to start any new tune.

One of the primary rules of composing is to base your melody on a specific scale. And, as you'll learn in Chapter 9, there are three notes in a scale which, when played together, create what we call a *major triad*. These three notes represent a good place to start for our first melody.

For simplicity's sake, let's start in the key of C, using the C Major scale. The three notes we want to use are the tonic, the third, and the fifth—C, E, and G. So let's start our melody with two half notes and a whole note, starting with C and progressing up to G on the whole note.

This gives us the first two measures of the melody:

The first two measures of our first melody.

Let's elaborate on these notes a bit. If you want to give the melody a little more of a flow, you can fill in the blanks between these three notes by adding notes in the step between each pitch. We'll do this by turning the half notes into quarter notes, and adding *passing tones* between the C and the E, and the E and G. (That means we'll go from C to D to E, and from E to F to G.)

The result looks like this:

The first two measures, with passing tones added.

Definition

A **passing tone** is a subsidiary tone you have to pass through to move from one important note to another. The passing tone is not part of the underlying chord structure, but is often situated between two of the notes in a triad.

Definition

You create a **neighboring tone** by starting on a pitch, moving up or down by a step (either half or whole) and then returning to the original pitch; the neighboring tone is the one that "neighbors" the original note. Like a passing tone, a neighboring tone typically is not one of the three notes in the underlying chord triad.

We're still left with that single whole note sitting there. It's okay to leave it like that, but doing so makes this part of our melody sound like nothing more than a simple major scale—which it actually is! Fortunately, we can choose to add a little more interest by using another technique called a *neighboring tone*, in which you land on the main note (in this case, the G), slide briefly to an adjacent note, and then return to rest on the main note (G, again). The result sounds a little like "doo-de-doo," which is slightly more interesting than a plain "doo."

You can place neighboring tones above or below the main tone; for our little melody, we'll use the neighboring tone above the G—which happens to be an A. Keeping the rhythm simple, we'll now start the second measure with a quarter note on G; then follow it by a quarter note on A and a half note on G.

The result looks like this:

Embellishing the melody with a neighboring tone.

This is a nice little melody—but it's really only half of a melody. Ending on the fifth note of the scale, as it does, actually sets up some melodic tension. When you hear this melody, you want to resolve the tension, and somehow get things back to where they started—on C.

There's an easy way to do this, of course. All you have to do is create a sort of mirror image of the first two measures, but with a downward motion from G to C.

The first thing we'll do is copy the first measure into a new third measure—except we'll copy it with the first note starting on G, and with the quarter notes moving down in a G F E D progression. (Note that this progression puts two of the C Major triad notes—G and E—on the primary beats of the measure: one and three.) Then we'll end the run with a whole note in the fourth measure, positioned on the tonic note: C.

Your completed melody looks like this:

Your completed melody—play it loud and proud!

That wasn't so difficult, was it? Granted, this melody won't win any Grammy awards, but it is a legitimate melody, and it's quite singable. (Trust me, I've heard worse.) The key thing is that you've seen that creating a melody isn't hard, as long as you know the basic theory involved.

What Makes a Melody Memorable?

All of this brings us to the key question: How exactly can you create a memorable melody?

It certainly helps to have a little soul and inspiration, of course, but you also can employ some very reliable techniques to ensure that you create a melody that works, and will stick in the listener's memory after he or she hears it. We'll go through a number of these techniques next, with the caveat that these aren't necessarily "rules"—it's possible to do just the opposite of what I recommend and still create a great-sounding melody. (Which means there must be *some* art involved, doesn't it?)

Center on a Pitch

You don't want your melodies wandering around all over the place, like a dog looking for a place to do his business. What you want is more of a hunting dog of a melody, one that knows where home is and, at the end of the day, finds its way back there.

The "home" of your melody needs to be a specific pitch. When you pick a home pitch, your melody can then revolve around the pitch. You can start on that pitch (although you don't have to), and you should end on that pitch. Equally important, the other notes in the melody can play around that pitch—and even land on it, occasionally.

Note that your home pitch doesn't have to be the tonic of the scale. You can make the third your home, or the fifth—but probably not the second or sixth or seventh, because they're less related to the tonic triad of 1-3-5.

For example, listen to the following melody. It's in the key of G, but revolves around the home pitch of B—the third of the scale.

A four-measure melody in the key of G, which hovers around the third of the scale (B).

What you want to avoid is having each measure of your melody center around a different pitch. If your melody wanders around in this type of fashion, with no central core, you won't know how to end the melody—you won't know where home is.

Make Sure You End Up at Home

Many of the most memorable melodies use the home pitch to lend logic to the melodic flow. In fact, it's good if your audience can listen to part of your melody and, based on the prominence of the home note, hum the end of the melody before they ever hear it.

When you don't end your melody on the expected note, you create an unresolved tension that can be unsettling to listeners. Although it's okay to insert that kind of tension in the middle of your melody, you don't want to end with that kind of tension. You want to resolve your melody so that there's a feeling of completion at the end.

What you want to avoid is a melody that wanders around aimlessly. Let your ear be your guide. Play over the melody and see if it holds together. It's a little bit like writing a good paragraph or a good stanza of a poem; when you're finished, the best thing to do is to read it aloud and see if it really works.

The wrong way to do it—you don't want to end your melody with unresolved tension.

Stay Within the Scale

When you're picking the specific notes for your melody, it's good to pick a particular scale—and stay within the seven notes of that scale. For example, if you decide to write in the key of F Major, your melody will include the notes F, G, A, B♭, C, D, and E. Used properly, none of these notes will sound out of place.

A melody that uses the F Major scale.

Conversely, if you're writing in F Major and throw a D♭ into your melody, that note will sound out of place. Although it's possible to use these nonscale (chromatic) notes in a melody, it's probably not something you, as a beginner, should try. Composing a melody using chromatic notes requires a degree of harmonic sophistication that seldom comes naturally—although it can be developed with practice.

> **Tip**
>
> Instead of basing your melody on a major or minor scale, you can base it on one of the church modes—Aeolian, Dorian, Lydian, and so forth—discussed back in Chapter 3.

By the way, when you choose a scale for your melody, it doesn't have to be a major scale. Let's say we're still in the key of F, but you want to write a less lively, more poignant-sounding melody. For this type of melody, you might choose to use the D minor scale (which uses one flat, as with the key of F). When you write this type of melody, you'll probably center on the tonic triad of D minor (D, F, and A) rather than the tonic triad of F Major (F, A, and C).

Use the Big Five

You can make things even simpler by sticking to five key notes within a given major scale—the first, second, third, fifth, and sixth of the scale. (In C Major, these notes are C, D, E, G, and A.)

> **Tip**
>
> On a piano, an easy way to see and play a pentatonic scale is to play strictly on the black keys. These five keys—G♭, A♭, B♭, D♭, and E♭—comprise the G♭ pentatonic scale.

These notes combine for what is called the *pentatonic* scale. (The word *penta* means five; five tones equal a pentatonic scale.) By using only these five notes, you avoid the two notes in the scale (the fourth and the seventh) that sometimes create harmonic tension.

When you use the five notes in the pentatonic scale, it's virtually impossible to insert a "wrong" note into your melody. However, you can overuse these notes and end up with a vaguely Oriental-sounding tune—or even something that sounds a little bit like the theme to an old cowboy movie!

A melody based on the C pentatonic scale.

Find the Hook

For a melody to be truly memorable, there needs to be a piece of your melody that really reaches out and grabs the listener's attention. In pop music this is called the *hook*, because it's the part of the song that hooks the listener. In more traditional music, this piece of the song is sometimes known as the *motif* (or *motive*)—and is repeated throughout the entire piece of music.

A motif is typically fairly short—a few notes (think of the five whistling notes in Sergio Leone's theme from the movie *The Good, the Bad and the Ugly*) or, at longest, one or two measures. When you hit on a good motif or hook, don't be afraid to use it—repeat it as often as you need, throughout your entire song.

A simple four-note motif, repeated throughout a longer melody.

Create Variations

You can also use your motif to create additional melodies in your music by varying the motif slightly, changing the rhythm, or moving the tones up or down in the scale. You should retain enough of the main motif so that listeners can tell where it came from, but add enough variation so that you create a new—but related—melody.

How can you vary a motif? You can reverse the rhythm, simplify the rhythm, or make the rhythm more complex. You can reverse the notes (so that the melody goes up instead of down, or down instead of up), or change the middle notes in the motif, or shift the notes up or down a third or a fifth. In short, just about any variation is fair game, as long as the initial motif isn't completely obliterated by the variations.

Take a look at the following example, in which the simple four-note motif from the previous example is run through a number of variations—both rhythmically and melodically.

The same four-note motif, with variations.

Remember that you want your variations to relate to the original motif. If you get too far away from the original motif, it isn't a variation anymore—it's a brand-new melody!

Write in Four—or Eight, or Sixteen

When you're composing a melody, it helps to keep the lengths of the parts of the melody (the motifs and phrases) relatively simple. In most Western music—popular music, especially—most melodies can be divisible by two. That means you probably want your melody to be two, four, eight, or sixteen measures long. You probably don't want to write a three- or five-measure melody; writing to an odd number of measures may feel wrong to some of your listeners.

When you write a longer melody, you can divide it up into two- or four- or eight-measure chunks. For example, the following sixteen-measure melody is constructed from four four-measure parts.

Note

One notable exception to this 2/4/8/16 rule is the genre we call the blues. Most blues music uses a twelve-measure form, with twelve-measure melodies. (To learn more about the blues form, see Chapter 11.)

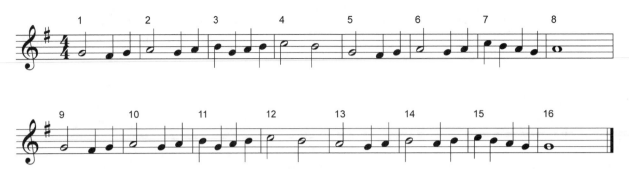

A sixteen-measure melody, consisting of four four-measure phrases.

Make It Move

A good melody doesn't just sit there; it goes someplace. You can propel a melody rhythmically, or tonally, through the "motion" of the tones. In this sense, motion refers to the progressive upward or downward direction of the pitches, or what some call the *contour* of a line of music.

A good way to think about the upward or downward motion of a melody is to look at the starting note and the ending note—while ignoring, for the time being, all the notes in between. To create an upward-moving melody, make sure the ending note is at least a third (and ideally a fifth or more) higher than the starting note. Same thing with a downward-moving melody; force the last note to be lower than the first one.

All the notes between the first and last notes help you move to that final note. The notes don't all have to go in the same direction, but they do have to gradually move up or down to where you want to end.

A melody with upward motion.

Note that it's okay to have a melody that starts and ends on the same note. What you can do is make the midpoint of the melody higher or lower than the starting/ending pitch. If you choose a higher midpoint, the first half of the melody will have upward movement, and the last half will use downward movement to return to the home pitch.

Take Small Steps

The most singable melodies progress in small steps, which means each note is only a step or two away from the previous note. The smaller the steps between the notes in your melody, the more lyrical your melody will sound.

Definition

A melody that progresses in half or whole steps uses what is called *step-wise* or *conjunct* motion. Melodies that progress by leaps larger than a whole step use what is called *disjunct* motion.

When you throw large jumps—of three or more steps—into your melody, it starts sounding random, and becomes much more difficult to play or sing. It's much better to use a series of passing notes within your chosen scale to move from one main note to another.

Obviously, this isn't a hard and fast rule. (And every rule is meant to be broken, anyway!) Think, for example, of "Somewhere Over the Rainbow," or "Moon River," or "When You Wish Upon a Star." All of these songs feature leaps of anywhere from a fifth to an entire octave in their melodies. So it's okay to leap, if you know what you're doing—although small steps are better suited for less-experienced songwriters.

Small steps and large leaps in a melody—the small steps sound more lyrical and are easier to sing.

Stay in Range

You don't want to cover too many notes in your melody. If the distance between the lowest note and the highest note is too wide, singers will have trouble singing all of your melody—and your melody will start to sound random and disjointed, without a home.

Consider, for example, America's national anthem, "The Star-Spangled Banner." Francis Scott Key put his words to one whopper of a tune—one that had a rather wide melodic range. Think of how hard this song is to sing—and how many well-trained vocalists have trouble hitting all the notes. The broad range in this song doesn't make it a bad song; it just makes it one of the more difficult songs to sing or play.

> **Note**
>
> Ironically, the melody of "The Star-Spangled Banner" comes from an English drinking song called "Anacreon in Heaven." Maybe the high notes are easier to hit after a few pints of Guinness!

Thus, if at all possible keep the lowest and highest notes in your melody within an octave of each other. (Or, at most, within an octave and a third.) You should also consider the absolute range of the voice or instrument you're writing for, and try to stay within that range. (To learn more about voice and instrument ranges, turn to Chapter 19.)

A melody with too wide a range—really hard to sing!

Avoid Unsingable Intervals

While we're on the topic of singability, certain intervals are easier to sing than others. Half steps and whole steps are easy to sing, as are seconds, thirds, and fifths. Some fourths, for some reason, are a little more difficult to sing, and sixths and sevenths are particularly problematic.

Octaves aren't by nature difficult—a C is a C is a C, whether it's high or low—although the shear distance between the notes adds a degree of difficulty for singers. Along the same lines, any interval over an octave should probably be avoided, just because it's such a big jump.

> **Tip**
>
> As with all things musical, the real test is in the singing. Whatever intervals you use, try to sing them, and then check what you sing against the piano. If you have trouble singing a particular interval, so will others—and the best melodies are the easiest to sing.

Chromatic intervals—notes that aren't in the underlying scale—are very difficult for most singers to sing. For example, if you're in the key of C and your melody jumps from an E to a G♭, a lot of singers won't be able to hit that second note. They'll want to sing either an F or G, both of which are in the scale; the G♭ takes a lot of concentration to hit, out of the blue.

There's another chromatic interval you should avoid at all costs, called a *tritone*; it's (depending on how you look at it) a raised (augmented) fourth or a flatted (diminished) fifth. The tritone just plain sounds wrong; some early music theorists considered this the "Devil's interval," and the musical equivalent of evil. (Go ahead, play a tritone—F to B, for example—and see how difficult it is to sing.)

Don't *put tritones in your melodies!*

Keep the Rhythm Simple

At least when you're starting out, it helps to keep the rhythm of your melody relative simple. That means sticking to quarter notes and half notes, and using sixteenth notes sparingly.

It also means avoiding, for the time being, what we call *syncopation*. Syncopation makes for a jumpy melody, and is hard for some singers to sing.

Definition

Syncopation means there's an emphasis in a place you're not expecting it—or when there *isn't* an emphasis where you *were* expecting it. You can create a syncopated rhythm by accenting something other than the downbeat—or by putting a rest on the downbeat. This type of change-up creates rhythmic patterns that might sound "off" to some listeners but often have kind of a funky or jazzy feel.

Syncopated rhythms may be created by using a short rest on the downbeat or other strong beats. If you find yourself writing a melody that sounds just a little too "jerky," consider simplifying the rhythm and using more straight eighth and quarter notes—on the beat.

Simplifying a rhythmically complex melody.

Stay in Time

It's also possible, especially when you're first starting out, to create a melody that doesn't strictly follow the pattern of your chosen time signature. For example, you could create a six-beat melody, which doesn't fit well in a four-beat 4/4 world.

A melody that doesn't follow the normal bar-line breaks.

You want to pace your melody so that it fits within your chosen time signature. That means creating a melody that can easily be divided into measures, without having extra beats left over. In fact, it's a good exercise to write out your melody without bar lines, and then make sure you can easily figure out where to draw the bars to create your measures. If you can't easily fit your melody into measures, think about rephrasing your rhythms, or changing the rest periods between sections of your melody.

Along the same lines, make sure you can easily tell where the first beat of the measure is throughout your melody—especially in the first and last measures. You don't want your melody to feel "offbeat," in the strictest sense of the phrase. You want your melody to end on a beat that feels right; otherwise your listeners will find themselves stumbling in place when "one" isn't where it's supposed to be.

> **Note**
>
> More-experienced composers are capable of changing time signatures within a melody, thus accommodating lines that don't fit within a steady time signature flow.

Set Up—and Resolve—Tension

One of the most common melodic techniques is to divide your melody into two parts, and set up a harmonic tension in the first part that is then resolved in the second part. This gives your melody a distinct form, and its own internal logic; it also helps to propel the melody from the first part to the second.

One way to create tension is to end the first part of your melody on something other than the tonic of the scale. (When you're factoring in the chord structure—which you'll learn in Chapter 10—you'll find that tension is achieved by ending the first part of the melody on a IV or V chord.) Practically, you can create tension by ending a phrase with the second, fifth, or seventh notes of the scale—which correspond to the notes in the scale's V chord, if you're reading ahead.

The half note in measure two creates tension; the next two bars resolve the tension.

You then have to relieve this tension by manipulating the second part of your melody back to the tonic of the scale—or to one of the notes in the tonic triad (the I chord). The notes in the tonic triad are the tonic, third, and fifth of the scale, although the tonic and the third probably work better for relieving tension. (That's because the fifth is an ambiguous note, used both in the I chord and the V chord; again, read ahead to Chapter 10 to learn all about chord progressions.)

In any case, you can hear the tension when you play a melody. Just look back to Dvořák's *New World Symphony* or "Michael, Row the Boat Ashore." For that matter, "Mary Had a Little Lamb" also has this type of internal tension, coming right after "Mary had a little lamb, little lamb, little lamb," and resolved with "Mary had a little a lamb, whose fleece was white as snow."

It's a popular technique—because it works!

Set Up a Call and Response

Another effective technique to employ in your melodies is that of *call and response*. This is where you set up a phrase in the first part of your melody, and then "answer" that phrase in the second part. This is slightly different from the technique of tension and release, although the call does set up a certain tension that demands a tension-relieving answer.

To create a call and response type of melody, it helps to think of a question—and its answer. For example, you might think of the question, "Where is my car?" and the answer, "It's in the street." When you put this call and response to music, you might get something like this:

A simple call-and-response melody.

Establish Symmetry

A technique that is somewhat implied in both the tension-and-relief and call-and-response techniques is that of symmetry. By this I mean that the second part of your melody should be somewhat of a mirror image of the first part of your melody.

You can achieve this symmetry by mirroring rhythms, or by mirroring tones. Take Dvořák's *New World Symphony*, for example. Measure 3 is identical to measure 1, thus setting up the symmetry between the two parts of the tune. "Michael, Row the Boat Ashore" has a rhythmic symmetry between the two parts, even though the tones used change a bit. (Sometimes the tones *have* to change, to relieve the harmonic tension or answer a melodic call.)

In any case, when you make the second part of your melody resemble the first part, you establish a familiarity in the mind and ear of the listener, so they know (pretty much) what to expect and feel comfortable when you deliver it to them.

The last two bars are a near–mirror image of the first two measures.

Balance Repetition and Variety

Repetition is part and parcel of symmetry—and of establishing motifs and hooks. You find a melodic or rhythmic figure that you like, and you repeat it throughout the course of the melody or song. This sort of repetition, such as that shown in the following example, helps to unify your melody; it's the melodic equivalent of a steady drumbeat, and serves as an identifying factor for listeners.

However, too much of a good thing can get annoying. If you repeat your figure too often, it will start to bore the listener. It's hard to say how much repetition is too much repetition, but chances are you'll be able to tell—or your listeners will tell you.

When you find yourself using too much repetition, it's time to trot out the variations—or to add completely new melodic or rhythmic figures. Balancing repetition and variety is an essential skill to learn, and marks a key difference between a novice and an experienced composer.

Follow the Chord Progressions

I've mentioned chords and chord progressions a few times in this chapter, because chords and progressions contribute significantly to the melodies you compose. However, I haven't presented chords yet, because I feel it's important to master a single melodic line before you start stacking multiple notes on top of each other.

That said, after you've read Chapters 9 and 10, you'll probably want to return to this chapter and apply what you've learned. That's because one very useful approach to composing melodies is to come up with a chord progression first, and then add a melody on top of that. Of course, you can't do this until you learn about chords.

After you've read Chapters 9 and 10, you'll better understand how to create—and resolve—harmonic tension in a melody, using certain chords. For example, you'll discover that the most common chord progression is I-IV-V, or some variation of that. (In the key of C, the chords would be C Major, F Major, and G Major.) The IV and V chords (the V chord, especially) are used to create tension; you often end the first part of your melody with the V chord. You resolve tension by getting back to the I chord, which is the reason you almost always end your tunes with the I chord. When your melodies follow these chords, you establish the kind of tension and relief that makes for a memorable melody.

Your melody needs to fit within the chord structure of your song, as you'll also learn in Chapter 10. This means that, within a specific measure, the main notes of your melody probably should fit within the three main notes of the underlying chord. For example, if you have an A minor chord, the main notes of the melody accompanying that chord should probably be A, C, or E—the three notes in the chord.

Again, you'll learn more about chords and progressions in the next two chapters, so be patient—it will all be explained, in due course!

Follow the Form

Most songs follow some sort of established song form. That means that your melodies should fit within that form, as well.

You'll learn more about song forms in Chapter 11, but here's a brief example: A lot of popular songs are divided into verses and choruses. The verse is the first melody, which is repeated throughout the song. The chorus is a second melody, often the main melody (containing the hook), which is played between verses. So a typical pop music song form might look like this: verse-verse-chorus-verse. That means you'll need to write two melodies for the song, which must be related in some way.

After you read Chapter 11, you should return to this chapter to apply what you've learned about form to your basic melodic skills.

Follow the Words

Another factor that can drive a melody is the presence of lyrics. If you're writing an instrumental, of course, you don't have to worry about following the words. But if you're writing a popular song, you have to deal with both music and words—and how they fit together.

You want your music to fit with your words. In the simplest sense, this means arranging the rhythm of the music so that it fits the natural rhythm of the words. You don't want your singers to be forced into awkward phrasing to fit all the syllables into a given space. Most words and phrases have a natural pace, and will suggest a rhythm to you. Make sure your music's rhythm fits this lyric rhythm—in particular, avoid putting an unaccented word or syllable on an accented part of the measure, like the downbeat.

You also want the flow of your melody to match the flow of the words. For example, if the words ask a question, you probably want the melody to flow upward, to imitate the way a human voice ends a question on a higher pitch.

In addition, you want the feel of the music to match the feel of the lyrics. If the lyrics are sad, you probably don't want to set them to a happy-sounding melody. There are exceptions to this rule, of course—mismatching words and lyrics can create a sense of musical irony that is appropriate in some situations—but in general, you want your melody to reflect the feel of the lyrics, even when played without vocals.

Note

See Chapter 19 for more information about instrumental and vocal ranges.

Write for a Specific Instrument, or a Voice

Finally, the type of melody you compose might be dictated by the specific voices or instruments you're writing for. For example, if you're writing for flutes, you probably don't want to create a booming, bombastic melody—they won't be able to play it. By the same token, writing too high a melody will be difficult for low male voices to sing. You need to find not only the right range for a given voice or instrument, but also the right *feel*. Match the requirements of your melody with the right voices and instruments to avoid an unpleasant listening experience.

The Least You Need to Know

- ♦ A melody consists of a logical progression of tones and rhythms.
- ♦ Melodies typically follow a two-, four-, eight-, or sixteen-measure form.
- ♦ Melodies typically conform to a specific scale or mode.
- ♦ The best melodies are often the simplest—in terms of both tune and rhythm.
- ♦ Longer melodies can typically be divided into two parts, with the end of the first part creating a tension that is resolved in the second part.
- ♦ You should make sure that your melodies are truly singable—and the only way to do this is to see if you can sing them!

Exercises

Exercise 8-1

Complete the last two measures of this four-measure melody.

Exercise 8-2

Complete the last two measures of this four-measure melody.

Exercise 8-3

Compose an eight-measure melody in the key of C, using the C Major scale, in 4/4 time. Use whole notes, half notes, quarter notes, and eighth notes; and begin and end your melody on the C note.

Exercise 8-4

Compose an eight-measure melody in the key of F, using the D minor scale, in 3/4 time. Use half notes, quarter notes, and eighth notes; and begin and end your melody on the D note.

Exercise 8-5

Compose an eight-measure melody in the key of G, using the G Major scale, in 4/4 time. Make this a rhythmically lively melody at a relatively fast tempo, using half notes, quarter notes, eighth notes, and sixteenth notes.

Chapter 9

Chords

In This Chapter

◆ Understanding major, minor, diminished, and augmented triads

◆ Extending chords to sevenths, ninths, and beyond

◆ Creating altered, suspended, and power chords

◆ Inverting the chord order

◆ Writing chords into your music

More often than not, music is more than a single melodic line. Music is a package of tones, rhythms, and underlying harmonic structure. The melody fits within this harmonic structure, is dependent on this harmonic structure, and in some cases dictates the harmonic structure.

The harmonic structure of a piece of music is defined by a series of *chords*. A chord is a group of notes played simultaneously, rather than sequentially (like a melody). The relationships between the notes—the intervals within the chord—define the type of chord; the placement of the chord within the underlying key or scale defines the role of the chord.

This chapter is all about chords—and it's a long one, because there are many, many different types of chords. Don't let all the various permutations scare you off, however; at the core, a chord is nothing more than single notes (typically separated by thirds) played together.

It's as simple as that. If you can play three notes at the same time, you can play a chord.

This chapter, then, shows you how to construct many different types of chords, with a particular emphasis on the type of harmonic structure you find in popular music. (This is important; the study of harmony in classical music is much more involved, with a slightly different set of rules.) And, when you're done reading this chapter, you can find a "cheat sheet" to all the different chords in Appendix B. This appendix is a quick yet comprehensive reference to every kind of chord imaginable—in every key!

Forming a Chord

Okay, here's the formal definition: A chord is a combination of three or more notes played together.

Let's do a little exercise: Sit down at the nearest piano and put your right thumb on one of the white keys. (It doesn't matter which one.) Now skip a key and put another finger on the third key. Skip another key and put a third finger on the fifth key. You should now be pressing three keys, with an empty key between each finger. Press down and listen to the music—you're playing a chord!

> **Note**
>
> The notes of a chord don't always have to be played in unison. You can play the notes one at a time, starting (usually, but not always) with the bottom note. This is called *arpeggiating* the chord, and the result is an *arpeggio*.

Basic chords consist of just three notes, arranged in thirds, called a *triad*. The most common triads are constructed from notes plucked from the underlying scale, each note two steps above the previous note. So, for example, if you want to base a chord on the tonic of a scale, you'd use the first, third, and fifth notes of the scale. (Using the C Major scale, these notes would be C, E, and G.) If you want to base a chord on the second degree of a scale, use the second, fourth, and sixth notes of the scale. (Still using the C Major scale, these notes would be D, F, and A.)

Building a three-note triad.

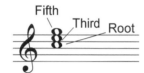

Within a specific chord, the first note is called the *root*—even if the chord isn't formed from the root of the scale. The other notes of the chord are named relative to the first note, typically being the third and the fifth above the chord's root. (For example, if C is the chord's root, E is called the third and G is called the fifth.) This is sometimes notated 1-3-5.

Different Types of Chords

Let's go back to the piano. Putting your fingers on every other white note, form a chord starting on middle C. (Your fingers should be on the keys C, E, and G.) Nice sounding chord, isn't it? Now move your fingers one key to the right, so that you're starting on D. (Your fingers should now be on the keys D, F, and A.) This chord sounds different—kind of sad, compared to the happier C chord.

You've just demonstrated the difference between major and minor chords. The first chord you played was a major chord: C Major. The second chord was a minor chord—D minor. As with major and minor scales, major and minor chords sound different to the listener, because the intervals in the chords are slightly different.

> **Warning**
>
> You should always spell a triad using every other letter. So Db-F-Ab is a correct spelling (for a Db Major chord), but the enharmonic spelling of C#-F-Ab is wrong.

In most cases, the type of chord is determined by the middle note—the third. When the interval between the first note and the second note is a major third—two whole steps—you have a major chord. When the interval between the first note and the second note is a minor third—three half steps—you have a minor chord.

It's no more complex than that. If you change the middle note, you change the chord from major to minor.

Read on to learn all about major and minor chords—as well as some other types of chords that aren't quite major and aren't quite minor.

Major Chords

A major chord consists of a root, a major third, and a perfect fifth. For example, the C Major chord includes the notes C, E, and G. The E is a major third above the C; the G is a perfect fifth above the C.

Here's a quick look at how to build major chords on every note of the scale:

Major triads.

There are many different ways to indicate a major chord in your music, as shown in the following table:

Notation for Major Chords

Major Chord Notation	Example
Major	C Major
Maj	C Maj
Ma	C Ma
M	CM
△	C△

In addition, just printing the letter of the chord (using a capital letter) indicates that the chord is major. (So if you see C in a score, you know to play a C Major chord.)

Minor Chords

The main difference between a major chord and a minor chord is the third. Although a major chord utilizes a major third, a minor chord flattens that interval to create a minor third. The fifth is the same.

In other words, a minor chord consists of a root, a minor third, and a perfect fifth. This is sometimes notated 1-♭3-5. For example, the C minor chord includes the notes C, E♭, and G.

Here's a quick look at how to build minor chords on every note of the scale:

> **Note**
>
> In this and other chord charts in this book, the accidentals apply only to the specific chord; they don't carry across to successive chords.

 Tip

When you play a chord based on the tonic note of a major scale or key, that chord is always a major chord. For example, in the key of C, the tonic chord is C Major.

Minor triads.

There are many different ways to indicate a minor chord, as shown in the following table:

Notation for Minor Chords

Minor Chord Notation	Example
minor	C minor
min	C min
mi	C mi
m	Cm

Diminished Chords

A diminished chord is like a minor chord with a lowered fifth. It has a kind of eerie and ominous sound. You build a diminished chord with a root note, a minor third, and a diminished (lowered) fifth. This is sometimes noted 1-♭3-♭5.

> **Note**
>
> Note the double flat on the fifth of the E♭ diminished chord.

For example, the C diminished chord includes the notes C, E♭, and G♭.

Here's a quick look at how to build diminished chords on every note of the scale:

Diminished triads.

There are many different ways to indicate a diminished chord, as shown in the following table:

Notation for Diminished Chords

Diminished Chord Notation	Example
diminished	C diminished
dimin	C dimin
dim	C dim
°	C°

Augmented Chords

An augmented chord is like a major chord with a raised fifth; thus an augmented chord consists of a root, a major third, and an augmented (raised) fifth. This is sometimes notated 1-3-#5.

For example, the C augmented chord includes the notes C, E, and G#.

Here's a quick look at how to build augmented chords on every note of the scale:

Augmented triads.

Note: Did you spot the double sharp on the fifth of the B augmented chord in the illustration of augmented chords?

There are many different ways to indicate an augmented chord, as shown in the following table:

Notation for Augmented Chords

Augmented Chord Notation	Example
augmented	C augmented
aug	C aug
+	C+

Chord Extensions

Chords can include more than three notes. When you get above the basic triad, the other notes you add to a chord are called *extensions*.

Chord extensions are typically added in thirds; so the first type of extended chord is called a *seventh chord* because the seventh is a third above the fifth. Next up would be the ninth chord, which adds a third above the seventh ... and so on.

Chord extensions are nice to know, but you can simplify most pieces of music to work with just the basic triads. The extended notes add more color or flavor to the sound, kind of like a musical seasoning. Like a good meal, what's important is what's underneath—and you can always do without the seasoning.

So if you see a piece of music with lots of seventh and ninth chords, don't panic—you can probably play the music without the extensions and still have things sound okay. Of course, for the full experience, you want to play the extended chords as written. But remember, the basic harmonic structure comes from the base triads; not from the extensions.

That said, it helps to have a full understanding of extended chords, just as a good chef must have a full understanding of all the different seasonings at his or her disposal. That means you need to know how to build extended chords—so you can throw them into the mix when necessary.

Sevenths

The seventh chord is the most common chord extension—in fact, it's so common that some music theorists categorize it as a basic chord type, not as an extension. In any case, you need to be as familiar with seventh chords as you are with triads. They're that important.

Creating a seventh chord within a specific key or scale is normally as simple as adding another third on top of the fifth of the base triad. This gives you a 1-3-5-7 structure—the equivalent of playing every other note in the scale.

There are actually three basic types of seventh chords: major, minor, and dominant. Major and minor seventh chords are kind of sweet sounding; the dominant seventh chord has its own internal tension.

Dominant Sevenths

The dominant seventh chord—sometimes just called the "seventh" chord, with no other designation—takes a major triad and adds a *minor* seventh on top. In other words, it's a major chord with a lowered seventh; the chord itself consists of a root, major third, perfect fifth, and minor seventh. This is sometimes notated 1-3-5-♭7.

For example, a C7 chord includes the notes C, E, G, and B♭.

The dominant seventh chord is an especially important—and frequently used—extension, as this is what you get if you play a seventh chord based on the fifth (dominant) tone of a major scale. As you'll learn in Chapter 10, the dominant chord is frequently used to set up the tension leading back to the tonic chord; when you add a seventh to the dominant triad (with its mix of major triad and minor seventh), you introduce even more tension to the music. Here's a quick look at how to build dominant seventh chords on every note of the scale:

Dominant seventh chords.

There's really only one way to notate a dominant seventh chord: by placing a single 7 after the name of the chord. For example, you notate a C dominant seventh chord like this: **C7**.

Major Sevenths

The major seventh chord takes a standard major chord and adds a major seventh on top of the existing three notes. This gives you a chord consisting of a root, major third, perfect fifth, and major seventh. For example, a C Major 7 chord includes the notes C, E, G, and B.

Here's a quick look at how to build major seventh chords on every note of the scale:

Major seventh chords.

There are several ways to indicate a major seventh chord, as shown in the following table.

Notation for Major Seventh Chords

Major Seventh Chord Notation	Example
Major 7	C Major 7
Maj7	C Maj7
M7	CM7
△7	C△7

Minor Sevenths

The minor seventh chord takes a standard minor chord and adds a minor seventh on top of the existing three notes. This gives you a chord consisting of a root, minor third, perfect fifth, and minor seventh. (This is sometimes notated 1-♭3-5-♭7.)

For example, a C minor 7 chord includes the notes C, E♭, G, and B♭.

Here's a quick look at how to build minor seventh chords on every note of the scale:

Minor seventh chords.

There are several ways to indicate a minor seventh chord, as shown in the following table:

Notation for Minor Seventh Chords

Minor Seventh Chord Notation	Example
minor 7	C minor 7
min7	C min7
m7	Cm7

Other Sevenths

When I said there were three basic types of seventh chords, I left the door open for other types of less frequently used seventh chords. Indeed, you can stick either a minor or a major seventh on top of any type of triad—major, minor, augmented, or diminished—to create different types of seventh chords.

For example, a major seventh stuck on top of a minor triad creates a "minor major seventh" chord. (That is, the base chord is minor, but the seventh is major.) This is notated 1-♭3-5-7; a C minor Major 7 chord would include the notes C, E♭, G, and B (natural).

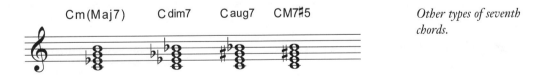

Other types of seventh chords.

A minor seventh on top of a diminished triad creates a diminished seventh chord, like this: 1-♭3-♭5-♭7. (This is the chord you get if you play a seventh chord based on the seventh tone of a major key.) A minor seventh on top of an augmented triad creates an augmented seventh chord, like this: 1-3-#5-♭7. A major seventh on top of an augmented triad creates a major seventh chord with a raised fifth (#5), like this: 1-3-#5-7 … and so on.

Other Extensions

While the seventh chord is almost as common as an unadorned triad, other chord extensions are less widely used. That doesn't mean you don't need to bother with them; when used properly, sixths and ninths and other extended chords can add a lot to a piece of music.

Let's look, then, at the other extensions you can use to spice up your basic chords.

Sixths

I said previously that all chords are based on notes a third apart from each other. There's an important exception to that rule: the sixth chord. With a sixth chord (sometimes called an *added sixth* chord), you start with a basic triad; then add an extra note a second above the fifth—or a sixth above the root. You can have major sixth and minor sixth chords, as well as sixths above diminished and augmented triads, as shown in the following figure:

Different types of sixth chords.

> ### Note
>
> Later in this chapter you'll learn about chord inversions, where the order of the notes in a chord is changed. Interestingly, a sixth chord can be viewed as nothing more than the first inversion of a seventh chord.
>
> For example, C Major 6 (C E G A) contains the same notes as A minor 7 (A C E G), just in a different order. For that reason, you sometimes might see sixth chords notated as seventh chords with a separate note (the third) in the bass. (C Major 6 could be notated like this: Am7/C.) This is a little advanced—come back to this sidebar after you've read the section on inversions. It'll make sense then.

> ### Note
>
> When you get up to the ninth chord, you assume that the chord includes both the underlying triad and the seventh.

Ninths

A ninth chord adds another third on top of the four notes in the seventh chord. That makes for five individual notes; each a third apart. You can have ninth chords based on both major and minor triads, with both major and minor sevenths. Here's just a smattering of the different types of ninth chords you can build:

Different types of ninth chords.

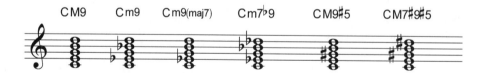

Seventh, ninth, and eleventh chords see frequent use in modern jazz music, which often employs sophisticated harmonic concepts.

Elevenths ... and Beyond

An eleventh chord adds another note a third above the ninth, for six notes total: 1-3-5-7-9-11. You can set an eleventh on top of any type of triad, along with all sorts of seventh and ninth variations—although the most common eleventh chord always uses the unchanged note from within the underlying key or scale.

As with the ninth chord, you have to make a few assumptions with the eleventh chord. You have to assume the underlying triad, of course, but you also have to assume the presence of both the seventh and the ninth.

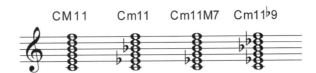

Different types of eleventh chords.

Above the eleventh, it's possible to construct both thirteenth and fifteenth chords. Just keep adding more notes; each a third above the last.

By the way, the fifteenth chord is pretty much the highest you'll find, because the new note for the next chord up—the seventeenth chord—is exactly two octaves up from the chord root. There's no point in calling it a new chord when all you're doing is doubling the root note.

Altered, Suspended, and Power Chords

To ensure that you have a comprehensive background in chord theory, there are three other chord types you need to know about. These are variations on the basic chord types that crop up from time to time—and can help you notate more complex musical sounds.

Altered Chords

When you get into seventh and ninth and eleventh chords, you run into the possibility of a lot of different variations. It's math again; the more notes in a chord, the more possible combinations of flats and sharps and such you can create.

This is why we have something called *altered chords*. Altered chords take standard, easy-to-understand chords and alter them. The alteration—a lowered fifth, perhaps, or maybe an added ninth—is typically notated in parentheses, after the main chord notation.

For example, let's say you wanted to write a C Major seventh chord, but with a lowered fifth. (I know … that's a really weird-sounding combination.) To notate this, you start with the basic chord—CM7—and add the alteration in parentheses, like this: CM7(♭5). Anyone reading this chord knows to start with the basic chord, then make the alteration shown within the parentheses.

Another example: Let's say you have a C minor chord and want to add the ninth but without adding the seventh. Now, if you wanted to include the seventh, you'd have a Cm9 chord, which is relatively standard. But to leave out the seventh takes a bit more planning. Again, you start with the underlying triad—in this case, Cm—and make the alteration within parentheses, like this: **Cm(add9).** Anyone reading this chord knows to play a C minor triad and then add the ninth—not to play a standard Cm9 chord.

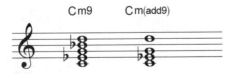

The difference between a ninth chord and a triad with an added ninth.

There are an endless number of possibilities you can use when working with altered chords. You can even include more than one variation per chord—all you have to do is keep adding the variations onto the end of the chord notation. Just remember to start with the base chord and make your alterations as clear as possible. (And, if all else fails, you can write out the notes of the chord on a staff—just to make sure everybody understands.)

Tip

Added notes can be notated by the word "add" plus the number, or just the number—within parentheses, of course.

Suspended Chords

We're so used to hearing a chord as a 1-3-5 triad that any change to this arrangement really stands out like a sore thumb to our ears. (Not that you should put your thumbs in your ears, but you know what I mean …) This is what makes a *suspended chord* so powerful, especially when used properly.

A suspended chord temporarily moves the normal major third of a major chord up a half step to a perfect fourth. This suspension of the second note of the triad is so wrong to our ears, we want to hear the suspension resolved by moving the second note down from the fourth to the third—as quickly as possible.

For example, a C suspended chord includes the notes C F G—instead of the C E G of C Major. This sets up an incredible tension, as the fourth (F) sounds really out of place; your ears want the F to move down to the E to create the more soothing C Major triad.

In fact, most often you do resolve suspended chords—especially at the end of a musical phrase. You can use the suspended chord to set up the desired end-of-phrase tension, but then quickly resolve the suspended chord to the normal major chord, like this:

Resolving a suspended chord—the F in the first chord drops down to the E in the final chord.

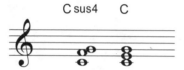

Note: As you can see from the example, you notate a suspended chord with the phrase "sus4"—or, more simply, "sus."

The resolution from the perfect fourth to the major third is just a half-step movement, but that little half step makes a world of difference; until you make the move, you're sitting on the edge of your seat waiting for that incredible tension to resolve.

> **Note**
>
> In classical music theory, a power chord is called an *open fifth*, and is technically an interval, not a chord.

Power Chords

If you want a really simple chord, one with a lot of raw power, you can play just the root and the fifth—leaving out the third. This type of chord is called a *power chord*; it is noted by adding a "5" after the chord note. (For example, a G power chord is notated G5, and includes only the notes G and D.)

Here's one bad thing about power chords: If you use a bunch of them in a row, you create something called *parallel fifths*. As you'll learn in Chapter 14, parallel fifths are frowned upon, especially in classical music theory. So use power chords sparingly and—if at all possible—not consecutively.

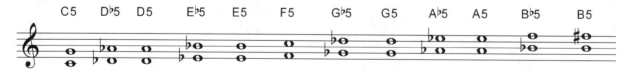

Power chords, up and down the scale.

Inverting the Order

Although it's easiest to understand a chord when the root is on the bottom and the fifth is on the top, you don't have to play the notes in precisely this order. Chords can be *inverted* so that the root isn't the lowest note, which can give a chord a slightly different sound. (It can also make a chord easier to play on a piano, when you're moving your fingers from chord to chord; inversions help to group the notes from adjacent chords closer together.)

When you rearrange the notes of a chord so that the third is on the bottom (3-5-1), you form what is called the *first inversion*. (Using a C Major chord as an example, the first inversion is arranged E G C.) The *second inversion* is where you put the fifth of the chord on the bottom, followed by the root and third (5-1-3). (Again using C Major as an example, the second inversion is arranged G C E.)

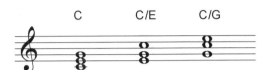

The first and second inversions of a C Major chord.

If you're working with extended chords, there are more than two possible inversions. For example, the third inversion of a seventh chord puts the seventh in the bass; the fourth inversion of a ninth chord puts the ninth in the bass.

The particular order of a chord's notes is also referred to as that chord's *voicing*. You can specify a voicing without writing all the notes by adding a bass note to the standard chord notation. You do this by adding a slash after the chord notation, and then the name of the note that should be played on the bottom of the chord.

For example, if you want to indicate a first inversion of a C Major chord (normally C E G, but E G C in the first inversion), you'd write this: C/E. This tells the musician to play a C Major chord, but to put an E in the bass—which just happens to be the first inversion of the chord. If you wanted to indicate a second inversion (G C E), you'd write this: C/G. This tells the musician to play a C Major chord with a G in the bass.

Warning

Don't confuse the chord/bass notation with the similar $\frac{chord}{chord}$ (like a fraction with a horizontal divider, as opposed to the chord/bass diagonal slash). Ther $\frac{chord}{chord}$ notation tells a musician—typically a pianist—to play one chord over another. For example, if you see $\frac{Cm}{Dm}$, you should play a Cm chord with your right hand, and a Dm chord with your left.

You can use this notation to indicate other, nonchord notes to be played in the bass part. For example, Am7/D tells the musician to play an A minor seventh chord, but to add a D in the bass—a note that doesn't exist within the A minor seventh chord proper.

An A minor seventh chord with a D in the bass—not your standard seventh chord.

Adding Chords to Your Music

When you want to indicate a chord in your written music, you add the chord symbol *above* the staff, like this:

Write the chord symbol above the staff.

The chord applies in the music until you insert another chord. Then the new chord applies—until the next chord change. For example, in the following piece of music you'd play a C Major chord in measure 1, an F Major chord in measure 2, a C Major chord in the first half of measure 3, a G7 chord in the second half of measure 3, and a C Major chord in measure 4.

Changing chords in your music.

If you're writing a part for guitar, or for a rhythm section (bass, piano, and so forth) in a pop or jazz band, you don't have to write out specific notes on the staff. A guitarist will know to strum the indicated chords, a piano player will know to *comp* through the chord progressions, and the bass player will know to play the root of the chord.

Definition

Comping is a technique used by jazz and pop musicians to play an improvised accompaniment behind a particular piece of music. A piano player might comp by playing block or arpeggiated chords; a guitarist might comp by strumming the indicated chords.

You write a comp part by using slashes in place of traditional notes on the staff. Typically, you use one slash per beat, so a measure of 4/4 will have four slashes, like this:

Writing chords for a rhythm section.

You can indicate specific rhythms that should be played by writing out the rhythm, but with slashes instead of note heads. The result looks something like this:

Indicating a specific rhythm for the chord accompaniment.

Note
A guitar part with tablature is sometimes called a guitar *tab*.

If you're writing specifically for guitar, you also have the option of including guitar tablature. Tablature shows the guitarist how to fret the chord, and is very useful for beginning-level players. More advanced players probably don't need this assistance, unless you're indicating a particularly complex chord.

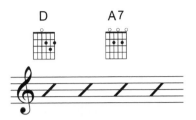

A guitar part with tablature added.

The Complete Idiot's Chord Reference

If you flip back to Appendix B of this book, you'll find "The Complete Idiot's Chord Reference." This is a comprehensive reference to just about every kind of chord you can think of—major chords, minor chords, extensions, you name it. You'll find out how to construct each chord, learn the guitar tablature, and discover alternate ways to describe the chord. Keep this appendix bookmarked—you'll get a lot of use out of it!

The Least You Need to Know

- A chord consists of three or more notes (called a triad) played simultaneously—with each note typically a third above the previous note.
- A major chord includes the root note, a major third, and a perfect fifth.
- A minor chord includes the root note, a minor third, and a perfect fifth.
- Extensions above the basic triad are typically added in thirds, and can be either major or minor.
- A minor seventh chord is a minor triad with a minor seventh; a major seventh chord is a major triad with a major seventh; a dominant seventh chord is a major triad with a minor seventh.
- When you play a chord with a note other than the root in the bass, you're playing a chord inversion.
- When you write for guitar, piano, or bass, you don't have to write out all the notes; all you have to do is specify the chord, along with rhythmic slashes on the staff.

Exercises

Exercise 9-1

Name the following major chords.

Exercise 9-2

Name the following minor chords.

Exercise 9-3

Write the following major chords on the staff.

A E♭ G B D♭ E F G♭ D A♭

Exercise 9-4

Write the following minor chords on the staff.

Cm Em A♭m Gm C♯m Fm B♭m F♯m D♭m B♭m

Exercise 9-5

Name the following extended chords.

Exercise 9-6

Write the following extended chords on the staff.

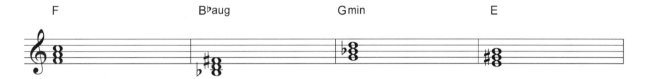

A 7   E♭m7   C 6   D Maj7   B♭m9   F 11   G 7   G m(maj7)   E Maj7   F m7

Exercise 9-7

Write the first and second inversions of the following chords.

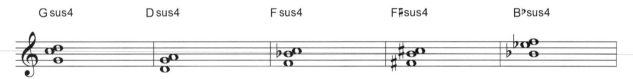

F   B♭aug   G min   E

Exercise 9-8

Resolve the following suspended chords by lowering the suspended note (the middle note of the chord) to the note a half step below.

G sus4   D sus4   F sus4   F♯sus4   B♭sus4

Chapter 10

Chord Progressions

In This Chapter

◆ Understanding scale-based chords

◆ Learning the rules of chord leading

◆ Figuring out how to end a progression

◆ Discovering the most common chord progressions

◆ Fitting chords to a melody—and a melody to a chord progression

In Chapter 9, you learned how to group notes together to form chords. Individual chords alone are interesting, but they become really useful when you string them together to form a succession of chords—what we call a *chord progression*. These chord progressions provide the harmonic under-pinning of a song, "fattening out" the melody and propelling the music forward.

Of course, to create a chord progression that sounds natural, you can't just string a bunch of chords together willy-nilly. Certain chords naturally lead to other chords; certain chords perform distinct functions within a song. You have to use your chords properly, and arrange them in the right order, to create a piece of music that sounds both natural and logical.

Chord progressions don't have to be complex, either. The simplest progressions include just two or three chords—which are easy enough for any beginning guitarist to play. How many songs, after all, do you know that use only the G, C, and D chords? (A lot, I bet.) Those three chords comprise one of the most common chord progressions—which should show you how easy all this is.

Chords for Each Note in the Scale

To better understand the theory behind chord progressions, you need to understand that you can create a three-note chord based on any of the seven notes of a major key or scale. You start with the note of the scale (one through seven) as the root of the chord; then build up from there in thirds—using only the notes within the scale.

Let's use the key of C as an example, because it's made up of only the white keys on a piano. When you play a triad based on C (the tonic of the scale), you play C E G—a C Major chord. Now move up one key, and play the next triad—D F A, or D minor. Move up another key, and you play E G B, the E minor chord. Move up yet another key, and you play F A C—F Major. Keep moving up the scale and you play G Major, A minor, and B diminished. Then you're back on C, and ready to start all over again.

This type of chord building based on the notes of a scale is important, because we use the position within a scale to describe the individual chords in our chord progressions. In particular, we use Roman numerals (I through VII) to describe where each chord falls in the underlying scale. Uppercase Roman numerals are used for major chords; lowercase Roman numerals are used for minor chords. To indicate a diminished chord, you use the lowercase Roman numeral plus a small circle. To indicate an augmented chord, use the uppercase Roman numeral plus a small plus sign.

Thus, within a major scale, the seven chords are notated as follows:

```
I        ii       iii      IV       V        vi       vii°
```

If you remember back to Chapter 2, each degree of the scale has a particular name—tonic, dominant, and so on. We can assign these names to the different chords, like this:

I	ii	iii	IV	V	vi	vii°
Tonic	Supertonic	Mediant	Subdominant	Dominant	Submediant	Leading Tone

Of these chords, the *primary chords*—the ones with the most weight—are the I, IV, and V. These also are the only major chords in the major scale—and often the only chords used within a song.

When describing chord progressions, we'll refer to chords by either their Roman numerals or their theoretical names (tonic, dominant, and so forth). You can figure out which specific chords (C Major, D minor, and so forth) to play, based on the designated key signature.

To make things easier, you can refer to the following table, which lists the seven scale-based chords for each major key signature.

Scale-Based Chords

Key Signature	Chords

continues

Scale-Based Chords (continued)

Key Signature	Chords

D

D E min F#min G A B min C#dim

I ii iii IV V vi vii °

E♭

E♭ F min G min A♭ B♭ C min D dim

I ii iii IV V vi vii °

E

E F#min G#min A B C#min D#dim

I ii iii IV V vi vii °

F

F G min A min B♭ C D min E dim

I ii iii IV V vi vii °

F#

F# G#min A#min B C# D#min E#dim

I ii iii IV V vi vii°

G♭

G♭ A♭min B♭min C♭ D♭ E♭min F dim

I ii iii IV V vi vii °

G

G A min B min C D E min F#dim

I ii iii IV V vi vii °

A♭

A♭ B♭min C min D♭ E♭ F min G dim

I ii iii IV V vi vii °

continues

Scale-Based Chords   (continued)

Key Signature	Chords						
A	A	B min	C#min	D	E	F#min	G#dim
	I	ii	iii	IV	V	vi	vii°
Bb	Bb	C min	D min	Eb	F	G min	A dim
	I	ii	iii	IV	V	vi	vii°
B	B	C#min	D#min	E	F#	G#min	A#dim
	I	ii	iii	IV	V	vi	vii°
Cb	Cb	Dbmin	Ebmin	Fb	Gb	Abmin	Bbdim
	I	ii	iii	IV	V	vi	vii°

Creating a Progression

Let's see how you can use these Roman numerals to create a chord progression. For the time being we won't pay attention to the underlying harmonic theory; we'll just concentrate on the mechanics of creating a progression.

I mentioned earlier the popularity of the G, C, and D chords. In the key of G Major, these chords happen to fall on the first (G), fourth (C), and fifth (D) notes of the scale. This makes these the I, IV, and V chords—or, more technically, the tonic, subdominant, and dominant.

If you've ever played any folk songs, you know that one of the more common chord progressions goes like this:

```
G / / /     C / / /     G / / /     D / / /
```

(Naturally, the progression repeats—or ends with a final G chord.)

Because you know that the G = I, C = IV, and D = V, it's easy to figure out the Roman numeral notation. It looks like this:

```
I           IV          I           V
```

There—you've just written your first chord progression!

The benefit of using this type of notation is you can apply the chord progression to other keys. Let's say you want to play this I-IV-I-V progression in the key of C. Referring back to the Scale-Based Chords table earlier in this chapter, you can translate the progression to these specific chords:

```
C / / /     F / / /     C / / /     G / / /
```

This definitely makes things simpler.

> **Note**
>
> The preceding example uses *slash notation*, where each slash (/) equals one beat. Measures are separated by spaces.

It's All About Getting Home

The goal of most major chord progressions is to get back to the home chord—the tonic chord, or I. All the other chords in the progression exist as part of a roadmap to deliver you back to the I chord. The route can be simple (just a chord or two) or complex (lots and lots of different chords), but ultimately you want to end up back on I.

If you're playing in a minor key, you want to end up on the home of that key—which is the vi chord of the relative major scale.

As you'll learn in the next section, certain chords naturally lead to the I key. In addition, you can employ multiple-chord progressions to get you back to I—these are called *cadences* and are also discussed later in this chapter.

> **Note**
>
> Technically, the vi chord of the major scale is actually the i chord of the relative natural minor scale—if you recall the relationship between major and minor keys, presented back in Chapter 4.

One Good Chord Leads to Another

Although you can write a song using any combination of chords that sounds good to your ears—even chords from other keys—in most cases chord progressions are based on a few simple rules. These rules come from a concept called *chord leading*, which says that certain chords naturally lead to other chords.

You can hear chord leading for yourself by playing some chords on the piano. To keep it simple, we'll stay in the key of C—so you don't have to play any of the black keys.

Start by playing a C Major chord (C-E-G). This is the I chord, which doesn't necessarily lead anywhere because, based on chord leading rules, the I chord can be followed by any chord in the scale.

Now play a G Major chord (G-B-D). This is the V chord in the scale, and it definitely wants to go somewhere. But where? You could follow it with an F Major chord (F-A-C), but that isn't fully satisfying. Neither is D minor (D-F-A) or E minor (E-G-B) or even A minor (A-C-E). The only chord that sounds fully satisfying— the chord that V naturally leads to—is the I chord, C Major.

The rule here is that the V chord naturally leads back to the I chord. Although you *can* write another chord after a V, the best resolution is to follow the V with the I.

Other chords also have related chords that they naturally lead to. Some chords can even lead to more than one chord. To learn which chords lead where, take a look at the following table.

Chord Leading Reference

These Chords ...	Lead to These Chords ...
I	Any chord
ii	IV, V, vii°
iii	ii, vi
IV	I, V, vii°
V	I
vi	ii, IV
vii°	I, iii

Although there are exceptions to these rules, you can create a pleasing chord progression by following the order suggested by this chart. This means if you have a iii chord, you follow it with either a ii or a vi chord. Or if you have a vi chord, you follow it with either a ii or IV chord ... and so on.

Let's put together some of these combinations. We'll start, of course, with the I chord. Because I leads to any chord, let's go up one scale note and insert the ii chord after the I. According to our chart, ii leads to either IV, V, or vii°. We'll pick V. Then, because V always leads to I, the next chord is a return to the tonic.

The entire progression looks like this:

```
I            ii            V            I
```

When you play this progression in the key of C, you get the following chords:

```
C / / /    Dm / / /     G / / /    C / / /
```

Sounds good, doesn't it?

Let's try another example. Again, we'll start with the tonic, but this time we'll use the vi chord as the second chord. According to the chart, vi can lead to either ii or IV; let's pick IV. Then, because IV can lead to either I, V, or vii°, we'll pick V as the next chord—which leads us back to I as our final chord.

The entire progression looks like this:

```
I            vi            IV            V            I
```

When you play this progression in the key of C, you get the following chords:

```
C / / /    Am / / /     F / / /     G / / /     C / / /
```

You should recognize that progression as the chords that drove thousands of doo-wop tunes in the 1950s and 1960s.

Let's return to that progression, and make an alternate choice for the third chord—ii instead of IV. Because ii also leads to V, we can leave the rest of the progression intact, which creates the following alternate progression:

```
I            vi            ii            V            I
```

This, when played in the key of C, results in these chords:

```
C / / /    Am / / /     Dm / / /     G / / /     C / / /
```

You can also work backward from where you want to end up—your final chord. Because in most cases you want the final chord to be the tonic (I), all you have to do is work through the options that lead to that chord. Consulting the Chord Leading Reference table, you find that three chords can lead to the I: IV, V, and vii°. The obvious choice is the V chord, so that's what we'll use. Now we have to pick a chord to lead to V; the choices are ii, IV, and I. Let's pick ii. Now we pick a chord that leads to the ii; the choices are I, iii, and vi. Let's pick iii. Now we pick a chord that leads to the iii; the choices are I and vii°. Let's pick I, which is also a good chord with which to start our phrase. When you put all these chords together, you get the following progression:

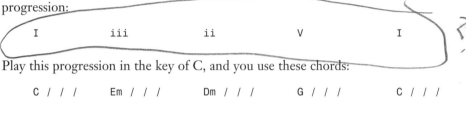

| I | iii | ii | V | I |

Play this progression in the key of C, and you use these chords:

C / / /   Em / / /   Dm / / /   G / / /   C / / /

Pretty easy, isn't it?

Ending a Phrase

When you come to the end of a musical phrase—which can be anywhere in your song, even in the middle of your melody—you use chords to set up a tension, and then relieve that tension. This feeling of a natural ending is called *cadence*, and there are some accepted chord progressions you can use to provide this feeling of completion.

Perfect Cadence

The most common phrase-ending chord progression uses the V (dominant) chord to set up the tension, which is relieved when you move on to the I (tonic) chord. This progression is notated V-I, and in the key of C looks like this:

G / / /   C / / /

You could probably see this cadence coming, from the chord leading shown in the table named Chord Leading Reference earlier in this chapter. There's no better way to get back home (I) than through the dominant chord (V).

Plagal Cadence

A slightly weaker ending progression uses the IV (subdominant) chord in place of the V chord. This IV-I progression is called a *plagal cadence;* in the key of C, it looks like this:

F / / /   C / / /

Although this is an effective cadence, it isn't nearly as strong as the perfect V-I cadence. For that reason, you might want to use a plagal cadence in the middle of your song or melody, and save the stronger perfect cadence for the big ending.

Imperfect Cadence

Sometimes, especially in the middle of a melody, you might want to end on a chord that isn't the tonic. In these instances, you're setting up an unresolved tension, typically by ending on the V (dominant) triad.

This type of ending progression is called an *imperfect cadence*, and you can get to the V chord any number of ways—I-V, ii-V, IV-V, and vi-V being the most common. In the key of C, these progressions look like this:

```
I-V:      C / / /        G / / /
ii-V:     Dm / / /       G / / /
IV-V:     F / / /        G / / /
vi-V:     Am / / /       G / / /
```

Interrupted Cadence

Even less final than an imperfect cadence is an ending progression called an *interrupted cadence*. In this progression, you use a V chord to trick the listener into thinking a perfect cadence is on its way, but then move to any type of chord *except* the tonic.

V-IV, V-vi, V-ii, and V-V7 progressions all are interrupted cadences—and, in the key of C, look like this:

Note
In classical music theory, an interrupted cadence is more often called a *deceptive cadence*.

```
V-IV:     G / / /        F / / /
V-vi      G / / /        Am / / /
V-ii:     G / / /        Dm / / /
V-V7:     G / / /        G7 / / /
```

Common Chord Progressions

Given everything you've learned about chord leading and cadences, you should be able to create your own musically sound chord progressions. However, just in case you get stuck, let's take a look at some of the most popular chord progressions used in music today.

Definition
Jazz musicians sometimes refer to chord progressions as chord *changes*—as in, "Dig those crazy changes, man!"

I-IV-V

You can't get any more popular than the old I-IV-V progression. This is the progression (in the key of G) you're playing when you strum the chords G, C, and D on your guitar.

There are many different variations on the I-IV-V progression. You can leave out the IV, insert an extra I between the IV and the V, and even tack on another I-V at the end to wrap things up with a perfect cadence. You also can vary the number of beats and measures you devote to each chord.

One example of I-IV-V in a four-measure phrase might look like this, in the key of C:

```
C / / /      C / / /      F / / /      G / / /
```

You could also bunch up the IV and the V into a single measure, like this:

```
C / / /      C / / /      C / / /      F / G /
```

The progression also could be used over longer phrases, as in this eight-measure example:

```
C / / /      C / / /      C / / /      C / / /
F / / /      F / / /      G / / /      G / / /
```

The point is these three chords are used in a huge number of modern songs—and make up the core of what many refer to as "three-chord rock-and-roll." They're not limited to rock, of course; many folk, country, jazz, rap, and even classical and show tunes are based on these three chords.

It's an extremely versatile progression.

Tip

This progression is often played with a dominant seventh chord on the fifth (V7), which provides increased tension before you return to the tonic.

I-IV-V-IV

This progression is a variation on I-IV-V. The variation comes in the form of a shift back to the subdominant (IV), which then forms a plagal cadence when it repeats back to the tonic. In the key of C, the progression looks like this:

```
C / / /      F / / /      G / / /      F / / /
```

It's a nice, rolling progression—not too heavy—without a strong ending feeling to it—which makes it nice for tunes that repeat the main melody line again and again.

I-V-vi-IV

This progression is another rolling one, good for repeating again and again. (That's because of the ending plagal cadence—the IV repeating back to I.)

In the key of C, it looks like this:

```
C / / /      G / / /      Am / / /      F / / /
```

I-ii-IV-V

This progression has a constant upward movement, resolved with a perfect cadence on the repeat back to I. In the key of C, it looks like this:

```
C / / /      Dm / / /      F / / /      G / / /
```

I-ii-IV

This is a variation on the previous progression, with a soft plagal cadence at the end (the IV going directly to the I, no V involved). In the key of C, it looks like this:

```
C / / /      Dm / / /      F / / /
```

As with all progressions that end with a plagal cadence (IV-I), this progression has a rolling feel, and sounds as if it could go on and on and on, like a giant circle.

I-vi-ii-V

This was a very popular progression in the 1950s, the basis of a lot of doo-wop and jazz songs. It's also the chord progression behind the song "I've Got Rhythm," and sometimes is referred to (especially in jazz circles) as the "I've Got Rhythm" progression.

In the key of C, it looks like this:

```
C / / /      Am / / /      Dm / / /      G / / /
```

I-vi-IV-V

This is a variation on the "I've Got Rhythm" progression, with a stronger lead to the V chord (IV instead of ii). It looks like this, in the key of C:

```
C / / /      Am / / /      F / / /      G / / /
```

This progression was also popular in the doo-wop era and in the early days of rock-and-roll. The defining factor of this progression is the descending bass line; it drops in thirds until it moves up a step for the dominant chord, like this: C-A-F-G. You've heard this progression (and that descending bass line) hundreds of times; it's a very serviceable progression.

I-vi-ii-V7-ii

This is another variation on the "I've Got Rhythm" progression, with an extra ii chord squeezed in between the final V and the return to I, and with the V chord played as a dominant seventh. In the key of C, it looks like this:

```
C / / /      Am / / /      Dm / / /      G7 / Dm /
```

By adding the ii chord between the V7 and the I, almost in passing, it takes the edge off the perfect cadence and makes the progression a little smoother.

IV-I-IV-V

As this progression shows, you don't have to start your chord progression on the tonic. In the key of C, it looks like this:

```
F / / /      C / / /      F / / /      G / / /
```

This progression has a bit of a rolling nature to it, but also a bit of an unresolved nature. You can keep repeating this progression (leading from the V back to the IV), or end the song by leading the progression home to a I chord.

Note
This progression is also frequently played at the end of a phrase in many jazz tunes. Used in this manner, it's called a *turnaround*. (See Chapter 16 to learn more.)

ii-V-I

This progression is quite popular in jazz, often played with seventh chords throughout. So you might actually play a ii7-V7-I progression, like this (in the key of C):

```
Dm7 / / /      G7 / / /      CM7 / / /
```

Sometimes jazz tunes cycle through this progression in a variety of keys, often using the circle of fifths to *modulate* through the keys. (That's the term you use any time you change key.)

Circle of Fifths Progression

There's one more chord progression that's fairly common, and it's based on the circle of fifths you learned about back in Chapter 9. Put simply, it's a progression where each chord is a fifth above the previous chord. The progression circles back around on itself, always coming back to the tonic chord, like this: I-V-ii-vi-iii-vii°-IV-I.

Here's what the progression looks like in the key of C:

```
C / / /    G / / /    Dm / / /    Am / / /    Em / / /    Bdim / / /    F / / /    C / / /
```

You can also play this progression backwards, creating a circle of fourths, but that isn't nearly as common as the one detailed here.

Singing the Blues

There's a unique chord progression associated with the genre of music we commonly call *the blues*. This blues form isn't relegated solely to blues music, however; you'll find this form used in many jazz and popular tunes, as well.

The blues progression is a 12-measure progression. (It's sometimes called a "12-bar blues.") This 12-measure progression repeats again and again throughout the melody and any instrumental solos.

The form is essentially a I-IV-I-V7-I-V7 progression, but spread over twelve measures, like this:

```
I / / /      I / / /      I / / /      I / / /
IV / / /     IV / / /     I / / /      I / / /
V7 / / /     IV / / /     I / / /      V7 / / /
```

In the key of C, the blues progression looks like this:

```
C / / /      C / / /      C / / /      C / / /
F / / /      F / / /      C / / /      C / / /
G7 / / /     F / / /      C / / /      G7 / / /
```

> **Note**
>
> The blues progression is sometimes played without the final V7 chord. That is, the final two measures stay on the I chord.

Although these are the basic blues chords, you can use lots of variations to spice up individual songs. (Turn to Chapter 16 to see some of these variations.)

Chords and Melodies

Although chords fill out a tune and provide its harmonic underpinning, you still need a melody to make a song.

The relationship between chords and melody is complex—and works a little like the proverbial chicken and the egg. You can start with one or the other, but in the end you have to have both.

This means you can write a melody to a given chord progression, or you can start with the melody and harmonize it with the appropriate chords. There's no set place to start; whether you start with the melody or the chords is entirely up to you.

Fitting Chords to a Melody

If you write your melody first, you then have to figure out which chords fit where. In many cases, it's a simple matter of applying one of the common chord progressions to your melody; more often than not, you'll find one that's a perfect fit.

To demonstrate, let's look at the chords behind some of the melodies we first examined back in Chapter 8.

Michael, Row the Boat Ashore

We'll start with "Michael, Row the Boat Ashore," which is a great example of a progression that relies heavily on the I, IV, and V chords—but with a few twists. Here's the song, complete with chords:

The chords to "Michael, Row the Boat Ashore."

The first twist in the chord progression comes in the fifth full measure (the start of the second phrase), which uses the iii chord (F#m) instead of the expected I. The second twist is the sixth measure, which moves down to the ii chord (Em). From there the melody ends with a perfect cadence (I-V-I), just as you'd expect.

So, if you started your hunt for the perfect progression for this melody by applying a standard I-IV-V progression, you'd be in the right neighborhood.

Bach's *Minuet in G*

Next, let's examine Bach's *Minuet in G*. Again, if you apply the standard I-IV-V progression, you'll be pretty much on the mark, as you can see here:

The chords to Bach's Minuet in G.

Old Johann was able to wring the most out of a very simple chord progression; in this case nothing more than I-IV-I-IV-I-V-I. Of course, this shows that you don't need a complex chord progression to create great music.

Dvořák's *New World Symphony*

Dvořák's *New World Symphony* uses another relatively simple chord progression, as you can see here:

The chords to Dvořák's New World Symphony.

The chord progression is basically I-V-I, with a neat little ii-V-I imperfect cadence at the end. There's also a very unique nonscale twist in the second half of the third measure, where the I chord (D♭) suddenly gets a raised fifth and goes augmented. (In the orchestral score, the fifth is in the bass in this measure, for a very dramatic effect.) The use of the augmented tonic sets up an unexpected tension, without messing up the harmonic structure by throwing in something like a IV or a V chord where it wouldn't really belong.

Pachelbel's *Canon in D*

Even more simple is the chord progression behind Pachelbel's *Canon in D*, as you can see here:

The chords to Pachelbel's Canon in D.

Note how the chords flow, one into the next, based on established chord leading rules—I-V-vi-iii-IV-I-IV-V—and then back to the I, again and again. You can play this progression all night long and not get tired of it; that's what makes it such a classic.

Mary Had a Little Lamb

Finally, let's figure out the chords to "Mary Had a Little Lamb." Just as the melody is a simple one, so is the accompanying chord progression—nothing more than I-V-I, repeated once. Sometimes the simplest progressions are the best!

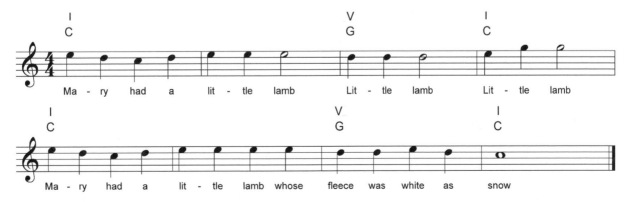

The chords to "Mary Had a Little Lamb."

Chord Writing Tips

When it comes to fitting a chord progression to an existing melody, here are some tips to keep in mind:

♦ Try some common chord changes first. You'd be surprised how many melodies fit with the I-IV-V progression!

♦ The main notes in the melody (typically the notes that fall on the first and third beats of a measure) are the first, third, or fifth note of the underlying chord.

♦ Try to simplify the melody by cutting out the passing and neighboring tones (typically the shorter notes, or the notes not on major beats); the main notes you have left often will suggest the underlying chord.

♦ Make sure you're in the right key. In most cases, the "home" note in the melody is the tonic note of the underlying key.

♦ Generally, the slower the tempo, the more frequent the chord changes. (So if you have a long whole note, or a note held over several measures, expect to find several different chords played behind that single note.)

♦ Work backward from the end of a melodic phrase, remembering that melodies almost always end on the I chord. You then can figure out the cadence leading to the I, and have half the song decoded fairly quickly.

♦ Chord changes generally fit within the measure structure, which means you're likely to see new chords introduced on either the first or third beat of a measure.

Writing a Melody to a Chord Progression

You don't have to start with a melody; you can base your tune on a specific chord progression and compose a melody that best fits the chords.

If you prefer to work this way, it helps to get a good feel for the chord progression before you start writing the melody. Play the chords again and again on either a piano or guitar. In many cases, you'll find a melody forming in your head; if this type of natural melody comes to you, you only have to figure the notes and write them down.

If no natural melody occurs, it's time to roll out the theory. While you don't want to work totally mechanically, there are some basic approaches you can use. Take a look at these tips:

♦ Stay within the notes of the chords—at least for the main notes in the melody. If you're holding an A minor chord in a specific measure, work with the notes A, C, and E for your melody.

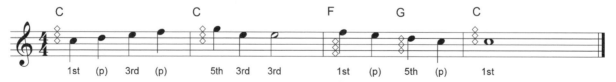

A simple melody for the popular I-IV-V chord progression—note the heavy use of chord notes in the melody. (The notes indicated with a (p) are passing tones.)

Note
In this example, the C in measure 3, beat 4 is technically an *anticipation*, not a passing tone. An anticipation is, in effect, an "eager" note—a note from the next chord that is sounded just a little earlier than the chord itself.

◆ Try to find a logical line between the main notes in different measures. For example, if your chord progression goes C-Am-F, realize that these chords have one note in common—the C. So you can base your melody around the C note. Conversely, if your chord progression goes C-F-G, you might want to pick three notes (one from each chord) that flow smoothly together—E to F to G, for example; or G to F to D.

◆ Use notes that emphasize the quality of the underlying chords. For example, when you're writing to a V7 chord, emphasize the tension by using either the root or the seventh of the chord in the melody.

◆ Once you pick your main tones, fill in the gaps with passing tones.

◆ Come up with an interesting rhythmic motif, and repeat that rhythm throughout the melody.

I wish there were a more complete set of rules for adding a melody to a chord progression, but we're getting into an area that is more art than science. The best way to hone your skill is simply to work at it—play a lot of chord progressions, and practice writing different types of melodies over the chords.

Over time, you'll figure out your own rules for writing melodies—and develop your own melodic style.

> **Note**
>
> Now that you know all about chord progressions, turn back to Chapter 8, and repeat some of the exercises with specific chord progressions in mind.

The Least You Need to Know

◆ Every note of the scale has an associated chord, notated by a Roman numeral (uppercase for major; lowercase for minor).

◆ Chord progressions naturally lead back to the tonic, or I, chord of the underlying scale.

◆ Every chord naturally leads to at least one other chord; for example, the V chord naturally leads to the I.

◆ The final chords in a progression—the ones that ultimately lead back to I—are called a cadence.

◆ The most common chord progressions include I-IV-V, I-IV-V-IV, I-V-vi-IV, I-ii-IV-V, I-ii-IV, I-vi-ii-V, I-vi-IV-V, I-vi-ii-V7-ii, IV-I-IV-V, and ii-V-I.

Exercises

Exercise 10-1

Write the following chords in the key of F.

I V ii vi IV iii V7 vii° IVM7 iim7

Exercise 10-2

Write the following chords in the key of D.

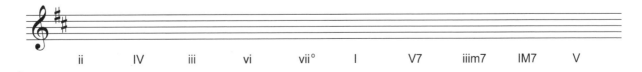

ii IV iii vi vii° I V7 iiim7 IM7 V

Exercise 10-3

Write the following chords in the key of E♭.

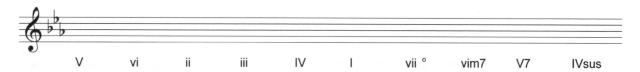

| V | vi | ii | iii | IV | I | vii° | vim7 | V7 | IVsus |

Exercise 10-4

Write the chords that lead from the following chords, in the key of C.

| ii | V | vi | IV | iii |

Exercise 10-5

Create the following types of cadences in the key of A.

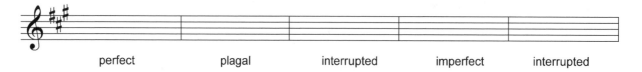

| perfect | plagal | interrupted | imperfect | interrupted |

Exercise 10-6

Figure out which chords go with the following melody. (Hint: There are two chords in every measure.)

Exercise 10-7

Write a melody to the following eight-measure chord progression.

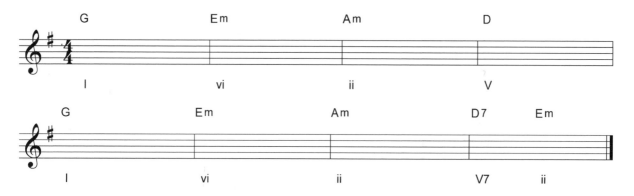

Chapter 11

Phrases and Form

In This Chapter

- Understanding the parts of a piece of music
- Analyzing song structure
- Discovering head tunes
- Learning longer musical forms

Now that you know all about melodies and chord progressions, it's time to think about the entire piece of music, from start to finish. A piece of music, after all, is more than just an eight-measure melody (and accompanying chords) played once. Most pieces repeat a melody several times, and often contain more than one melody.

When you're constructing a song (or a longer piece of music), you have to consider the overall form of the piece. If you have a main melody, do you need to repeat that melody—and if so, where, and how many times? Do you need to add a second, contrasting melody? What about some sort of buffer or break between the two melodies? And how do work your way into the main melody—and how do you wrap things up at the end?

All these questions pertain to what we call *song form*. Song form is the sum of all the parts that make up your song, usually in some sort of logical order.

Think of song form as the grammar you use when writing music. Just as you can analyze the pieces and parts of a sentence, you can also analyze the pieces and parts of a song and, not surprisingly, there are some common parts you probably want to use.

There are also some established forms you might want to use; especially if you're writing classical music—symphonies, cantatas, minuets, and the like. We'll discuss these classical forms in this chapter, too, for when you're ready to take on some *serious* composing tasks!

Parts of a Song

When you're writing popular music, there are accepted parts of a piece of music that you have to work with. Not that you have to use each song part in each and every song you write; these parts are more like building blocks you can use (at your discretion) to construct your own individual piece of music.

> **Note**
>
> In popular music, most any piece of music is typically called a song. In other types of music, however, the word "song" has more specific connotations regarding length and form and use of instruments and voices. To be more universal, you could use the word *composition*, or (less formally) the words *piece* or *tune*. Since this book, however, deals primarily with popular music, we'll continue to use the word song—as long as you realize that we're talking about any formal musical composition, not just something played by four guys with guitars.

Introduction

The introduction, or intro, to a piece is typically some sort of instrumental lead-in. The introduction can be of any length, and doesn't even need to exist—a song can start cold on the first note of the first verse. The introduction may include a theme based on the song's main melody, played by one of the instruments; or maybe just a chord progression from either the verse or the chorus. In any case, the introduction is used to set up the first verse of the song, and then is quickly forgotten.

Verse

The verse is the first main melody of the piece. It's an important melody, and often is repeated several times throughout the course of the song.

Harmonically, the melody might end on the tonic chord (I), or it might end on the dominant (V), creating a tension that is resolved when you proceed to the chorus.

If your song has words, each instance of the verse typically has a different set of lyrics. The lyrics to the first verse are sometimes repeated in the final verse. In all cases, the verse should relate to and lead into the song's chorus.

Pre-chorus

Some, but not all, popular songs have a short (four- to eight-measure) instrumental break between the verse and the chorus. This section serves as kind of a buffer or buildup to the chorus.

Chorus

The chorus is the second main melody of the song, and the emotional high point of the piece. The chorus should contain the main melodic theme, as well as any hook you might have to grab the listener. The hook can be in the melody, chords, rhythm, or lyric—something unique and memorable that sets this song apart from all others. Choruses are often shorter than verses, often lasting just four or eight measures.

Bridge

The bridge is kind of a break in the middle of the piece. Most bridges sound completely different from the verse and chorus, and are often based on a different harmonic structure. For example, a bridge might be based around the IV chord instead of the I chord.

Bridges typically are short—only about eight measures. (That's why a bridge is sometimes called the "middle eight" of a song.)

Instrumental Solo

If you're writing a song with lyrics, you might want to give the singer (and the audience) a break by inserting an instrumental section after the chorus or bridge. This section should probably be based on the chords of the verse, or maybe the verse and chorus combined. When the instrumentalist is done soloing, you return to either the verse or the chorus and pick up the lyric where you left off.

This section is relevant only if you're writing a song with lyrics; otherwise the entire song is instrumental!

Ending

The ending isn't necessarily a separate section of the song. Sometimes you end the song after the last chorus; either by stopping on the I chord or (if you're in a recording studio) fading out the volume. More sophisticated songs have unique ending sections tacked on to the end of the song, which typically use some sort of cadence or *turnaround* (explained in Chapter 16). You might even want the ending to mirror the song's intro, or otherwise reflect the melodic or harmonic nature of the piece.

> **Note**
>
> An extended chorus played during the fadeout of a song is called the *out chorus*.

Putting It All Together

Most popular and jazz music is based on eight-measure phrases. Your verse might be one eight-measure phrase; your chorus, another. We keep track of the different parts of a song by assigning them letters—which shouldn't be confused with the letters we used to label the notes in a scale. (These letters have nothing to do with individual notes or pitches.)

The very first eight-measure phrase in your song—which is typically the first verse—is labeled "A." If the verse is repeated anywhere in the song, it retains its "A" labeling.

The second eight-measure phrase—typically the chorus—is labeled "B." If the chorus repeats later in the song, the repeated chorus is still labeled "B."

The third eight-measure phrase—the bridge, if you have one—is labeled "C." Additional phrases build on this lettering scheme.

Let's look at a song that has a verse, a chorus, a verse, and another chorus. The form of this song would look like this:

> **Note**
>
> The eight-measure phrase rule isn't hard and fast, although the concept of being divisible by eight is somewhat rigidly followed. This means that, in addition to the standard eight-measure phrases, you can also have 16- and 32-bar phrases, both of which are divisible by 8. (Although if a phrase gets to be 32 bars long, it's probably more of a section than a phrase, if you want to be technical about it.)

    A   B   A   B

Note that when the verse repeats, we don't give it a new letter; it keeps the "A" designation—even if the lyrics change. Same thing with the chorus; the B section is always B, no matter how many times it repeats.

Now let's look at a song that has two verses, a chorus, and a final verse. The form of this song looks like this:

    A   A   B   A

Things get more interesting when you add a bridge to the mix. Consider a song with two verses, a chorus, a bridge, and a final chorus:

    A   A   B   C   B

Or how about a song with two verses, a chorus, another verse, a bridge, a final verse, and a final chorus:

A   A   B   A   C   A   B

Tip

When you have variations of a single section like this, you can label each instance of the section by a number after the letter, as in A1, A2, A3, and so on.

It's not really that hard to follow, once you know what letters stand for what.

Incidentally, some songs are all A. This is fairly common in folk music, where you have one melodic phrase repeated over and over, each time with a different set of lyrics. Think of "If I Had a Hammer," or "Where Have All the Flowers Gone?" as good examples. Neither song has a chorus, per se; they're all verses, and lots of them.

Head Cases

There's a unique musical form associated with jazz music, and with some rock-and-roll "jam" bands. This form, called the *head arrangement*, is ideally suited for extended improvisation.

In this type of music you play the "head"—the main melody, or sometimes both verse and chorus—relatively straight, and then repeat those chord progressions for a series of instrumental solos. (Jazz musicians call this "soloing over the changes.") The head is then repeated, straight after the soloists blow themselves out.

In terms of form, this type of tune might look like this:

A(head)   A(solos)   A(head repeat)

If a more complex song (complete with both verse and chorus) is used as the head, the form might look something like this:

ABA(head)   ABA(solos)   ABA(head repeat)

Classical Music Forms

Within the genre that most of us know as "classical" music, several distinct forms exist. If you plan to take a more traditional path in your musical career, you'll need to explore each of these forms in more depth:

- **Anthem**   An anthem is a piece of choral music, generally with a religious text. Most anthems are for four voices, and some even include instrumental parts; most often for string instruments.

- **Aria**   An aria is a vocal piece (a song, operatic in nature) that can be either standalone, or part of a larger work. Over time, arias have become longer and more complex, serving as a type of showcase for the vocalist.

- **Canon**   The canon is a musical form in which the melody is imitated by various parts at regular intervals. Canons typically are instrumental in nature.

- **Cantata**   A cantata is a type of chamber music, Baroque in style. It comes primarily from Lutheran church music, and is written for either soloists and instrumental accompaniment or soloists, chorus, and instrumental accompaniment.

- **Chorale**   A chorale is a congregational hymn of the Lutheran church, typically for four vocal parts or organ.

- **Concerto**   A concerto is a piece of ensemble music for voices and instruments, typically with a solo instrument or voice in contrast with an orchestral ensemble.

- **Fugue**   The term *fugue* describes a piece of music that incorporates imitative counterpoint. (See Chapter 14 to learn more about counterpoint.) Most fugues are instrumental in nature.

◆ **Madrigal**   A madrigal is a piece of vocal music based on a fourteenth-century Italian form. Madrigals are secular in nature.

◆ **March**   A march is an instrumental piece, based on a regular and repeated drum rhythm, originally developed for military bands.

◆ **Minuet**   A minuet is a French dance in triple time (3/4, 3/8, 6/8, and so forth).

◆ **Opera**   An opera is a long, complex dramatic work, incorporating both voices and instruments. You can think of an opera as the classical equivalent of today's popular musicals, mixing music with a dramatic plot.

◆ **Operetta**   Literally, a "little opera." More commonly, a shorter or less ambitious stage work than a full-blown opera, typically with just a single act.

◆ **Oratorio**   An oratorio is an extended vocal work based on a sacred text.

◆ **Sonata**   A sonata is a piece of instrumental music, performed in several distinct sections (called *movements*). Sonatas typically are written for a soloist and small ensemble.

◆ **Song**   A song, in classical music, is a short and self-contained piece for one or more voices; it can be accompanied or not, and either sacred or secular in nature. In popular music, however, just about any musical composition (vocal or instrumental) is called a song.

◆ **Suite**   A suite is an ordered set of instrumental pieces meant to be performed at a single sitting.

◆ **Symphony**   A symphony is an extended work for orchestra, typically in three or four distinct movements. The symphony is generally regarded as the central form of orchestral composition—this is the big dog of classical instrumental music.

If you're serious about continuing your music education, you'll study each of these forms in much more detail. For now, though, it's probably enough to know the names of these forms; you can learn more about each form when the time comes.

The Least You Need to Know

◆ Most popular songs consist of a short instrumental intro, one or more verses, a chorus, a bridge, and an ending.

◆ Each part of the song is assigned a letter; the form of the song is notated by a combination of letters. For example, a song with two verses, a chorus, and a final verse is designated AABA.

◆ Jazz musicians and jam bands often play head arrangements, in which the main melody (the head) is played straight; then used for a series of instrumental solos.

◆ There are several forms specific to classical music, including the opera, the sonata, and the symphony.

Exercises

Exercise 11-1

Compose a 32-measure song in the ABCA form: verse, chorus, bridge, and verse. Use the key of G, in 4/4 time, and label each section of the piece.

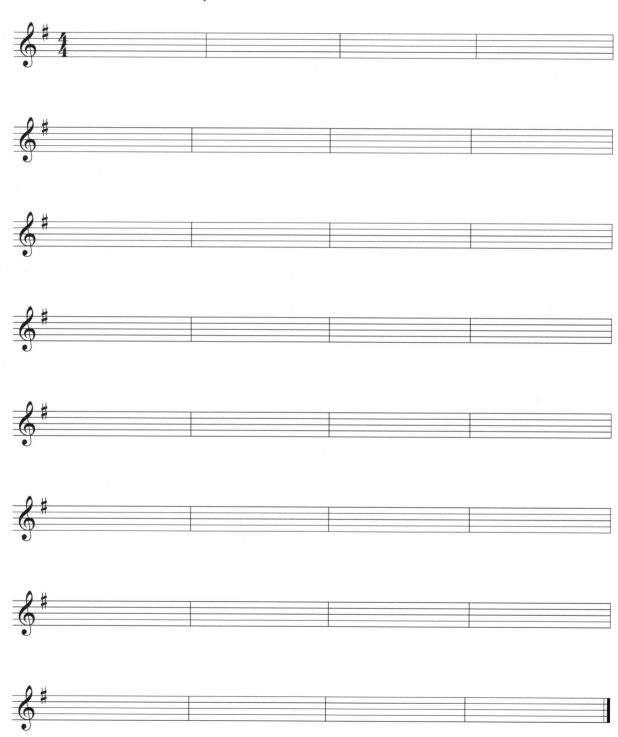

Part 4 Accompanying

Learn how to train your ears so you can write down the music you hear; then discover how to create simple accompaniment parts on piano or guitar. Finally, learn how to take a song in one key and transpose it to a totally different key—no math required!

Chapter 12

Transcribing What You Hear

In This Chapter

◆ Understanding why ear training is important

◆ Discovering how to actively listen

◆ Developing your tonal memory

◆ Learning how to transcribe songs from CDs and tapes

In an ideal world, everything you need is served up to you on a silver platter. As a musician, that means you'll always get perfectly noted pieces of sheet music from which to read, with all the chords and melodies and rhythms clearly written out.

Unfortunately, we don't live in an ideal world: You won't always get sheet music for the songs you have to play; sometimes you'll be expected to "play by ear" and figure out the music on your own.

How do you write down a piece of music, note for note, based on a few listens to a CD or tape? It's a particular skill, that's for sure; one that involves a technique called *ear training*. That means you have to train your ears to recognize certain rhythms and intervals, and be able to transfer what you hear to the written page.

Training Your Ear

Consider the following: You're in a band that plays the latest hit songs, and the band leader gives you a CD and asks you to learn a new tune—by tomorrow night. No sheet music, no one to answer your questions, no one to practice with you and help you figure it out—you're completely on your own, just you and your CD player.

Or you're working with a songwriter who doesn't read music. Your friend sings a melody, and asks you to write it down so he can send it to a music publicist. He doesn't know what key the song is in, or what notes he's singing; he leaves those details up to you to figure out.

Maybe you're playing organ in the church choir. The guest vocalist this week approaches you just before Sunday's service, and says she'll be singing "Amazing Grace," in the key of G. She doesn't have any sheet music for you—"You know the song," she says—and if you don't, you'll have to learn it, fast.

Perhaps you're playing saxophone in a pickup band at your local bar. It's open mike night, and the next performer wants you to add some horn accompaniment to his tune. "It's a 12-bar blues," he says, "in the key of A. You have a solo after the second chorus." No music, no nothing—just you, onstage, winging it.

All of these situations require you to think on your feet—or, more properly, to play by ear. You need to be able to hear a song and figure out what chords and notes are being played, without benefit of any written music.

Definition

Transcribing is the art of writing down melodies and chords by ear, without the benefit of any other written notation.

This might sound daunting to you, but it's a skill you need to develop. You have to be able to hear a melody or chord progression, and then *transcribe* what you hear. With practice, you'll be able to do this quickly and accurately; it can even become second nature. All you have to do is train your ears.

Transcribing music involves three distinct steps:

1. Listen
2. Process
3. Document

You begin by listening to the music—not for passive enjoyment, but more actively, so that you clearly hear every note. Then you process what you've heard, figuring out what notes and chords and rhythms are being played. Finally, you document the music you've processed, either by writing down the notes on paper, or using the processed music as a basis for live playing or improvisation.

With practice, you'll move through the listen-process-document system almost subconsciously; the notes will come to you automatically when you hear them, without a lot of work on your part. So warm up your ears—it's time for the training to begin!

Note

Ear training is a difficult skill to learn. Developing your listening skills takes time and guidance, and for most people is best accomplished in a classroom setting, or with an experienced teacher.

Still, there are many steps you can take to train your ears on your own, several of which I include in this chapter. If you want to continue in this self-paced fashion, pick up a copy of Ron Gorow's *Hearing and Writing Music: Professional Training for Today's Musician* (September Publishing, 2000).

Better still, head down to your local community college and sign up for an ear-training class. The personal feedback and guidance you'll receive from the instructor will be worth the effort.

Listening—Actively

Before we get into ear training proper, you need to learn how to actively listen to music. This isn't listening for enjoyment; it's listening to remember, and to analyze.

Start by isolating yourself from the hurly burly of your day-to-day life. Turn off the TV, close the windows, and block out all extraneous noises—the air conditioner, the refrigerator, the hum of the air pump in your fish tank. Create an environment in which you can focus on the music, without any distractions.

Prepare the music. This means setting up your audio system, with a good pair of speakers, or even a quality set of headphones. Make sure the music source can be easily accessed; you'll be doing a lot of rewinding and fast forwarding. And use a high-quality source; compact discs are better than cassette tapes or vinyl records.

Now get yourself comfortable—but not *too* comfortable. Find a comfy chair, or a couch, or even a place on the floor, surrounded by pillows. Don't get relaxed; instead, remain alert and ready for input. And don't squirm. When you're fully prepared, it's time to listen. Select a song, one of your favorites; then press the play button … and listen.

Begin by listening to the overall form of the song. Determine where one phrase ends and another begins. Figure out where the verses are, and the chorus, and even the bridge, if there is one. Get a feel for how the song is constructed, for its internal logic, for the way it flows from one point to another.

Now listen to the song again, but this time focus carefully on the melody line. Listen hard, and listen critically. Note where the melody goes up, and where it goes down. Note where the melody changes; where the verse ends and the chorus begins; and where any variations occur. Listen to it as many times as you need, until you're sure you can sing it back, verbatim.

Return to the start of the song, and this time *don't* listen to the melody. Instead, listen to the bass line. Listen to the tones played, and to the rhythms. Note how the bass notes relate to the melody, and to the other parts. Listen to the bass part and *memorize* the bass part; then play the song back again and sing along with the bass, from memory.

Again, return to the start of the song. This time listen to another part—the lead guitar, or the piano, or the saxophone. It doesn't matter; pick a part, and follow it from start to finish. Listen critically, and hear how this part fits with the bass and the melody and all the other parts. Listen until you have the part memorized.

Repeat this process until you *know* all the parts of the song. Get to the point where you can sing back any given part, without prompting. Let that song get inside your brain; become one with the music.

Tip

When you're isolating the bass line, you might want to turn up the bass (and turn down the treble) on your audio system, to better hear the low notes.

Finally, listen to the entire song again and try to figure out where the chord changes are. There might be a new chord every 4 beats, or 8, or even 16. Figure out the time signature (probably 4/4), and then try to lay a map of the chord changes over the form of the song.

This is how you actively listen to a song. You're not listening for enjoyment (you can do that separately); you're listening to *learn*—and to remember. Once you can recall a part exactly, from memory, you're one step closer to figuring out the notes behind the part, and transcribing it to paper.

Developing Superhearing

As part of your active listening, you have to be able to discern the component parts of the music. You have to be able to hear discrete pitches and intervals, hear different rhythms, and even hear the individual pitches within each chord. Sound difficult? It is—which is why you need to practice.

Hearing Pitch

The first part of the music you need to hear is the pitch. You need to be able to listen to a pitch, isolate it, and then replicate it. In plain English, that means you need to be able to sing back any specific pitch you hear in a song. To do this, you have to develop what is called *tonal memory*, or *pitch memory*. This is simply the ability to recall a specific pitch, outside the context of the song or melody.

You can develop your tonal memory with this simple exercise. Take a half-full glass of water and hit it (gently!) with the edge of a spoon. The glass will produce a distinct pitch. Listen to the pitch, and fix it in your head. Wait until the glass stops ringing, then wait a few seconds more, then sing or hum the note that you heard. While you're singing (or humming), hit the glass again; if your tonal memory was on target, the second tone generated by the glass will be the same as the tone you're singing. If not, try it again—and pay more attention this time.

Repeat this exercise, adding more time between hitting the glass and singing the note. The longer you can hold the note in your head, the better developed your sense of tonal memory will be.

> **Note**
>
> When you hear notes or melodies inside your head (in your inner voice), you're *internalizing* the music.

Next, try to find that pitch on your instrument. (Use whatever instrument you like—piano, guitar, trumpet, whatever—it doesn't matter.) Hit the glass, wait a minute, sing the pitch, and then try to play that pitch on your instrument. Don't worry if you can't find the pitch right off. You might need to poke around a few related notes until you find the one that matches what you're singing. That's natural. With practice, you'll be able to more quickly identify individual tones.

Obviously, you want to verify the note you're playing with the source—the ringing glass. Play the note on your instrument while you hit the glass; if you have the right note, they'll be in unison.

You can extend this exercise by generating different notes with different objects. (You can also fill the glass to different levels to produce different pitches.) When you're comfortable with your progress, put on a CD and pick a single note from the melody. Repeat the exercise, this time trying to reproduce that melody note. Rewind the CD to replay the melody and check your accuracy.

> **Note**
>
> Interestingly, about 5 percent of musicians (just musicians—not the general population) have something called *absolute pitch*, which means they can wake up in the morning and, with no prompting or assistance, correctly sing or identify any given pitch. Some people claim to be able to help you develop this skill, but in general it is virtually impossible for anyone over the age of five or so to learn perfect pitch. (Not 100 percent impossible, but almost.)
>
> In any case, you don't really need this kind of long-term pitch memory to transcribe music. You can get along fine with the short-term pitch memory that we all possess, along with a good interval memory, which we'll discuss next.

Hearing Intervals

If you can hear and reproduce a single note, what about two of them?

That's right: The next step is to develop your tonal memory to decipher and reproduce pitch intervals.

Before you begin your exercises, you need to develop an internal database of relative interval relationships. That means internalizing all the different intervals within a given object—remembering what each interval sounds like.

The best way to do this is to sit down at your instrument and play each interval until it's burned into your brain. Play a minor second, and a major second, and a minor third, and a major third, and so on; until you have each interval committed to memory. Can you sing a minor third? If not, you need to study some more.

Of course, there are shortcuts you can take. If you can remember specific snatches of melody, you can associate those melodies with particular intervals. The following table provides some melodic shortcuts for your interval training:

Intervals Found in Popular Melodies

Interval		Song-Specific Phrase
ASCENDING		
Minor second	Theme from *Jaws*	**Dum-dum** ... (bass line)
	"As Time Goes By" (from *Casablanca*)	**YOU MUST** remember this ...
	"Bye Bye Blackbird"	**BYE-BYE** blackbird ...
Major second	"Frere Jacques"	**FRE-RE** Jacques ...
	"Happy Birthday"	Hap-**PY BIRTH**-day to you ...
	"I Left My Heart in San Francisco"	**I LEFT** my heart in San Francisco ...
Minor third	"To Dream the Impossible Dream"	**TO DREAM** the impossible dream ...
	Brahm's Lullaby	**LULLA-BY** and goodnight ...
Major third	"Have Yourself a Merry Little Christmas"	**HAVE YOUR**-self a merry little Christmas ...
	"Oh Susanna"	**WELL I** come from Alabama ...
	"Oh When the Saints Come Marching In"	**OH WHEN** the saints ...
Perfect fourth	"Here Comes the Bride"	**HERE COMES** the bride ...
	"Amazing Grace"	**A-MAZ**-ing grace ...
	"We Wish You a Merry Christmas"	**WE WISH** you a merry Christmas ...
Tritone	"Maria" (from *West Side Story*)	**MA-RI**-a ...
Perfect fifth	Theme from *Goldfinger*	**GOLD-FIN**-ger ...
	"My Favorite Things" (from *The Sound of Music*)	**RAIN-DROPS** on roses ...
	"Twinkle Twinkle Little Star"	**TWINKLE TWINKLE** little star ...
	Chant of the Wicked Witch's guardsmen in *The Wizard of Oz*	**YO-EE**-oh ...
Minor sixth	"Sunrise, Sunset" (from *Fiddler on the Roof*)	**IS THIS** the little girl ...
Major sixth	"NBC" chime	**N-B-C** (first two notes)
	"Jingle Bells"	**DASH-ING** through the snow ...
	"It Came Upon the Midnight Clear"	**IT CAME** upon the midnight clear ...
Minor seventh	"There's a Place for Us" (from *West Side Story*)	**THERE'S A** place for us ...
	Theme from *Star Trek*	**Doo-doooo** ... (first two notes)
Major seventh	"Cast Your Fate to the Wind"	(first two notes of the melody)
Octave	"Somewhere Over the Rainbow"	**SOME-WHERE** over the rainbow ...
	"A Christmas Song"	**CHEST-NUTS** roasting on an open fire ...
	"Let It Snow"	Oh, **THE WEA**-ther outside is frightful ...

continues

Intervals Found in Popular Melodies   (continued)

Interval		Song-Specific Phrase
DESCENDING		
Minor second	"Joy to the World" (Christmas carol)	**JOY TO** the world, the Lord is come …
	"O Little Town of Bethlehem"	O **LITTLE TOWN** of Bethlehem …
	"Spinning Wheel" (Blood, Sweat and Tears)	**RIDE A** painted pony …
Major second	"Three Blind Mice"	**THREE BLIND** mice …
	"Mary Had a Little Lamb"	**MA-RY** had a little lamb …
	"Yesterday" (The Beatles)	**YES-TERDAY**, all my troubles seemed so far away …
Minor third	"Jesus Loves Me"	**JE-SUS** loves me this I know …
	"The Star-Spangled Banner"	**OH-OH** say can you see …
	"Hey Jude" (The Beatles)	**HEY JUDE** …
Major third	"Swing Low, Sweet Chariot"	**SWING LOW**, sweet chariot …
	"Good Night Ladies" (from *The Music Man*)	**GOOD NIGHT** ladies …
	"Summertime" (from *Porgy and Bess*)	**SUM-MER**-time, and the livin' is easy …
Perfect fourth	"Born Free"	**BORN FREE** …
	"I've Been Working on the Railroad"	**I'VE BEEN** working on the railroad …
	"My Girl" (The Temptations)	**MY GIRL**, talkin' 'bout my girl …
Tritone	European police siren	
Perfect fifth	Theme from *The Flintsones*	**FLINT-STONES,** meet the Flintstones …
	"Feelings"	**FEEL-INGS,** whoa, whoa, whoa, feelings …
Minor sixth	Theme from *Love Story*	**WHERE DO** I begin …
Major sixth	"Over There"	**O-VER** there …
	"Nobody Knows the Trouble I've Seen"	**NO-BOD**-y knows …
Minor seventh	"Watermelon Man"	Water-**MEL**-on **MAN**
Major seventh	"Have Yourself a Merry Little Christmas"	So **HAVE YOUR**-self a merry little Christmas now …
Octave	"Salt Peanuts" (Dizzy Gillespie)	Salt **PEA-NUTS**, salt peanuts …

Exercise your interval memory the same way you did your tonal memory. Start by listening to a song and picking two adjacent notes in the melody—the first two notes are often the best to work with. Wait a few seconds; then try to sing the two notes. Verify your accuracy by playing the song again.

Once you can internalize the interval, try to determine what interval it is that you're singing. Is it a second? A third? Is it major or minor? Determine the interval, and then try to reproduce the interval on your instrument. Once you can accurately play the interval, you can verify the specific interval you guessed. (For example, if you find yourself playing a G and then a B, you know you're playing a major third.)

Tip

When you first start listening to intervals, you should focus on the relative distance between the two notes. Is it a wide span between the pitches? If so, the interval is a larger one; maybe a fifth or a sixth or something even larger. Is it a narrow span between the pitches? If so, the interval is a smaller one; maybe some sort of second or third. Narrow the possibilities down as much as possible before you determine the precise interval.

Hearing Rhythms

We'll set aside pitches for a moment and instead focus on note durations—in other words, your *rhythmic memory*. Use the same technique as you did before, but this time listen to the rhythm of a song's melody. Start by figuring out the time signature of the song and breaking the melody (in your head) into measures. Now pick the first few beats of the melody's first measure. Stop the playback, fix that rhythm in your head, and then pound it out with your hand on a table. Repeat this process until you can hold the rhythm in your head for half a minute or longer.

Once you can repeat a short rhythmic phrase, it's time to up the ante. Try repeating the rhythm for an entire measure; then two, then four, then for the entire melody. Always check your accuracy by pounding the table in time to the original song.

With the entire rhythm of the melody committed to memory, use the theory you've learned and try to transcribe the rhythm. Start small, a beat or two at a time. Make sure the rhythm you write is mathematically sound; for example, if the song is in 4/4, all the notes have to add up to a full whole note. (That means four quarters, or two quarters and eight eights, or whatever.)

Once you've written down the entire rhythm, play back the song again, this time reading the rhythm you've written. If you notice a discrepancy, correct it; otherwise, repeat the exercise with another song; this time one that is more rhythmically complex.

Hearing Melodies

Now that you can hear individual notes, intervals, and rhythms, you should be able to hear and transcribe complete melodies. All you have to do is put together everything you hear, in the right order, to develop your melodic memory.

While you can piece together a melody one note or interval at a time, it's easier if you try to grasp the big picture first. That means figuring out how many measures long the melody is, and how it's broken up into phrases. Once you can dissemble a melody into its component parts, you should focus on each part separately.

On what pitch does this part of the melody start? On what pitch does it end? On what pitch does the middle of the phrase end? If you try to pinpoint individual parts of the melody, it should be relatively easy to connect the dots and fill in the empty spaces with the proper passing and neighboring tones.

Once you've written out the entire melody—including both pitches and rhythmic notes—remember to verify your accuracy by playing back the melody you've written. Compare the melody you play with the melody you first heard; the better you get, the closer they'll match up.

> **Note**
>
> If you don't have any spare music paper lying around the house, feel free to photocopy the pages of blank staves located in the back of this book.

Hearing Keys

Once you can notate a melody, you should be able to determine what key the song is in. For example, if your melody incorporates a B♭—but no other flat or sharp notes—it's a good guess that the song is written in the key of F. (As you probably remember from Chapter 4, the key of F has a single flat.) If the melody has an F# and a C#, you're probably in the key of D.

Another way to determine the key is to fix the home pitch of the melody. If the melody keeps resolving to G, chances are you're in the key of G. (Unless, that is, the melody is minor—in which case, you could be in the key of G minor.)

Test your guess by using your instrument to play a major scale in the designated key, while the original song is playing. If all the notes fit, you've guessed right. If not, try a related key—a key one or two steps away on the circle of fifths.

Hearing Chords

The last piece of the puzzle concerns the underlying chord structure. You need to hear when the chords change, and what they change to.

When determining chords, it helps to listen to the song's bass line. If you listen to the notes the bass is playing, 9 times out of 10 the main notes—all embellishment aside—will be the root notes of the underlying chords. For example, if you know the song is in the key of C and the bass player plays, in successive measures, C, A, F, and G, it's a good guess that the chord progression is C-Am-F-G.

You should also listen carefully to determine whether you're hearing a major or a minor chord. Remember, major chords are happy sounding; minor chords are a little sad.

Tip

If you're having trouble hearing the chords, you can always try to figure out the chords from the notes of the melody, which you learned how to do back in Chapter 10.

Once you've figured out the chords in the song, you should test your chord transcription against the melody you've previously transcribed. Make sure the notes of the melody fit within the chord structure; if not, you probably need to rethink a few chords.

The real test comes when you play your chords against the original recording. Be especially careful to match where your chords change with where the chords change in the original song. It's not uncommon to accidentally skip a chord change or two, so listen closely to make sure you picked up on all the changes.

Writing It All Down

If you've followed the exercises carefully, you've ended up with a complete transcription of the melody and chords for a specific song. Congratulations! It's a lot of work, I know, but this newfound skill is one you'll use again and again as you progress in the music field.

You can further develop this skill by transcribing other parts of the song, not just the melody. If the song has a horn section, try to figure out and transcribe each individual horn part. If there's an orchestral backing, work on transcribing the string parts. If there's a fancy rhythm section, isolate and transcribe the rhythms played by each individual percussionist.

Further developing your transcribing skill is especially important if you choose to pursue the fields of composing or arranging. You can certainly challenge yourself by transcribing an entire big-band arrangement for your high school jazz band, a full choral arrangement for your church choir, or a string quartet for your community orchestra. There's value in this skill—and a great sense of accomplishment when you get it right.

> **Note**
>
> As the final assignment for a college music theory class, I transcribed the entire arrangement of Weather Report's "Birdland." It wasn't easy—it's a complex song, with a lot of different parts—but I was able to use the transcription to create a full arrangement for my band to play. So I learned some interesting points about music theory, got a good grade on my assignment, and added a new song to our band's repertoire—all in one fell swoop!

The Least You Need to Know

♦ Ear training is necessary for those times when you don't have written music to work with—or when you want to figure out a song you've recently heard.

♦ The key to transcribing a song is to listen, process what you've heard, and then document what you've processed.

♦ To accurately analyze a piece of music, you have to learn how to actively listen—to isolate and then remember the individual parts of the song.

♦ As part of the ear training process, you must develop your intrinsic tonal, interval, and rhythmic memory, so that you can remember and replicate the pitches, rhythms, and melodies you hear.

♦ Once you've transcribed the entire melody, you can more easily figure out the song's key signature and its underlying chord structure.

Exercises

Exercise 12-1

Play each of the following notes on your instrument, wait for thirty seconds, and then sing them back.

Exercise 12-2

Sing each of the following ascending intervals, starting on any note you like.

♦ Major third   ♦ Minor second

♦ Perfect fifth   ♦ Minor third

♦ Perfect fourth   ♦ Octave

♦ Major second   ♦ Tritone

Exercise 12-3

Sing each of the following descending intervals, starting on any note you like.

♦ Minor third   ♦ Perfect fourth

♦ Major second   ♦ Major seventh

♦ Perfect fifth   ♦ Major third

♦ Major sixth   ♦ Minor sixth

Exercise 12-4

Sing all the notes of the following chords, one after another. (Start on any root note you like.)

- ◆ Major chord
- ◆ Minor chord
- ◆ Diminished chord
- ◆ Augmented chord
- ◆ Major seventh chord
- ◆ Minor seventh chord
- ◆ Dominant seventh chord
- ◆ Major ninth chord

Exercise 12-5

Transcribe the rhythm (only) of "I Got Rhythm."

Exercise 12-6

Transcribe the melody of "This Land is Your Land."

Exercise 12-7

Use the blank music paper at the back of this book to transcribe the melody and chords to your favorite popular song.

Accompanying Melodies

In This Chapter

- ◆ Working with a lead sheet
- ◆ Figuring out what to play
- ◆ Understanding different types of accompaniment
- ◆ Adding a more interesting bass part
- ◆ Accompanying on guitar

If you play piano or guitar, at some point in time you will be asked to accompany another musician or group of musicians. Maybe it's playing behind a singer at church, or backing up your children's choir at school, or even vamping behind a harmonica soloist in a blues band. Whatever the situation, you'll be expected to provide at least rudimentary backing to the primary musicians.

If, along with this request, you also are handed a page of detailed sheet music, you're set. All you have to do is read your part, play the notes, and take your bows.

However, if there's no written music accompanying the request, you have your work cut out for you. Depending on the gig, you might have to transcribe the melody, figure out the chords, and compose your own part—all of which you can do, if you have the proper grounding in music theory.

What's the Score?

When you're asked to accompany someone on piano (or guitar, for that matter), you should first figure out how much homework you need to do. This is determined by the amount of written music you're given.

The best of all possible situations is that you receive a complete musical score. If this is the case, you don't need to read any further in this chapter—you're set!

However, it's more likely that you'll be provided with only sketchy written information—or none at all. If this is the case, you need to apply the skills you've learned in the previous chapters to figure out just what you need to play.

Working from a Lead Sheet

Here's the 411: You're given a sheet of music that includes the melody and the chords—what musicians call a *lead sheet*. It will look something like this:

A typical lead sheet—melody and chord symbols.

With this lead sheet in hand, what do you play?

The temptation for many novice musicians is to play the melody with your right hand and form the chords with your left hand.

You should resist this temptation.

> **Note**
>
> Learn more about lead sheets and other types of arrangements in Chapter 19.

When you read a lead sheet, the melody (also known as the *lead*) is provided for your reference only. Unless you're playing solo piano in a cocktail bar, you're not expected to play the melody—except, maybe, during instrumental breaks.

No, what you're expected to play are the *chords*—along with any kind of embellishment or harmony you can create to play behind the melody.

But the main thing you need from this situation is to play the chords, which you have—printed in big, bold letters on your lead sheet. Play the chords themselves with your right hand, while you play the root note of the chord (the bass line) with your left hand.

That's all you have to play, and it isn't hard at all.

> **Tip**
>
> When you're playing chords with your right hand, try to avoid playing every chord in the standard 1-3-5 inversion. Try different inversions—different *voicings*—to better group the notes from adjacent chords together. (Turn back to Chapter 9 for more information on chord inversions.) For example, if you're alternating between the C and the F chord, you might play the C chord C-E-G, but then play the F chord C-F-A (first inversion), which lets you leave your thumb on the C note for both chords.

Working from a Chord Sheet

A chord sheet is like a lead sheet, but without the melody written out. Working from a chord sheet is just like working from a lead sheet—play the chords with your right hand and the root of the chord with your left. A typical chord sheet looks like this:

A chord sheet—no melody.

Working from a Melody

Sometimes you get the melody (in the form of a lead sheet) *without* chords. All you have to go from is the melody—no chords, no bass line, no anything else.

A melody sheet—no chords.

What do you do now?

First, don't panic. Second, remember back to Chapter 10, in which you learned how to create a chord progression based on a melodic line. That is the skill from which you need to draw now.

Take the melody you were given and go off by yourself for a half-hour or so. Play the melody on the piano, and try to figure out what chords sound good with that melody. If it's a familiar song, the chords might come easily to you; if you've never heard the song before, you have your work cut out for you. In any case, apply the rules you learned back in Chapter 10, and write out your own chord progression for this melody.

> **Tip**
>
> When you're trying to figure out the chords behind a melody, there are several different approaches you can take. The best approach, as you learned in Chapter 10, is to try some common chord progressions. See if I-IV-V fits the melody; if not, try I-ii-V, or I-vi-IV-V, or the "circle of fifths" progression. Chances are, one of the common chord progressions will fit—or at least come close.

The key thing here is that the chords you write are now your chords. Even if they're not quite the established chords for this melody, you can get away with it by claiming that this is your unique harmonization. You're at the piano, and you're in charge, so what you play must be right!

Now, if you're playing along with other musicians—perhaps a bass player or a guitarist—you don't want to end up with three different sets of chords to this single melody. If you're playing in a group, put your heads together and work out the chord progressions as a group. Heck, maybe one of you actually knows the chords already! In any case, three heads are better than one, and together you should be able to come up with just the right chord progression for this song.

Working from Nothing

Now we visit the worst-case scenario. You're asked to play piano accompaniment and you're given no music at all. All you have are your ears and your fingers, and all the skills you've picked up from reading this book.

Now you can panic!

In this situation, it's okay to ask for help. Ask the person in charge if he or she has *anything* to give you—a lead sheet, a lyric sheet, an old trumpet part—anything at all. (Anything is better than nothing in this scenario.) Ask what key the song is in. Ask if there's anyone who knows the chords and can either teach them to you or write them down for you. Ask if anyone has a recording of the song you can take home and listen to.

In short, ask for all the help you can get.

Whatever meager help you get, you're now on your own. It's time to fall back on the ear-training skills you learned back in Chapter 12. You'll need to figure out the melody, figure out the key, and figure out the chords. In short, you have to reconstruct the song from memory and hope you get it right.

Then, when you start to play and the vocalist says "Those aren't the right chords!" make sure you have something small but heavy nearby—because you'll want to throw it!

Working the Form

Once you get the chords written down, you'll need to write down some sort of "cheat sheet" to help you remember the form of the song. Do you play one or two verses before the first chorus? How long is the introduction? Is there an instrumental break in the middle—and for how many measures? Do you fade out at the end, or stop cold?

You'll need to figure all this out and write it down, so you'll remember when to start, when to stop, and what to do in between. Use the form notation (AABA, ABCA, and so forth) you learned back in Chapter 11 to help you keep your place.

Playing the Part

Once you have the chords written down, you have to play the song. Because there's no formal piano part, you're on your own in terms of figuring out what type of part to play. Fortunately, you can employ some common accompaniment techniques; you don't have to reinvent the wheel.

Block Chord Accompaniment

The easiest type of accompaniment to play is the *block chord* accompaniment. This approach is exactly as it sounds: Whenever there's a chord change, you put all your fingers on the keyboard (at the same time) and play the chord.

That's it. You don't play any special rhythms, you don't arpeggiate the chord, you don't do anything except *plunk!* the notes of the chord all at once.

All you have to do is put the three (or more) notes of the chord in your right hand and double the root of the chord with your left hand, like this:

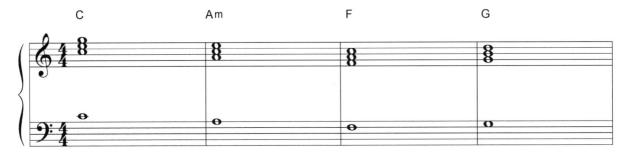

Accompanying a melody with block chords.

The primary benefit of playing a block chord accompaniment is that it's easy—for you, anyway. The drawback is that it's a rather sparse accompaniment; it really doesn't add anything to the music, except to provide only the most basic harmonic underpinning to the melody.

Still, if block chords are all you can master, that's what you should play. No one will ever accuse you of getting in the way or covering up the melody!

Rhythmic Accompaniment

There's another way to play chords that isn't quite as boring as the block chord approach. You play the block chords, but with a more interesting rhythmic pattern.

What kind of pattern am I talking about? There are several you can choose from, including these:

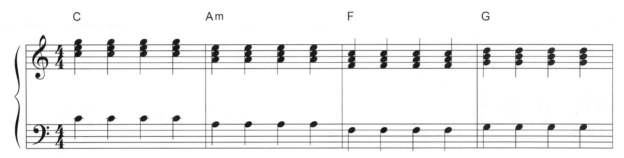

Rhythmic accompaniment in quarter notes.

Rhythmic accompaniment with a syncopated rhythm.

Rhythmic accompaniment with a syncopated dotted quarter note rhythm—kind of a Latin feel.

You can even break up the rhythm slightly by playing your left hand (the bass) on beats one and three, and your right hand (the chords) on two and four, like this:

Playing the chords on the backbeat.

Or, if you want a more lively sound, play the bass on each beat and the chords as eighth notes on each upbeat (plus the downbeat of one), like this:

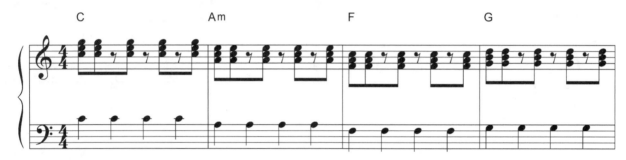

Playing the chords on the upbeat.

The benefit of this approach is that it provides a driving pulse for the song. The drawback is that you have to pick the right kind of pulse, which requires you to have some sense of rhythm.

If you don't have any natural rhythm, you might want to stick to block chords.

Definition

An **arpeggiated accompaniment** also is often called a *broken chord* accompaniment because you break the chord apart and play each note separately.

Arpeggiated Accompaniment

If you're playing a slower song, you might want to break up the chords and play the individual notes in a sequence, like an arpeggio. You can create a simple *arpeggiated accompaniment* by playing straight eighth notes over two beats, with the root of the chord on beat one, the third of the chord on the first upbeat, the fifth on beat two, and the third (again) on the second upbeat.

Written out, it looks something like this:

Playing an arpeggiated accompaniment.

You can vary this accompaniment by changing up the order of the chord tones, varying the rhythm, or even adding passing notes, like this:

An arpeggiated accompaniment with passing tones in addition to the main chord tones.

If you make sure you play the root of the chord in the bass, you have a quick and easy accompaniment for all types of music.

Moving Bass

Once you get good at these simple types of accompaniment, you can spice things up by playing a more complex bass part.

So far, all you have to do is play the root of the chord—in time!— with your left hand. However, if you listen to just about any song from the pop era, starting with the Beatles, you'll hear a lot more in the bass than just the root. That's because bass guitarists in the '60s upped the ante and started playing some really interesting bass parts.

If you want to add more bass to your piano accompaniments, start by adding passing tones between the root notes of consecutive chords, like this:

> **Note**
>
> Paul McCartney was one of the pioneers of this new style of bass playing, as was James Jamerson at Motown. One of the most influential bass parts ever recorded was on the Four Tops' hit "Bernadette"—which is James Jamer-son at the top of his form.

Passing notes in the bass.

You're not limited to the root in the bass, either. Many bass parts provide interest by stopping on the third or the fifth of the chord, instead of on the root. If you expand on this concept you end up with a *walking bass line*, such as that found in a lot of jazz music. A walking bass line goes beyond simple passing tones by "walking" up and down the scale, like this:

A walking bass line.

As you develop your accompanying skills, you can elaborate on the bass or the chords in lots of different ways. Just remember to listen to the song and play a part that's appropriate.

One Good Strum Deserves Another

Pianos aren't the only accompanying instruments, of course. If you play guitar, you have to face many of the same challenges a piano player does when asked to provide accompaniment to others.

Chief of these challenges, of course, is figuring out what chords to play—which, you now know, is within your grasp. All you have to do is use the skills you learned previously in this book.

Once you've figured out the chords, you have to play them. In most instances, you can get by with simple strumming. You can strum on the first beat of every measure, you can strum on every beat, you can strum a backbeat on two and four, or you can strum in a more complex rhythm. Depending on the song, you can even break up the chords by playing one string at a time in an arpeggiated pattern. The important thing is to use your ears and play what fits the music.

And make sure you keep up with the chord changes!

The Least You Need to Know

♦ If you're given a lead sheet with chord notation, play the chords as written.

♦ If you're given a melody sheet with no chords noted—or no music at all—you have to figure out the chords before you play.

♦ When accompanying other musicians, play the chord with your right hand and the root of the chord with your left.

♦ You can play many different types of accompaniment—block chords, simple rhythms, broken chords, and so on—depending on the mood and tempo of the song itself.

♦ Before you play a new song, make sure you sketch out the form of the song (verse, chorus, and so forth) so that you don't get lost in the middle of things.

Exercises

Exercise 13-1

Play a block chord accompaniment based on the following lead sheet.

Exercise 13-2

Play a rhythmic accompaniment based on the following lead sheet.

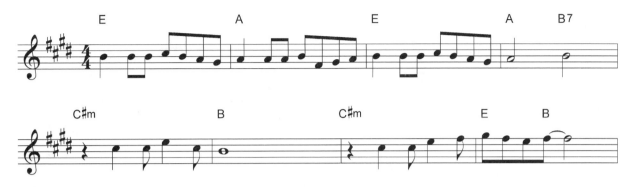

Exercise 13-3

Play an arpeggiated accompaniment based on the following lead sheet.

Exercise 13-4

Play an accompaniment with a moving bass part, based on the following lead sheet.

Chapter 14

Transposing to Other Keys

In This Chapter

◆ Understanding transposition

◆ Discovering when you need to transpose a song

◆ Learning different methods of transposition

◆ Using computerized music notation programs to transpose your songs automatically

You're sitting at your piano, on stage, ready to play the next tune, when the female vocalist walks over to you.

"This song's a little high for me in B♭," she says. "Take it down to A."

Huh?

Or maybe you're just starting to play guitar, don't know all the chords yet, and just got the sheet music for one of your favorite songs. You blanch when you discover that the song is in the key of G♭. G-flat! Who plays in G-flat? You don't know any chords in G-flat—not a one!

But you *do* know all your chords in G; maybe there's a way to change the song from G♭ to G.

Perhaps you're arranging a Christmas carol for your church choir, which will be accompanied by a solo trumpet. You hand the trumpet player his part and he plays what you thought was supposed to be a C—but it comes out as a B♭ instead, according to the notes on your piano.

What gives?

All three of these examples are situations in which you need to know how to *transpose* a piece of music from one key to another—which is what this chapter is all about.

Move Your Notes Around

Transposition is the art of translating a note or chord from one key to another. It's really a math exercise—this note in this key equals that note in that key. When you transpose a note or a melody or a chord, you take it from one key, and instead play the equivalent note, melody, or chord in another key.

For example, let's say you're playing the note C in the key of C—the key's tonic note. When you transpose that note to the key of F, you now play an F—which is the tonic note for the key of F.

Sounds easy enough, doesn't it?

Let's look at a more complex example: Let's say you're in the key of C and you play a melody that moves from C to D to E—the first three notes of the C Major scale. When you transpose that melody to the key of F, the new notes (the first three notes of the F Major scale) are F, G, A.

Getting the hang of it yet?

Here's another example: Let's say you're in the key of C, and you're playing the I-vi-IV-V chord progression—C-Am-F-G. When you transpose that chord progression into the key of F, the new chords are F-Dm-B♭-C. It's still I-vi-IV-V; just in a different key.

You can transpose from any one key to any other key. That means you could move the notes anywhere from a half step to a major seventh up or down from where you started. (You also can move notes up or down by whole octaves—what is called *octave transposition*—but you're really not altering any notes; you're just changing octaves.)

Why You Need to Transpose

As you saw in the introduction to this chapter, there are many different reasons you might need to transpose a song. Here are some of the most common:

- The song, as written, is out of the range of a vocalist or instrumentalist. If a singer can't hit the high notes in the key of C, maybe the key of B or B♭, or even A might be friendlier.

- You or another musician don't know how to play the song in the given key. This is especially a problem with beginning guitarists who don't always know the chords in some of the more extreme flat or sharp keys—but they do know the chords for G and A and C and F. If you can transpose the song to one of these keys, everyone can play their parts. (You have the same problem with any instrument that has to deal with a lot of sharps and flats in the key signature; it's easier to play in C, G, D, F, and B♭ than it is to play in the other, more complex, keys.)

- You're writing or arranging for one of the many instruments that don't play in what we call *concert key*. For example, trumpets always sound one whole note lower than what is written—so you have to transpose all trumpet players' music up a step so they'll be in the same key as the other musicians. (So if the concert key is C, you write the trumpet part in D; when a trumpet plays a D, it actually sounds as concert C.)

Definition

Concert key is the underlying key of a piece of music, as determined by the pitches when played. The piano is always in concert key.

Warning

Many instruments do not play in concert key. See Chapter 18 to learn which instruments play in what keys.

These scenarios are more common than you'd think—which means you better learn how to transpose—and fast!

Four Ways to Transpose

When you have to transpose a song from one key to another, there are four ways to go about it. You can …

- Put your math skills to work and manually move each note up or down the required number of steps.

- Put your music theory skills to work and utilize degree-wise Roman numeral notation.

- Use your music theory skills again and mechanically transpose each note based on the interval from the previous note.

- Put technology to work and let a computerized music notation program do the job for you.

Step-Wise Transposition

Step-wise transposition is the grunt work of the arranging and composing world. In this method, you count the half steps between the first key and the second, and then move each note and chord up or down the necessary number of steps.

For example, let's say you have the following melody in the key of D:

Your original melody, in the key of D.

You need to transpose this melody to the key of F. When you do the counting, you find that F is three half steps above D. So you have to move all the chords and notes up three half steps like this:

1. Take the first note of the melody—an A. If you move this note up three half steps, it becomes a C.
2. Move to the second note of the melody—a B. If you move this note up three half steps, it becomes a D.
3. Move to the third note of the melody—a C#. If you move this note up three half steps, it becomes an E.

And so on, and so on. You do the same thing with the chords:

1. The first chord is D Major. If you move this chord up three half steps, it becomes an F Major chord.
2. The second chord is a G Major. If you move this chord up three half steps, it becomes a B♭ Major chord.

When you get done transposing all the notes and chords, you get this:

The same melody, transposed to the key of F.

It's grunt work, that's for sure—but it gets the job done.

Degree-Wise Transposition

If you've done a good job reading this book—and developing your music theory skills accordingly—there's another approach you can take to transposition. This approach requires you to break all the chords and notes down to their degrees of the underlying scale; you can then apply those degree representations to the new key.

The easiest way to understand this approach is to look at chords—in this case, the chords from our previous key-of-D melody:

The original chord progression, in the key of D.

To get the ball rolling, we've noted the chord type below each chord—I, IV, V, and so forth. For the next few minutes, we're going to work strictly with this degree notation and forget (for the time being) about the original chords.

The chord progression in Roman numerals only.

With the chord progression broken down by Roman numeral, you can write out each of the chords in your new key—in this case, the key of F. When you write out the new chords, you get this:

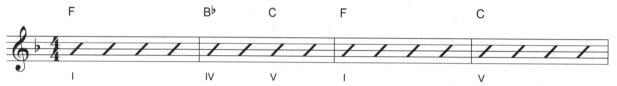

The chord progression transposed to the key of F.

Tip

If you're not sure which chords to use, refer back to the Scale-Based Chords table in Chapter 10.

Voilà! You've just transposed the entire chord progression—and you didn't have to count any half steps to do it.

You can apply this same technique to the notes in the melody. Work through the original key-of-C melody and put the degree of the scale (1, 2, 3, and so forth) under each note of the melody, like this:

Marking up the original melody, write the degree of the scale under each note.

Now get a blank sheet of music paper and, in the key of F, write out the scale degrees above the staff. If you fill in the actual notes for each scale degree, you end up with the completed melody:

Your transposed melody, by the numbers.

This method is a little more work for melodies than it is for chords, but it definitely works.

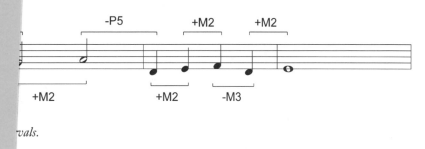

ve to transpose the first note from one key to another, but then you
etely in the new key. You do this by noting the intervals between each
se intervals to "compose" the transposed melody on the fly.

, and note the intervals between each note in the melody, like this:

vals.

Now, you start composing your "new" melody in the new key. The first note in the new key (which you have to manually figure out) is a C, and the interval between that note and the second note is a major second—which makes the second note a D. The next interval is another major second, which makes the next note an E. The next interval is a major second down, which makes the next note a D. And so on, until you're done.

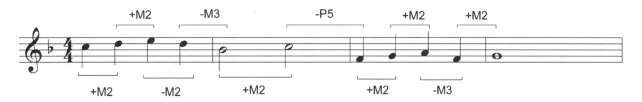

Transposing your melody one interval at a time.

This method doesn't work as well when you're transposing chords, because it doesn't tell you what *type* of chord comes next—major, minor, or other. I suppose you could augment this interval-based approach by noting the chord type from the original version, but that gets a tad complex; there are easier ways to transpose chord progressions.

Software-Based Transposition

Thanks to modern computer technology, you may be able to avoid manual transposition completely. Almost all computerized music notation programs let you enter your music in concert key; then click a button (or select a menu item) to automatically transpose one or more staves to another key.

For example, the Finale program (from Coda Music Technology) enables you to determine whether a given part is noted in concert key or the instrument's native key. Depending on the option you select, your score can show all instruments in concert key, or the specific keys for each instrument.

Programs such as Finale enable you to do your original composing in concert key and then automatically transpose the parts to their own keys when you're done writing. You can also write a single melodic or chord line, change keys, and have all the notes and chords automatically switch to the new key. These programs are great writing aids—no counting necessary!

> **Note**
>
> Learn more about music notation programs in Chapter 19.

Finale's Key Signature dialog box; the Transposition Options section lets you choose between transposing the notes when you change keys and holding the notes to their original pitches.

The Least You Need to Know

◆ Transposition is the art of moving notes and chords from one key to another.

◆ You need to learn transposition for those times when a singer requests a song in a different key, you or other musicians can't play in the original key, or you're composing or arranging for instruments that don't play in concert key.

◆ You can transpose a melody by counting the half steps from one key to another, noting the scale degrees of the original melody and chords, or using the intervals between the notes of the melody.

◆ Many computerized music notation programs will automatically transpose your music for you with the click of a mouse.

Exercises

Exercise 14-1

Use the step-based method to transpose this melody from the key of F to the key of G. (Watch the change from flats to sharps!)

Exercise 14-2

Use the degree-based method to transpose this chord progression from the key of A♭ to the key of E.

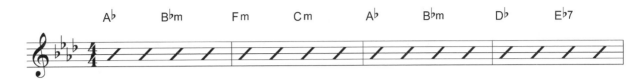

Exercise 14-3

Use the interval-based method to transpose this melody from the key of B♭ to the key of A.

Exercise 14-4

Use whatever method you like to transpose the following chords and melody from the key of C to the key of E.

Part 5

Embellishing

Discover how to fill out your music with lush harmonies and interesting counterpoint, and how to jazz up a tune with fancy chord substitutions. Bonus chapter: more fiddly notation marks!

Chapter 15

Harmony and Counterpoint

In This Chapter

◆ Understanding the differences—and similarities—between harmony and counterpoint

◆ Creating pleasing background harmonies

◆ Using different chord voicings

◆ Composing interesting two-part counterpoint

◆ Learning effective voice leading technique

A song doesn't have to be anything more than a melody and chords. Think of a folk singer and her guitar, or a solo violinist accompanied by piano. Melody and chords are all you need. However, when you turn on the radio you don't hear a lot of solo folk singers. What you typically hear is a full arrangement, complete with keyboards and bass and drums, background vocals, and other types of instrumental backing.

Of course, these background vocals and instruments are doing nothing more than playing the notes in the song's chord progression. But they also help to fill out the sound and make the piece of music more interesting.

To fill out your songs, you need to add harmony parts. These harmony parts can be either vocal or instrumental, and there can be any number of them. What they do is simple: They follow separate lines within the underlying chord progression, thus buttressing the harmonic structure of the song.

If you want to get really fancy, your backing parts can represent new and contrasting melodies when played against your original melody. When you create this type of complex harmony, it's called *counterpoint;* it's widely used in many forms of classical music.

Note

This chapter presents harmony and counterpoint from a popular music perspective. Classical musicians have a much different—and more formal—take on these concepts.

Two Ways to Enhance a Melody

Two notes sounded together make a harmonic interval; three or more notes sounded together make a chord; and two or more *melodies* sounded together make counterpoint. Intervals and chords are used to construct harmony; counterpoint exists as separate melodic lines.

Another way to think of it is that harmony is a vertical (up and down) combination of notes, whereas counterpoint operates horizontally (side to side).

Harmony is vertical.

Counterpoint is horizontal.

In reality, harmony and counterpoint are related concepts; both involve "vertical" combinations of notes and both involve a "horizontal" movement of individual voices or instruments. Still, harmony is more about singing or playing parts of a chord; counterpoint is more about creating a second (or third or fourth) melody line—albeit one that adheres to the underlying harmonic structure.

Note

Technically, the study of harmony includes chords and chord progressions—basically, anything that combines two or more notes simultaneously. Because we already covered this basic material in Chapters 9 and 10, in this chapter we're covering the use of multiple voices or instruments to enhance melodies, based on the underlying harmonic structure (chord progression) of a piece of music.

Living in Harmony

Harmony is like playing chords behind a melody, only using other instruments or voices. In fact, the art of adding chords to a melody is a harmonic exercise.

We add harmony parts to our music because harmony lends richness to a song. It fills out a single melody line and reinforces the underlying chord structure.

A song with backing harmonies is the difference between a solo vocalist and a full chorus. It's the difference between a folk singer with an acoustic guitar and a pop singer with a group of backup vocalists. It's the difference between a jazz trio and a big band.

In other words, harmony makes music bigger.

You create harmony parts by using the notes in the underlying chord progression. If all you do is assign specific notes of a chord to specific instruments or voices, you've created harmony.

It doesn't have to be much harder than that. Harmony parts, whether vocal or instrumental, are typically less rhythmically complex than the main melody. It's not uncommon to find harmony parts consisting of whole notes or half notes while the melody maintains a more complex rhythm.

Harmony parts can also mirror the rhythm of the melody; in these instances, the harmony resembles classical counterpoint—which you'll learn about later in this chapter. Harmony can also be used to punctuate the melody, fill in breaks in the melody, and function as a kind of call and response mechanism. (Think of the classic pop tune "Midnight Train to Georgia"; Gladys Knight is the call and the Pips are the response.)

In terms of harmonic complexity, you can have everything from a single accompanying voice to choruses and string sections with two and three and more voices. The more voices you have, the more challenging it is to create distinct harmony parts without doubling or duplicating other parts. Of course, writing a single harmony part is also challenging, but in a different way; that single part has to include just the right notes, suggesting the underlying chord without distracting from the main melody.

For the purposes of learning basic theory, we're going to concentrate on simple two- and three-part backing harmony, without a lot of rhythmic or melodic complexity. Once you master this type of rudimental harmony, you can expand to include more complex types of vocal and instrumental backing.

Voicing and Inversions

The order of the notes of a chord (top to bottom) is referred to as the chord *voicing*. (It's also called the chord *inversion*, as you learned in Chapter 9.) Voicing is very important when you're writing harmony parts, because you have to employ different voicings to avoid parallel motion between parts.

Let's consider the harmony you play as piano accompaniment. If you recall, we used the following chord progression as an example back in Chapter 13:

A common chord progression that needs harmonized.

As learned back in Chapter 13, a simple block chord piano accompaniment (right hand only) to this chord progression looks something like this:

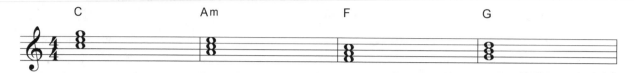

Simple block chord harmonies.

The triads you play as accompaniment represent three-voice harmony; you just happen to play all three voices with one hand. All the chords are in the root (noninverted) form of 1-3-5—which represents a problem. When you change from chord to chord, all the harmony notes move in parallel to each other. In terms of voice leading, this is often frowned upon.

It's also boring.

You can prove this by isolating the top note of this chord accompaniment. Now sing the succession of top notes as if you were singing backup vocals:

Isolating the top voice in the I-vi-IV-V chord progression.

Like I said: pretty boring—and not particularly melodic, either.

A better approach is to vary the voicings of the chords so that the harmony parts don't have to move in parallel.

For example, you might keep the C chord in its normal root position, but change the Am to the first inversion (C-E-A), the F to the second inversion (C-F-A), and the G to the first inversion (B-D-G), like this:

Inverting the chords to vary the internal voicings.

Tip

The succession of root position, first inversion, second inversion is fairly common—and one you can apply to any number of chord progressions. (Also common is the succession of first inversion, second inversion, root position.)

Not only does this make the chord progression easier to play (all the notes are closer together on the keyboard) it also makes any individual part easier to sing. Take the top note part again: Instead of moving G-E-C-D as it did originally, it now moves G-A-A-G, like this:

The new top voice harmony part, thanks to revoicing the chords.

The voice is fairly consistent, now; it doesn't jump all over the place like it did before. And if you check out the other voices, you find that they're also a lot more singable. (The middle voice moves E-E-F-D, and the bottom voice moves C-C-C-B.)

When you write out each of these parts separately, you use three different staves, like this:

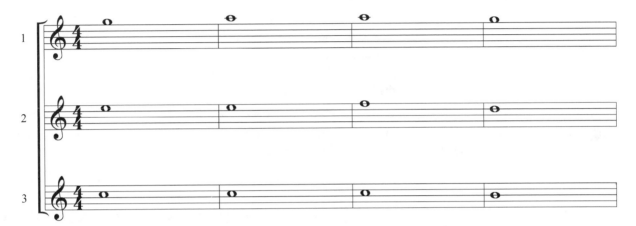

Three-voice harmony—on three different staves.

These principles apply when you're playing piano accompaniment; they also apply when you're writing vocal or instrumental harmony parts. If you vary the voicings, you open up a lot of possibilities as far as which voice goes where.

Making Harmony Parts More Melodic

Of course, you're not limited to having your voices follow the strict chord pattern. What if we start swapping the top two notes of our harmony between two different voices? There are lots of ways to do this, but one particularly good-sounding one looks like this:

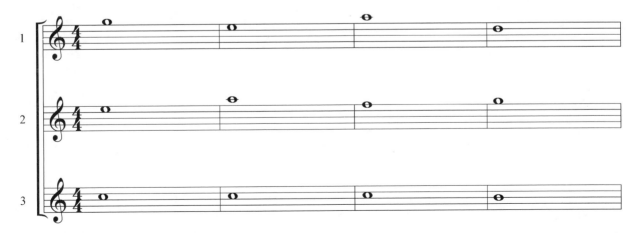

Swapping a few notes between the top two harmony parts.

See what we did here? We swapped the second and fourth notes between the parts, so that the first part now goes G-E-A-D, and the second part goes E-A-F-G. You're still representing all the notes in the chord, but you're making each individual line more melodically interesting.

Tip

It's helpful to think of a chord progression as nothing more than a group of simultaneous melodies. This will help you create singable harmony parts, as opposed to parts that correspond only to notes within the underlying chord structure.

Tip

If you follow these voice-leading conventions, you'll create chord progressions that sound good in both popular and classical music. When you're working in the popular and jazz styles, however, you'll discover that you can be a lot freer with your voice leading; let your ear guide you to what works best.

A good tip when you're creating either vocal or instrumental harmony is to physically sing each part yourself. If the part is boring or hard to sing, consider different inversions or swapping notes between parts. The best harmony parts sound great on their own!

Voice Leading

Voice leading is what you get when you follow one harmony part from start to finish; the different intervals between the notes follow a set of conventions and act to create a pseudo-melody out of the harmony line. You have to make sure that one note properly leads to the next to avoid having the harmony line sound like a bunch of totally unconnected tones.

When you're writing harmony, there are two key voice leading conventions to keep in mind. When you follow these conventions, the creation of harmony parts becomes somewhat easy:

◆ In general, voices should move the shortest distance possible, and retain common tones between successive chords in the same voice.

◆ Avoid moving voices in parallel "perfect" intervals—fourths, fifths, or octaves. Voices *can* move in parallel thirds and sixths.

Here's an example of bad voice leading. Notice how the two parts move in parallel, and how each voice has huge leaps from note to note?

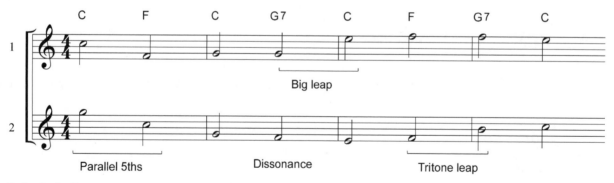

Bad voice leading …

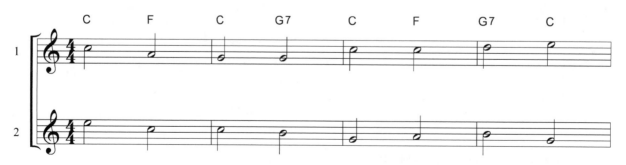

… corrected.

The second example shows how to fix the voice leading problems, merely by swapping a few notes from voice to voice or by picking other notes within the chord. It isn't that hard when you realize that any note can be assigned to any voice; all you have to do is pick the right notes to create the best-sounding musical lines.

Making a Point—with Counterpoint

Counterpoint is simply the art of combining two or more simultaneous musical lines. Unlike the art of harmony, where the harmony parts are subsidiary to the main melody, both melodic parts in counterpoint have equal weight.

The two voices in traditional counterpoint must not only sound melodic when played separately; they also must fit together harmonically to suggest the chord structure of the song. That means if you play the underlying chords against the counterpoint, the melodic lines mustn't sound dissonant; it also means you should be able to deduce the underlying chord structure from the melodic lines alone.

> **Definition**
> The word "counterpoint" comes from the Latin *punctus contra punctum*, which means "note against note." When a second melodic part is added to an existing one, the new part is said to be "in counterpoint" to the first part.

Sounds like a tall order, doesn't it? Creating effective counterpoint is kind of like working with a musical puzzle, creating two melodies that not only fit with the song's chord progression, but also sound good when played together. Mastery of contrapuntal technique is definitely something that separates novices from more experienced musicians.

Key to successful counterpoint is the interaction of the different voices. (And when I say "voices," I mean melodic lines; counterpoint can be used in both vocal and instrumental music.) The two lines have to work together; not fight with each other. The second line has to be the melodic equal of the first, and neither line should dominate.

All of this is harder to do than you might think.

> **Note**
> The dean of contrapuntal writing was J.S. Bach, although many classical composers utilized this particular musical form. Bach was known for his three- and four-part counterpoint, in which any of the parts could be the lead part.

It's also important that both lines be singable. That means either melody should be able to stand on its own as a main melody against the underlying chord progression. A melody in counterpoint should not be just a combination of notes to fit the chords; it has to be melodic, it has to have its own internal musical logic, *and* it has to fit with the other melody.

When composing melodies for counterpoint, call upon the skills you learned back in Chapter 8. Make sure each melody has a shape and a destination, as well as a coherent form. Also make sure each melody makes sense within the song's general chord structure, it fits within a comfortable vocal or instrumental range (generally no more than an octave range), and the intervals within the melody are small and singable.

When you put your two melodies together, you should make sure they both fit within the notes of the underlying chord, and stay within the confines of the underlying scale. The two melodies should also not duplicate each other; if you have two identical melodies, you're writing in unison; not in counterpoint. That means each melody should have its own motion—which should complement, but not interfere with, the motion of the other melody. The notes within each melody also should not interfere or clash with the notes in the other melody; avoid dissonant vertical intervals.

> **Definition**
> Two melodies in counterpoint that move in opposite directions (one up; the other down) are said to have *contrary motion*.

It's okay for the two melodies to have their own rhythmic patterns. In fact, in classical music it's expected. (If your two melodies have identical rhythmic structure you have what is called a 1:1 rhythmic ratio, which in some ways is easier to work with than more rhythmically complex forms.)

Creating Your First Counterpoint

The best way to learn about counterpoint is to dive into the deep end—and start composing!

For our first counterpoint, we'll start by defining some parameters. These are not necessarily hard and fast rules for the contrapuntal form, but they do make it easier for beginners to create a working counterpoint.

Here are the parameters:

- Use a 1:1 rhythmic ratio; both melodies should use the same rhythmic patterns.
- Only consonant harmonic intervals are allowed; no dissonant harmonies.
- The lower part must begin and end on the tonic of the key.
- The upper part must begin on either the first or the fifth of the key, and end on the tonic—either in unison with the bass part or an octave above.
- Between the melodies, rely heavily on intervals of thirds and sixths. Avoid octaves and unisons, except for the final note.
- Move each voice the shortest distance possible.

Now let's get started.

> **Note**
>
> These general principles are similar to the ones established by Johann Joseph Fux in his classic counterpoint book *Gradus ad Parnassum* ("steps to perfection"), published in 1725. Many great composers throughout history have used this book to learn counterpoint.

Some composers like to write both melodic parts simultaneously; this enables them to employ various advanced techniques, such as sharing a contrapuntal melody between the two parts. However, for beginners it's a lot easier to write the first part first; then complete the puzzle by adding the second, counterpoint, melody.

Which is exactly what we'll do.

We'll start from the bottom up and create our first melody for the lower voice. (This is the staff labeled "2," in bass clef.) Our melody is in 3/4 time, in the key of F Major. Because counterpoint works best when both parts have a lot of rhythmic and melodic movement, the melody is fairly lively, with a lot of eighth notes; it also starts and ends on the tonic note, F.

The lower voice—the first of two parts in counterpoint.

Now things get interesting. We need to come up with a second, higher, melody that doesn't clash with the lower melody—in fact, it should complement the first melody. You can't create this second melody in a vacuum; counterpoint is more than just putting two unrelated melodies together. The two melodies have to fit together logically, and have to work together to suggest the underlying chords.

So let's start at the start. The lower part started on an F, which is the tonic of the underlying key. According to our parameters, the upper melody can start either on the tonic or the fifth. We don't want to get too fancy with our first counterpoint, so we'll start the upper melody (the treble clef labeled "1") on the F two octaves higher.

In the first measure, the lower melody has a slight upward progression. To distinguish the upper melody from the lower part, we'll give this second melody a slight downward progression. Remember, we want the intervals between the two voices to be pleasant-sounding, which means emphasizing the thirds and sixths, and avoiding dissonant intervals. We also want to avoid parallel movement, so we'll leave the second note of the upper melody on F, which sounds good against the D on the bottom. (It's a nice minor third.)

For the third note, it's time to introduce some motion—in this case, a downward motion, to contrast with the upward motion in the lower melody. We'll move down from F to C, which is a nice singable fourth. It also forms a pleasing minor sixth against the E in the lower melody.

The fourth and final note in the first measure also needs to show downward movement, so we'll continue down from C to A, an easily singable minor third. The A also creates a pleasing major third against the F in the lower melody.

Now, if you look closely, you'll see that not only did we introduce contrary motion in the upper melody (down, in contrast to the upward-moving lower melody), but we also used the upper melody to suggest the underlying chord (F Major). The downward melody is actually an arpeggiated F Major chord, in its first inversion (F to C to A).

What we have so far is shown here:

Starting to add counterpoint to the first voice.

As you can see, creating counterpoint requires a lot of logical thinking—it's a lot like thinking through the moves in a game of chess. The conventions are there and it's all very logical, but you have to work hard to make it all fit together as it should.

We'll continue adding to the upper voice line, following the conventions note by note. When we're finished, we have two complete melodies, in counterpoint to each other, like this:

Your first counterpoint!

Your first counterpoint is a good example of simple 1:1 rhythmic counterpoint. Of course, classical counterpoint requires that the rhythms differ between the two voices, so let's continue to work with this example to create some rhythmic variations.

How do you introduce different rhythms into the top melody? In this example, you can do it by essentially scooting all the notes to the left one beat. That is, you put the eighth-note figure on beat one instead of beat two of each measure, and extend the measure-ending quarter note into a half note.

Here's what this looks like:

Your first counterpoint—but with different rhythms in the top melody.

Note that this approach created eighth notes in the top part when the bottom part is using quarter notes, and vice versa. This provides a simple rhythmic variation without going whole-hog on complex interrelated rhythms.

What to Avoid

Whether you're writing harmony or counterpoint, there are certain combinations of notes that you want to avoid. In most cases, you'll avoid these combinations because they don't sound right; still, it's good to know the conventions in advance so you can keep from making rookie mistakes.

Avoid Parallel Movement

Parallel movement is when two or more voices move in the same direction by the exact same interval. Parallel movement is frowned upon in some types of music—but perfectly acceptable in others. For example, in classical music you want to avoid parallel movement in perfect fourths or fifths and octaves; in popular music, however, it's permitted (even if it does sound a little boring if carried on for too long).

In any case, if you try hard, you can generally come up with something that sounds more interesting than extended parallel voices.

Avoid parallel movement.

Avoid Big Leaps

Whether you're writing harmony or counterpoint, you should follow one of the key conventions used when creating melodies—keep the intervals between notes as small as possible. Avoid big leaps between notes; they not only sound disconnected, they're also hard to play and sing.

Avoid big leaps.

Avoid Dissonant Intervals—Unless They Resolve

In this case we're talking about the intervals between different voices—and this is as much a practical consideration as anything else. If you're fitting voices to chords, you probably won't have much in the way of dissonance to work with; there's nothing dissonant within an F Major chord, for example.

But what if you're harmonizing an F Major seventh chord—in which two of the notes are E and F, which are just a minor second apart? The voicing you want to avoid is putting the two notes together on two close voices; for example, having the first soprano sing the F and the second soprano sing the adjacent E. Not only will this sound harsh; it will also be difficult for each voice to sing—the notes are too close together. A better approach would be to put one of the notes in a lower voice, so that there's an octave or so space between the two notes.

Avoid unresolved dissonances.

The tritone is another interval to avoid in your harmony. This is simply the hardest interval in the world to sing, or for instruments to hit. When you put a tritone in your harmony, you're just asking for trouble—specifically, for one of the voices to miss the note!

Now, it's okay to introduce this kind of dissonance, if you then resolve it. That means you can include dissonance in passing tones, or even at the end of phrases, but only if one of the voices then resolves to a more pleasing interval. For example, in that F Major seventh chord, the voice with the E might quickly resolve to either an F or a C. In the tritone example, you can move one of the voices up or down a step to create either a perfect fifth or a third.

Tip

For some good examples of close harmony, listen to some old Beach Boys albums. Of particular note is the classic *Pet Sounds* album, which contains some terrific close harmony on songs like "God Only Knows" and "Wouldn't It Be Nice."

Realize, however, that this is one rule that's definitely meant to be broken. There are so many instances of close harmony out there that it's hard to argue against the practice. The problem is that this type of close harmony is difficult to pull off; especially for beginners. Wait until you're more comfortable with your harmony and counterpoint before you try writing voices this close together.

The Least You Need to Know

- Harmony is a vertical combination of notes within the underlying chord structure; counterpoint is an integrated series of horizontal melodies relating to the underlying chords.
- Harmony is facilitated when you vary chord voicings throughout a progression.
- Each harmony part must be singable on its own and follow established voice leading conventions.
- Each melody within a counterpoint should be able to function as a standalone melody, and at the same time complement the other melodies.
- Whether you're creating harmony or counterpoint, you should generally avoid movement in parallel fifths or octaves—especially in classical music. (Popular music typically has fewer—and looser—conventions.)

Exercises

Exercise 15-1

Find and correct the voice leading errors in the following piece of harmony.

Exercise 15-2

Create two-voice harmony for the following melody, using half notes and quarter notes.

Exercise 15-3

Create a second melody part in counterpoint to the following melody.

Exercise 15-4

Based on the following chord progression, create a two-voice counterpoint.

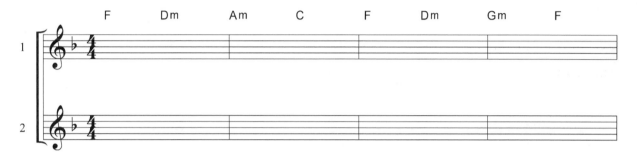

Chapter 16

Chord Substitutions and Turnarounds

In This Chapter

♦ Learn how to spice up boring chord progressions with extensions

♦ Discover how to alter a chord's bass note and play two chords simultaneously

♦ Master the art of chord substitution

This section of the book is all about embellishing your music. You can embellish your melody with harmony and counterpoint (as you learned in the last chapter); embellish individual notes (as you'll learn in the next chapter); and embellish your chords and chord progressions.

Which is what this chapter is all about.

Even if you're stuck with a boring I-IV-V progression, there is still a lot you can do to put your own personal stamp on things. For example, you don't have to settle for precisely those chords; you can extend the chords, alter the bass line, and even substitute other chords for the originals. You'll still maintain the song's original harmonic structure—more or less—but you'll really jazz up the way things sound.

All this will impress your listeners and fellow musicians. A few key chord alterations and substitutions will make folks think you have the right touch—and that you really know your music theory!

Extending a Good Thing

The simplest way to spice up a boring chord progression is to use seventh chords, or even add a few extensions beyond that. As you learned back in Chapter 9, the basic chord is a triad consisting of the 1-3-5 notes. When you start adding notes on top of the triad—sevenths, ninths, and elevenths—you're extending the chord upward.

Chord extensions can make a basic chord sound lush and exotic. There's nothing like a minor seventh or major ninth chord to create a really full, harmonically complex sound.

Seventh chords—especially dominant seventh chords—are common in all types of music today. Sixths, ninths, and other extended chords are used frequently in modern jazz music—and in movie and television soundtracks that go for a jazzy feel. Pick up just about any jazz record from the 1950s on, and you'll hear lots of extended chords. There are even a lot of rock and pop musicians—Steely Dan comes to mind—who embrace these jazz harmonies in their music.

So why not use this technique yourself?

> ### Note
>
> Seventh chords have been part of the musical vocabulary from about the seventeenth century. There is a tendency to use the V7 and ii7 chords as much as or more than the triads on those degrees of the scale—even for the simplest musical genres, such as hymns and folk songs. In the blues, it is common to use seventh chords on every scale degree—even the tonic.
>
> Extended chords (ninths, elevenths, and so forth) came into widespread use in the nineteenth century. (Chopin is often cited as one of the first composers to extensively use extended chords.) For example, in most forms of jazz the ninth, eleventh, and thirteenth chords are used more often than triads and seventh chords.

Here's an example of how extended chords can make a simple chord progression sound more harmonically complex. All you have to do is take the standard I-vi-IV-V progression in the key of C (C-Am-F-G) and add diatonic sevenths to each triad. That produces the following progression: CM7-Am7-FM7-G7—two major sevenths, a minor seventh, and a dominant seventh. When you play this progression—and invert some of the chords to create a few close voicings—you get a completely different sound out of that old workhorse progression. And it wasn't hard to do at all!

The standard I-vi-IV-V progression (in C) embellished with seventh chords (and some close voicings).

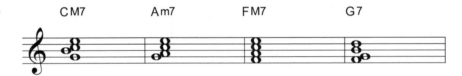

You can get the same effect by adding ninths and elevenths to your chords while staying within the song's underlying key. The more notes you add to your chords, the more complex your harmonies—and the fuller the sound.

Altering the Bass

Here's another neat way to make old chords sound new—and all you have to do is change the note on the bottom of the chord.

Back in Chapter 9 we touched briefly on the concept of *slash chords*, more properly called *altered bass chords*. With an altered bass chord, the top of the chord stays the same; but the bass, as the name implies, is altered.

Some folks call these chords slash chords because the altered bass note is indicated after a diagonal slash mark, like this: G/D. You read the chord as "G over D," and you play it as an G chord with a D in the bass.

Examples of slash chords.

You can use altered bass chords to achieve several different effects, including the following:

◆ By putting one of the three main notes (but not the root) in the bass, you dictate a particular chord inversion.

◆ By treating the bass note as a separate entity, you can create moving bass lines with increased melodic interest.

◆ By adding a nonchord note in the bass, you create a different chord with a different harmonic structure.

Slash chords are used a lot in jazz, and also in more sophisticated popular music. Listen to Carole King's *Tapestry* album and you'll hear a lot of altered bass (she's a big fan of the minor seventh chord with the fourth in the bass); the same thing with a lot of Beach Boys songs, especially those on the legendary *Pet Sounds* album.

Two Chords Are Better Than One

An altered bass chord uses a diagonal slash mark to separate the chord from the bass note. When you see a chord with a horizontal line between two different notes, like a fraction, you're dealing with a much different beast.

This type of notation indicates that two chords are to be played simultaneously. The chord on top of the fraction is placed on top of the pile; the chord on the bottom is played underneath. For example, when you see $\frac{C}{G}$ you know to play an C Major chord on top of a full G Major chord.

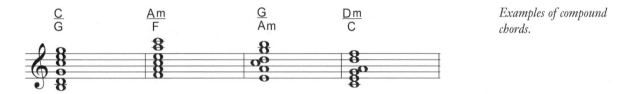

Examples of compound chords.

When you play two chords together like this, you have what's called a *compound chord*. You use compound chords to create extremely complex harmonies—those that might otherwise be too complex to note using traditional extensions.

One Good Chord Can Replace Another

When you're faced with a boring chord progression, you may have no alternative but to substitute the chords as-written with something a little less boring. The concept of *chord substitution* is one that is common in jazz (those jazz musicians get bored easily!) and other modern music.

Chord substitution is a simple concept. You pull a chord out of the song, and replace it with another chord. The substitute chord should have a few things in common with the chord it replaces, not the least of which is its place in the song's underlying harmonic structure. So if you replace a dominant (V) chord, you want to use a chord that also leads back to the tonic (I). If you replace a major chord, you want to replace it with another major chord or a chord that uses some of the same notes as the original chord.

The key thing is to substitute an ordinary chord or progression with one that serves the same function, but in a more interesting manner.

Diatonic Substitution

The easiest form of chord substitution replaces a chord with a related chord either a third above or a third below the original. This way you keep two of the three notes of the original chord, which provides a strong harmonic basis for the new chord.

This type of substitution is called *diatonic substitution*, because you're not altering any of the notes of the underlying scale; you're just using different notes from within the scale for the new chord.

For example, the I chord in any scale can be replaced by the vi chord (the chord a third below) or the iii chord (the chord a third above). In the key of C, this means replacing the C Major chord (C-E-G) with either A minor (A-C-E) or E minor (E-G-B). Both chords share two notes in common with the C chord, so the replacement isn't too jarring.

Replacing the I chord (C Major) with the vi (A minor) and the iii (E minor)—lots of notes in common.

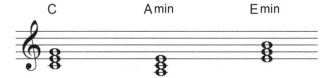

You can replace extended chords in the same manner, and actually end up with more notes in common. For example, you can replace CM7 with either Am7 or Em7, both of which have three notes in common with the original chord.

Major Chord Substitutions

Diatonic substitution is the theory; you'd probably rather know some hard-and-fast rules you can use for real-world chord substitution. Don't worry; they exist, based partially on diatonic substitution theory.

The following table presents four different substitutions you can make for a standard major chord. Remember that the root of the substitute chord must stay within the underlying scale, even if some of the chord notes occasionally wander about a bit.

Major Chord Substitutions

Substitution	Example (for the C Major chord)
Minor chord a third below	Amin
Minor 7 chord a third below	Amin7
Minor chord a third above	Emin

The first substitution in the table is the standard "down a third" diatonic substitution. The second substitution is the same thing, but uses an extended chord (the minor seventh) for the substitution. The third substitution is the "up a third" diatonic substitution, as discussed previously.

Minor Chord Substitutions

Substituting a major chord is relatively easy. So what about substituting a minor chord?

As you can see in the following table, some of the same substitution rules work with minor as well as major; especially the "up a third" and "down a third" diatonic substitutions.

Minor Chord Substitutions

Substitution	Example (for the A minor Chord)
Major chord a third above	C
Major chord a third below	F
Major 7 chord a third below	F Maj7
Diminished chord with same root	A dim

The last substitution falls into the "more of a good thing" category. That is, if a minor chord sounds good, let's flat another note and it'll sound even more minor. Some folks like the use of a diminished chord in this fashion; others don't. Let your ears be the judge.

Dominant Seventh Substitutions

Okay, now you know how to substitute both major and minor chords; but what about dominant seventh chords? They're not really major and they're not really minor—what kind of chords can substitute for *that*?

The answer requires some harmonic creativity. You *can* do a diatonic substitution (using the diminished chords a third above or below the dominant seventh), but there are more interesting possibilities, as you can see in the following table:

Dominant Seventh Chord Substitutions

Substitution	Example (for the G7 chord)
Major chord a second below	F
Diminished chord a third below	E dim

continues

Dominant Seventh Chord Substitutions (continued)

Substitution	Example (for the G7 chord)
Diminished chord a third above	B dim
Minor 7 chord a fourth below— over the same root	D m7/G

The more interesting substitutions here are the first one and the last one. The first substitution replaces the V7 chord with a IV chord; the use of the subdominant (IV) chord results in a softer lead back to the I chord. The last substitution uses an altered chord, so that you're leading back to tonic with a iim7/V—what I like to call a "Carole King chord." (That's because Ms. King uses this type of harmonic structure a lot in her song-writing.) So if you're in the key of C, instead of ending a phrase with a G or G7 chord, you end with a Dm7/G instead. It's a very pleasing sound.

Turnarounds

Chapter 10 also presented a concept of the phrase-ending *cadence*. Well, in the fields of jazz and popular music, you find a similar concept called a *turnaround*. A turnaround typically is a two-bar phrase, with two chords per measures, that functions much the same as a traditional cadence, "turning around" the music to settle back on the I chord at the start of the next phrase.

There is a wide variety of chord combinations you can use to create an ear-pleasing turnaround, some of which go outside the underlying key to circle back around to the tonic.

Here are just a few you might want to try:

> **Note**
>
> Some jazz musicians refer to turnarounds as *turnbacks*.

Common Chord Turnarounds

Turnaround	Example (in C)				
I-IV-iii-ii	C	F	E min	D min	C
I-vi-ii-V	C	A min	D min	G	C
iii-VI-ii-V	E min	A min	D min	G	C
I-vi-♭vi-V	C	A min	A♭min	G	C

continues

Common Chord Turnarounds   (continued)

Turnaround	Example (in C)
I-♭VII-iii-ii	C B♭ E min D min C
IV-iii-ii-♭ii	F E min D min D♭min C
I-vi-♭vi-♭II	C A min A♭min D♭ C
I-VI-♭V-♭III	C A G♭ E♭ C
I-♭III-♭VI-♭II	C E♭ A♭ D♭ C
I-♭VII-♭III-♭II	C B♭ E♭ D♭ C

Note that some of these outside-the-key chords take traditionally minor chords and make them major, so pay close attention to the uppercase and lowercase notation in the table. (For example, the III chord is an E Major chord in the key of C; not the expected E minor.)

Also pay attention to flat signs before a chord; this indicates to play the chord a half step lower than normal. For example, a ♭vi chord in the key of C is a half step lower than the standard A minor vi chord, which results in the A♭ minor chord instead.

You can use these turnarounds in any of the songs you write or arrange. It's an easy way to add harmonic sophistication to your music, just by changing a few chords at the end of a phrase!

The Least You Need to Know

◆ When you don't want to play a boring old chord progression, you can use one of several techniques to make the chord progression sound more harmonically sophisticated.

◆ The easiest way to spice up a chord progression is to change triads to seventh chords or extended chords (such as sixths, ninths, elevenths, or thirteenths), and add sevenths and other extensions to the basic chords.

◆ Another way to change the sound of a chord is to alter the bass note—to either signal a different inversion, or to introduce a slightly different harmonic structure.

◆ Substituting one chord for another also can make a chord progression more interesting. The most common chord substitutions are diatonic, in which you replace a chord with the diatonic chord either a third above or below the original chord.

◆ You can add interest to a chord progression by introducing a two-measure turnaround at the end of the main phrase; these chords circle around and lead back to the I chord at the start of the next phrase.

Exercises

Exercise 16-1

Write out the notes for the following slash chords.

Exercise 16-2

Write out the notes for the following compound chords.

Exercise 16-3

Write two substitute chords for each chord shown.

Exercise 16-4

Rewrite the following chord progression (on the second staff), using extended chords.

Exercise 16-5

Rewrite the following chord progression (on the second staff), using various types of chord substitutions.

Exercise 16-6

Add a two-measure turnaround to the following chord progression.

Chapter 17

Special Notation

In This Chapter

- ◆ Discover how to note phrasing with slur marks
- ◆ Find out how to write and play embellished notes, including turns, trills, and grace notes
- ◆ Learn how to play music with a swing feel
- ◆ Figure out how to fit words to music

There are some aspects of music theory that don't fit neatly within traditional categories. Still, you need to know about them, so I have to include them somewhere in this book.

That somewhere is this chapter. It's kind of a grab bag of more advanced techniques, mainly relating to notation, that you need to have at your fingertips—even if you won't use them every day.

So settle back and read about some of the oddball aspects of music theory, and that popular musical style we call *swing*.

Throwing a Curve

When you're writing music, you sometimes need to connect two or more notes together. You might literally connect them together to form a single, longer note; or you might simply want them played together as a smooth phrase. In any case, whenever you connect two or more notes together, you use a notation effect that looks like a big curve—and is called, alternately, either a *tie* or a *slur*.

Ties

You learned about ties back in Chapter 5. When two notes of the same pitch are tied together—either in the same measure, or across measures—the notes are played as a single note.

A tie is made with a small curve, either above or below the note, like this:

Two identical notes tied together equal one long note.

Slurs

A *slur* looks like a tie between two notes of different pitches, but really indicates that the notes are to be played together as a continuous group. Although you can't play two different tones as a continuous note, you can run them together without a breath or a space in between. This is called "slurring" the notes together; it looks like this:

Two different notes tied together are slurred together.

Definition

The curved line used in a slur is called a **slur** mark.

There's a subtle difference between two notes that are slurred together and two notes that aren't. The notes without the slur should each have a separate attack, which ends up sounding like a slight emphasis on each note. The second of the two slurred notes doesn't have a separate attack, so the sound is much smoother as you play from note to note.

Phrases

When you see a curved line above several adjacent notes, it's not a slur—it's a *phrase*. You use phrase marks to indicate separate ideas within a longer piece of music. When one idea ends, you end the phrase mark; when a new idea begins, you start a new phrase mark.

Lots of notes grouped together are played as a smooth phrase.

Note

Technically, a phrase mark indicates that a passage of music is played *legato*—which means to play smoothly.

Often, wind instruments (trumpets, clarinets, and so forth) base their breathing on the song's phrases. They'll blow during the phrase and breathe between the phrase marks.

Bowed instruments (violins, cellos, and so forth) use phrases to time their bowing. They'll use a single, continuous movement of the bow for the duration of the phrase; at the end of the phrase mark, they'll change the direction of their bowing.

The Long and the Short of It

Back in Chapter 7, you learned about some of the embellishments you can make to individual notes—accents, marcatos, and so on. There are a few more marks you can add to your notes; they're presented here.

Tenuto

A straight horizontal line over a note means to play the note for its full duration. In other words, stretch it out for as long as possible.

This mark is called a *tenuto* mark, and it looks like this:

The tenuto mark means to play a long note.

Staccato

The opposite of a long note is a short note; the opposite of tenuto is *staccato*. A dot on top of a note means do not play it for its full duration; just give it a little blip and get off it.

A staccato mark looks like this:

The staccato mark means to play a short note.

When Is a Note More Than a Note?

There are other marks you can add to your notes that indicate *additional* notes to play. These notes are kind of musical shorthand you can use in place of writing out all those piddly smaller notes.

Grace Notes

> **Note**
>
> Drummers call a grace note a *flam*, because (on a drum) that's what it sounds like—"fa-lam!"

A *grace note* is a short note you play in front of a main note. In mathematical terms, a grace note might have the value of a sixteenth or a thirty-second note, depending on the tempo of the music. Basically, you play the grace note just ahead of the main note, at a slightly lower volume level. When you note a grace note, write it as a smaller note just in front of the main note, like this:

A grace note is like a little preview note before the main note.

Grace notes are typically written as small eighth notes, with a line drawn through the stem and flag. The grace note can be on the same tone as the main note, or on an adjoining tone. (You play whatever note the grace note is on.)

Turns

A *turn* is an ornament used primarily in Baroque and classical music. In a turn the neighboring notes turn to the main note, "turning it around."

Let's look at how a turn works: When you see the turn mark (which looks like a line turned around on itself), you play the diatonic note above the main note, then the main note, then the note a step below the main note, and then the main note again. Here's how it looks on paper, and how you play it in practice:

A turn "turns around" the main note.

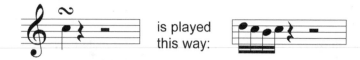

is played
this way:

When you're playing a turn, you have a bit of latitude for how fast you actually play it. You can play a turn as written in the example, as a pure mathematical subset of the note's noted duration; or you can whip through the turn really quickly, landing back on the main pitch until the note is done. It's all a matter of interpretation.

Tip _____

If you're unsure how to play a turn in a piece of music, ask your conductor for the proper interpretation.

Trills

A *trill* is a way to extend a single note by alternating between two neighboring tones. In particular, you alternate between the main note and the note one step above, like this:

Play a trill with a whole bunch of neighboring notes.

is played
this way:

As with turns, there are many different ways to play a trill. The most common approach is to alternate between the two notes as rapidly as possible, although technically a trill can have a *preparation* in which you play the main note straight before you enter into the "shake." (You can also terminate the trill—or just trill right into the next note.)

Glissandos

Whereas turns and trills alternate between two or three neighboring notes, a *glissando* packs a lot more notes into a short space. To be precise, a glissando is a mechanism for getting from one pitch to another, playing every single pitch between the two notes as smoothly as possible.

Depending on the instrument, a glissando can be a continuous glide between the two notes (think trombone) or a run of sequential chromatic notes (think piano). Glissandi (*not* glissandos!) can move either up or down; typically, both the starting and ending notes are specified, like this:

Glissando up—and down.

Arpeggiated Chords

When you want an instrument to play a chord as an arpeggio, but you don't want to write out all the notes, you can use the symbol called the *role*. The role indicates that the instrument is to play an arpeggio—but a rather quick one. This squiggly line tells the musician to play the written notes from bottom to top, in succession, and to hold each note as it is played. The effect should be something like a harp playing an arpeggiated chord, like this:

The quick and easy way to notate an arpeggiated accompaniment.

is played
this way:

Getting Into the Swing of Things

The last bit of notation I want to discuss concerns a feel. If you've ever heard jazz music, particularly big band music, you've heard this feel; it's called *swing*.

Traditional popular music has a straight feel; eighth notes are played straight, just as they're written. Swing has a kind of triplet feel; it swings along, all bouncy, percolating with three eighth notes on every beat.

What's that, you're saying—*three* eighth notes on every beat? How is that possible?

It's possible because swing is based on triplets. Instead of having eight eighth notes in a measure of 4/4, you have *twelve* eighth notes—four eighth-note triplets. So instead of the basic beat being straight eighths, the first and third beat of every triplet combine for a *spang-a-lang-a-lang-a-lang* kind of rhythm.

What's confusing is that instead of notating swing as it's actually played (with triplets), most swing music uses straight eighth notation—which you're then expected to translate into the triplet-based swing.

So if you're presented a swing tune and you see a bunch of straight eighths, you should play them with a triplet feel, like this:

 is played this way: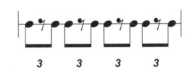

In swing, straight eighths are played with a triplet feel.

Some arrangers try to approximate the swing feel within a straight rhythm by using dotted eighth notes followed by sixteenth notes, like this:

 is played this way:

In swing, dotted eights and sixteenths are played with a triplet feel.

Whatever you do, don't play this precisely as written! Again, you have to translate the notation and play the notes with a triplet feel.

The swing feel is an important one, and you find it all over the place. Swing is used extensively in jazz music, in traditional blues music, in rock shuffles, and in all manner of popular music old and new. Learning how to swing takes a bit of effort; it's normal to play the stiff dotted-eighth/sixteenth rhythm instead of the rolling triplets when you're first starting out. But that effort is worth it—a lot of great music is based on that swinging feel.

Getting the Word

Before we end this chapter, let's take a look at one other notation challenge: how to add words to your music.

Notating lyrics is something that all songwriters have to do, and it isn't that hard—if you think logically. Naturally, you want to align specific words with specific notes in the music. More precisely, you want to align specific *syllables* with specific notes.

This sometimes requires a bit of creativity on your part. You might need to split up words into awkward-looking syllables. You also might need to extend syllables within words where a note is held for an extended period of time. This requires a lot of hyphens in the lyrics, as you can see in the following example:

Notating lyrics; split words in syllables, and extended syllables.

Just remember to position your lyrics underneath the music staff. If you have multiple verses, write each verse on a separate line; then break each word into its component syllables and carefully match up each syllable with the proper musical note.

The Least You Need to Know

♦ Curved marks are used to *tie* identical notes together, *slur* neighboring notes together, and indicate complete musical *phrases*.

♦ A dot above a note means to play it short (staccato); a line above a note means to play it long (tenuto).

♦ You play grace notes lightly and quickly before the main note.

♦ Turns and trills ornament a main note by the use of rapidly played neighboring notes.

♦ A glissando indicates a smooth glide from one pitch to another.

♦ Swing music is played with a rolling triplet feel; not straight eighth notes.

♦ Lyrics must be broken down into syllables to fit precisely with notes in the music.

Exercises

Exercise 17-1

Write out how you would play each of these marked-up notes.

Exercise 17-2

Add grace notes to every quarter note in this melody.

Exercise 17-3

Add slurs to each pair of eighth notes in this melody.

Exercise 17-4

Use phrase marks to divide this melody into four natural phrases.

Exercise 17-5

Translate the following straight rhythm into a swing feel using triplet notation.

Exercise 17-6

Compose and play a four-measure melody with a swing feel, in the key of B♭.

Exercise 17-7

Write the following lyrics under the appropriate notes in the melody: "Tangerine elephants high in the sky, crocodile tears in my beer."

Part 6

Arranging

Learn how to write for specific voices and instruments, how to create good-looking master scores and lead sheets, and how to conduct your music in front of a choir, band, or orchestra.

Chapter 18

Composing and Arranging for Voices and Instruments

In This Chapter

- Learn about the different voices in the choir—and all the instruments in the orchestra
- Discover the playable (and singable) ranges of each instrument and voice
- Uncover the best—and the worst—keys to write in
- Find out which instruments don't sound in concert pitch—and how to transpose their music

You know the theory; now it's time to put that theory to practice.

The most common application of music theory comes when you compose or arrange a piece of music for multiple voices or instruments. That could be a simple presentation for your church choir, a new song for your rock band, a sophisticated piece for your high school jazz band, or a multipart symphony for a full orchestra.

Whatever size group you're writing for, you have to deal with the same issues of theory, and call on the same set of skills. You also have to know a little bit about the ranges of each instrument or voice, and how each instrument will play the notes you write.

This chapter deals with the particular skills necessary for vocal and instrumental arranging. I recommend you bookmark this chapter; if you do a lot of arranging, you'll find the information about ranges and transposition very useful!

Vocal Arranging

A vocal ensemble is probably the easiest type of group to arrange for. That's because all the voices reproduce exactly what you write, with absolutely no transposition. (Well, except for the fact that the tenor voice sounds an octave lower than written—but that's an easy one to deal with.)

Voice Characteristics

When you're writing for a choir, you have to know the voices that are available at your disposal. In general, you have two female voices and two male voices, with an optional third male voice to work with.

- ◆ **Soprano**   This is the highest female voice. The soprano typically sings the lead part, as the highest voice naturally stands out from the rest. Some sopranos can sing quite high, although you might want to avoid the very upper reaches of the range; these high parts often sound shrill, especially with younger or less-experienced singers.

- ◆ **Alto**   The alto is the lower female voice, with a deep and resonant tone. The alto range overlaps the soprano range, but know that an alto will sound strained at the top of her range—just as a soprano will sound strained at the bottom of hers.

- ◆ **Tenor**   The tenor is the highest male voice; it overlaps significantly with the range of the female alto. Tenor parts are written in treble clef, but actually sound an octave lower than written.

- ◆ **Baritone**   The baritone is an optional male part; most choruses don't have separate baritone lines. The baritone falls smack between the tenor and the bass, but typically has more of a bass-like sound—without the very low notes.

- ◆ **Bass**   The bass is the lowest male voice. It's natural to assign bass notes to the bass voice, which works out okay most of the time. At the low end of the bass range, the sound gets a tad rumbly.

Vocal Ranges

It's important that you write vocal parts that can actually be sung. It's no good to write a bass part that sounds forced—if the poor fellow can hit the note at all.

For that reason, pay close attention to the ranges listed in the following table and stick within these ranges when writing your vocal parts.

Vocal Ranges

Voice	Range
Soprano	
Alto	
Tenor (sounds one octave lower)	
Baritone	
Bass	

Instrumental Arranging

When you move on to instrumental arranging, you have a lot of different instruments at your disposal. You need to know a little bit about how each instrument works; in particular the range of the instrument and whether it sounds in concert pitch or is somehow transposed.

Instrument Characteristics

Instruments are typically organized into several major groups. For our purposes, we'll look at strings (both bowed and plucked), brass, woodwinds, keyboards, and percussion.

Strings

When you think of stringed instruments, you typically think of the violin and its close cousins: the viola, cello, and double bass (sometimes called the string bass or upright bass). Each of these instruments works on the same principle, with four strings stretched over a hollow body. Music is made when a bow is pushed and pulled over the strings, or when the strings are plucked.

The highest string voice is the violin, followed (in descending order) by the viola, cello, and double bass. The violin is written with the treble clef, cello and double bass use the bass clef, and the viola—the oddball of the group—uses the alto clef, as shown in the following figure. (Remember: The pointy part of the alto clef points at C.)

The alto clef; used primarily by the viola.

Tip

On a symphonic score (discussed in Chapter 19), the instruments are displayed in the following top-to-bottom order: woodwinds, brass, percussion, special instruments (like piano or harp), and, finally, strings.

Guitars and Other Plucked Instruments

The guitar is technically part of the string family, although most folks differentiate it from the violin-type instrument. That's because the guitar is never bowed; it's always plucked or strummed. (The guitar also has six strings, compared to the four strings of the violin instruments.)

There are several other instruments that fit within the guitar category. The mandolin and ukulele are smaller and higher pitched than the guitar, whereas the electric bass is more like a traditional double bass, but in a guitar-like configuration with just four strings.

Guitars, of course, can be either acoustic or electric—and the electric ones can have either solid or hollow bodies. The different configurations produce different types of sound, although the notation is the same for all the different guitars.

Guitar parts can be notated with notes on staves or, if you just want a strummed rhythm, by using chord notation. You can also spell out the fingering of each chord by using guitar tablature, as shown in the following.

Tip

Guitar tabs can be automatically derived from traditional chord notation when you use a computerized music notation program, such as those discussed in Chapter 19.

Guitar tablature.

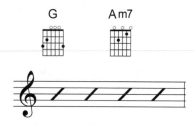

Oh, and while we're talking about plucking strings, we can't forget the harp. The harp isn't really a guitar (it's kind of like a piano, but more vertical), but it does work when you pluck its strings.

Brass

Brass instruments typically are made of brass. However, so are saxophones and cymbals and timpani, and they're not part of the brass family; so that really isn't a good indicator, is it? Nope, what makes brass instruments unique is that length of brass tubing wound up into a tight little package, the open mouthpiece you blow into, and the three or four valves you use (in conjunction with changing the shape of your lips) to create different tones.

The trumpet is the brash and annoying younger brother of the brass family, the trombone is the more stable older brother, and the tuba is the not-always-serious uncle. Also hanging around is the weird foreign relation, the French horn; and a few other unusual relatives, such as the baritone. All in all, it's a rather loud and brassy bunch—pun intended.

Brass instruments use either the treble or bass clefs, depending on their predominant pitch.

Woodwinds

Some woodwinds are made of brass; some are made of wood. But all (except the flute) use a wooden reed to produce their sound; you put the reed in your mouth and blow until it vibrates.

The flute produces sound when you blow across an open hole; kind of like blowing across a soda bottle. But it's still classified as part of the woodwind family, probably because it has a similar valve structure and fingering for determining individual notes.

There are lots of different woodwind instruments. You have flutes and piccolos; at least four different types of saxophones; a variety of clarinets; those odd-sounding oboes and bassoons; and even the not-so-common English horn (which isn't a horn and isn't even English—it's an alto version of the oboe).

Woodwind instruments primarily use the treble clef, although the bassoon and contrabassoon both use the bass clef.

Keyboards

Depending on whom you ask, keyboard instruments are really string instruments or percussion instruments. In reality, they're a little of both. The sounds are produced by internal strings, which are struck by tiny hammers—much like percussion instruments are struck.

There are many different types of keyboards, and they all have fairly wide ranges. The piano, of course, is the big dog, but you can't forget about organs, or harpsichords, or any number of electronic synthesizers. A full piano has 88 keys; some smaller instruments can have shorter keyboards. Without exception, all modern keyboard instruments sound in concert pitch.

Percussion

When you talk percussion, you're talking about a lot of different instruments. Percussion instruments make noise when you hit them or shake them, so the family includes everything from snare drums and cymbals to marimbas and timpani. Most percussion instruments are of indefinite pitch—that is, although they make a noise when you hit them (or shake them), that noise isn't associated with a specific pitch. Other percussion instruments, such as timpani and the mallet family, do produce a definite pitch (or pitches).

When you're writing for an indefinite pitch instrument, you don't have to follow standard staff notation. For example, when you write for drum set, you assign different parts of the staff to different drums and cymbals in the set. In the following example, the bass drum is the bottom space on the staff; the snare drum is the third space up. Cymbals are at the top, notated by X-shaped note heads.

Writing for drum set.

Of course, you can save yourself a lot of time and trouble by just telling the drummer how many measures there are in each section of your song and letting him (or her) make up his (or her) own part. That's particularly common when you're arranging for a rock or jazz band.

Transposition

Many instruments read one note and play another—at least compared to concert pitch (the actual notes as played on a piano). For example, a trumpet reads a C but plays a B♭. These so-called *transposing instruments* need to have their music transposed to a different key to play in the same concert key as all the other instruments.

Let's take the trumpet again. Because the trumpet always sounds a major second lower than written, you need to write the trumpet part a major second *higher* than the pitch you actually want to hear. So if you want the trumpet to play a concert C, you have to write a D; the trumpet reads D, sounds C, and everything is right with the world.

You learned about transposition back in Chapter 14, and you'll need to apply those skills here. That's because there are a lot of instruments that don't play in concert key; all these instruments need their parts transposed.

Most transposing instruments fall into three groups, and are named according to how they relate to C:

◆ B♭ instruments, like the trumpet, sound a major second below concert pitch. So if the concert pitch is C, they sound B♭.

◆ E♭ instruments, like the alto sax, sound a major sixth below (or a minor third above) concert pitch. So if the concert pitch is C, they sound E♭.

◆ F instruments, such as the French horn, sound a perfect fifth below (or a perfect fourth above) concert pitch. So if the concert pitch is C, they sound F.

The following table details which instruments fall into which group:

Transposing Instruments

Transposition Range	Sounds	Instruments
Concert pitch	As written	Bass flute
		Bassoon
		Cello
		Contrabassoon
		Double bass
		Electric bass
		Flute
		Guitar
		Harp
		Oboe
		Marimba and other mallet instruments
		Piano and other keyboards
		Piccolo
		Trombone
		Tuba
		Viola
		Violin
B-flat instruments	Major second lower	Baritone horn
		Bass clarinet (actually a Major ninth lower)
		Bass saxophone
		Clarinet (B♭)
		Cornet
		Flugel horn
		Soprano saxophone
		Tenor saxophone
		Trumpet
E-flat instruments	Major sixth lower	Alto clarinet
		Alto saxophone
		Baritone saxophone
		Clarinet (E♭)
F instruments	Perfect fifth lower	English horn
		French horn

What does all this mean in terms of actual transposition? The next table details how each type of instrument transposes each of the possible concert keys:

Concert Key Transpositions

Concert Key	B♭ Instruments	E♭ Instruments	F Instruments
C	D	A	G
D♭	E♭	B♭	A♭
D	E	B	A
E♭	F	C	B♭
E	G♭ (F#)	D♭ (C#)	B
F	G	D	C
G♭	A♭	E♭	D♭
G	A	E	D
A♭	B♭	F	E♭
A	B	G♭ (F#)	E
B♭	C	G	F
B	D♭ (C#)	A♭	G♭ (F#)

Note

There are actually many more transpositions than listed in this table, especially among the instruments used in classical music. For example, trumpets in D were very often used by Mozart, Haydn, and other composers of their time.

One of the reasons for these different transpositions is that early trumpets and horns had no valves, so there were only a limited number of notes available on them. A composer would then chose a transposition that gave him the best selection of available notes for each instrument.

Good Keys and Bad Keys

Because of the need to transpose the nonconcert key instruments, you can end up with some instruments reading a whole bunch of sharps and flats, which of course is problematic. For example, the concert key of A has three sharps, and is relatively easy to read. But for B♭ instruments, such as trumpets, the transposed key is B, which has five sharps and is a bear to read. For that reason, you probably want to avoid composing in the concert key of A—unless you want to give your trumpet section a real workout!

In general, you want to arrange things so no instrument is reading more than three sharps or flats. Taking this challenge into account, the following table shows the best—and the worst—keys to compose in:

Good and Bad Concert Keys

Good Keys	Acceptable Keys	Bad Keys
E♭	C	D♭
F	G	D
B♭	A♭	E
	G♭	
	A	
	B	

Instrumental Ranges

> **Note**
>
> The notation 8va means to play the note an octave above what's written. The notation 8vb means to play the note an octave below what's written.

Just as with voices, each instrument has its own particular range. There are certain notes that a trumpet, for example, just can't play.

For that reason, you need to know the playable range for each instrument in the orchestra, which is where the following table comes in. For each instrument listed (they're grouped by family and alphabetized), you'll find the actual range (in concert pitch), and how you have to transpose those notes when you're writing for that instrument. (Mark my words: You'd better bookmark this table now!)

Instrument Ranges

Instrument	Range (Concert Pitch)	Write It ...
Strings (bowed)		
Cello		Concert pitch
Double bass		Octave higher than concert pitch
Viola		Concert pitch
Violin		Concert pitch
Strings (plucked)		
Banjo		Octave higher than concert pitch
Electric bass		Octave higher than concert pitch
Guitar		Octave higher than concert pitch

continues

Instrument Ranges   (continued)

Instrument	Range (Concert Pitch)	Write It ...
Harp		Concert pitch
Mandolin		Concert pitch
Ukulele		Concert pitch

Brass

Instrument	Range (Concert Pitch)	Write It ...
Baritone horn		Major ninth higher than concert pitch
Bass trombone		Concert pitch
Bass trumpet (B♭)		Major ninth higher than concert pitch
Cornet		Major second higher than concert pitch
Flugelhorn		Major second higher than concert pitch

continues

Instrument Ranges   (continued)

Instrument	Range (Concert Pitch)	Write It ...
French horn		Perfect fifth higher than concert pitch
Piccolo trumpet		Major sixth lower than concert pitch
Trombone		Concert pitch
Trumpet (B♭)		Major second higher than concert pitch
Tuba		Concert pitch
Woodwinds		
Alto clarinet		Major sixth higher than concert pitch
Alto saxophone		Major sixth higher than concert pitch
Baritone saxophone		Octave and a major sixth higher than concert pitch
Bass clarinet		Major ninth higher than concert pitch
Bass flute		Octave higher than concert pitch

continues

Instrument Ranges (continued)

Instrument	Range (Concert Pitch)	Write It ...
Bass saxophone		Octave and a major sixth higher than concert pitch
Bassoon		Concert pitch
Clarinet (B♭)		Major second higher than concert pitch
Clarinet (E♭)		Minor third lower than concert pitch
Contrabassoon		Octave higher than concert pitch
English horn		Perfect fifth higher than concert pitch
Flute		Concert pitch
Oboe		Concert pitch
Piccolo		Octave lower than concert pitch
Soprano saxophone		Major second higher than concert pitch

continues

Instrument Ranges   (continued)

Instrument	Range (Concert Pitch)	Write It ...
Tenor saxophone		Major ninth higher than concert pitch

Mallets

Instrument	Range (Concert Pitch)	Write It ...
Chimes		One octave lower than concert pitch
Glockenspiel		Two octaves lower than concert pitch
Marimba		Concert pitch
Timpani		Concert pitch
Vibraphone (vibes)		Concert pitch
Xylophone		Octave lower than concert pitch

Keyboards

Instrument	Range (Concert Pitch)	Write It ...
Organ		Concert pitch

continues

Instrument Ranges (continued)

Instrument	Range (Concert Pitch)	Write It ...
Piano		Concert pitch

The Least You Need to Know

◆ In descending order, the four main voices in the choir are soprano, alto, tenor, and bass (SATB).

◆ The main families of instruments are strings (both bowed and plucked), brass, woodwind, keyboards, and percussion.

◆ Transposing instruments don't sound in concert pitch; they sound a specified interval above or below the written note. Their parts must be transposed so that the note they play is the proper note in concert pitch.

◆ B♭ instruments (trumpet, clarinet, and soprano and tenor saxes) sound a major second lower than concert pitch; E♭ instruments (alto and baritone saxes) sound a major sixth lower than concert pitch; and F instruments (English horn and French horn) sound a perfect fifth lower than concert pitch.

Exercises

Exercise 18-1

Transpose the following melody for trumpet. (Remember to set the transposed key signature!)

Exercise 18-2

Transpose the following melody for alto sax. (Remember to set the transposed key signature!)

Alto Sax

Exercise 18-3

Transpose the following melody for French horn. (Remember to set the transposed key signature!)

Fr. Horn

Exercise 18-4

Transpose the following trumpet melody back into concert pitch. (Remember to set the transposed key signature—and watch those accidentals!)

Trumpet

Chapter 19

Lead Sheets and Scores

In This Chapter

◆ Create clear and readable written music by the rules

◆ Understand the differences between lead sheets, chord sheets, and scores

◆ Learn how to create a full score for choir, big band, or orchestra

◆ Explore easy-to-use music notation software for your computer

Once you've written a piece of music, you need to present it in a way that other musicians can easily read. There are many different approaches to creating written music; which ones you use depends in part on the type of music you've written and who will be playing it.

If you've written a song for a rock or country band, the music you write can be fairly simple—chords and melody will generally suffice. If, on the other hand, you've written a full-blown symphony (good for you!), you'll need to create a detailed score containing the individual parts for each and every instrument in the orchestra.

Whatever type of written music you create, you need to keep it neat and make it easily understandable. Musicians have to be able to read the music at first pass (called *sight reading*), which means it helps to follow certain established parameters. There's no point in being unique if nobody can read your music!

Follow the Rules

Whatever type of music you prepare, you need to follow certain notation rules. These rules include the following:

◆ The first instance of each staff for each instrument or voice must have its own clef sign, key signature, and time signature.

◆ Typically, the time signature is shown only in the very first measure—and wherever a time change appears.

◆ You don't have to repeat the clef on every staff (after the first one, of course); you can simply indicate the key signature by using sharps and flats without a clef. (Although with today's music notation programs, it's easy enough to have the software insert the clef and key signature on each staff automatically.)

- Each instrument should be clearly marked at the beginning of each staff. (The first instance typically has the full instrument name spelled out; subsequent staves can use abbreviations.)

- In band and orchestral *scores*, group like instruments together (all the trumpets together, for example).

- For instruments that use the grand staff (both bass and treble clef), group the two staves by using braces.

- Measure lines should be drawn through all the instruments belonging to the same section—but not through *all* the instruments in the score.

- If you want, you can combine all like instruments on a single staff (all the trumpet parts on one staff, for example).

Definition

The master piece of music—the one that contains all the individual parts—is called the **score**.

- If an instrument or voice will be resting for an extended period of time, you don't have to include the staff for that instrument or voice during the rest period.

- Use letter markings to notate individual sections of the music. (For ease of reading, letter markings are typically enclosed in a box or circle.)

- Number your measures—or at least the first measure of every line. (Alternately, you can insert a number mark every 5 or 10 measures.)

It goes without saying that the music you create should also be *readable*. If you're writing it all out by hand, make sure you produce clear and distinct notes, and they're easily distinguishable on the staff. If you have poor penmanship (like I do!), consider taking a calligraphy course to improve your handwriting, or use a computerized music notation program to create great-looking music on your computer printer. (See the "Use the Computer" section later in this chapter.)

These rules apply to the score you compose and that the conductor uses. As for the music that the musicians themselves read, you have to create individual parts for each instrument. (This is not a requirement for vocal scores.) So if you've written a piece for a big band, you have to create a separate first trumpet part, and a separate second trumpet part, and a separate third trumpet part, and so on. When you write out the individual parts, include only that instrument's part—the conductor is the only person who gets to see all the parts together on the master score.

Warning

A lead sheet is not commercial sheet music. Sheet music typically includes full piano parts, whereas lead sheets contain melody and chords only. In addition, lead sheets are not available commercially, unlike sheet music.

Take the Lead

The most common form of written music is the *lead sheet*. A lead sheet doesn't include any individual instrumental parts; all you get is the song's melody, chords, and lyrics.

As you can see in the example on page 226, a typical lead sheet consists of one staff for the melody line, with lyrics under the staff and chords above it.

Lead sheets are simple to create, and they're ideal for noting popular songs. If you play in a rock or country band (or even a jazz trio or quartet), you can use lead sheets to present much of the music you play.

Make It Simple

Even simpler than the lead sheet is a piece of music that contains only chords; no melody lines and no lyrics. There are two different approaches to this type of music, and we'll look at both.

Chord Sheets

The *chord sheet* is just what it sounds like: a sheet of music containing only the chords of a song (see the example on page 227). The chords are presented measure by measure, so that members of the rhythm section (piano, bass, and guitar) can play through the song with minimal effort.

The Nashville Number System

In the field of country music, especially among studio musicians, there's a different type of chord sheet used. This method of writing chords is called the *Nashville Number System*, and it uses numbers instead of letters.

In the Nashville Number System, everything revolves around the tonic chord of a given key. That tonic chord is assigned the number 1. The chord based on the ii of the key—a minor chord—is assigned the number 2m (The m tells the musician it's a minor chord.) The chord based on the iii of the key—also a minor chord—is assigned the number 3m. And so on up the scale, up to chord number 7.

As you can see, major chords are distinguished by number only; minor chords have an m added. Extensions are added as superscripts to the right of the number, so that a dominant seventh chord based on the fifth of the scale is noted as 5^7.

A chord chart using the Nashville Number System looks something like the example on page 228.

Because the Nashville Number System doesn't use traditional notes, it is ideal for musicians who don't know how to read music. It also makes it very easy to change key—just play the 1 or 2 or 3, or whatever chord in whatever key you want; it's as easy as that.

> **Tip**
>
> If you prepare a chord sheet using a music notation program, you may choose to include guitar tablature in additional to the standard chord symbols. This is particularly useful if you're writing for beginning-level guitarists.

> **Note**
>
> The Nashville Number System is very much like the Roman numeral notation system, except it uses regular numbers (1, 2, 3) instead of Roman numerals (I, II, III).

Sing It Loud

Arranging for choirs is a bit more complicated than sketching out chords for a rock band. Choral music normally has four or five parts, and each part has to have its own line in the score.

Let's look at a typical four-part choral score (see the example on page 229). The parts are arranged with the highest voice (soprano) at the top, and the lowest voice (bass) at the bottom. The four vocal parts (soprano, alto, tenor, and bass) are grouped together with braces, and a piano accompaniment is included below the vocal parts. The top three parts use the treble clef; the bass line uses the bass clef. Lyrics are included below each staff.

When you create a choral score—or any score with multiple parts, for that matter—make sure a measure within one part aligns vertically with the same measure in all the other parts. In fact, the notes within each measure also should align between parts. If it helps, use a ruler to help keep the notes in alignment when you're writing the score.

> **Note**
>
> Charts for choruses are sometimes called *SATB* scores, for the soprano, alto, tenor, and bass parts.

>
>
> **Tip**
>
> If there are additional backing instruments, they can also be included in the score—below the vocals, just like the piano part.

A typical lead sheet.

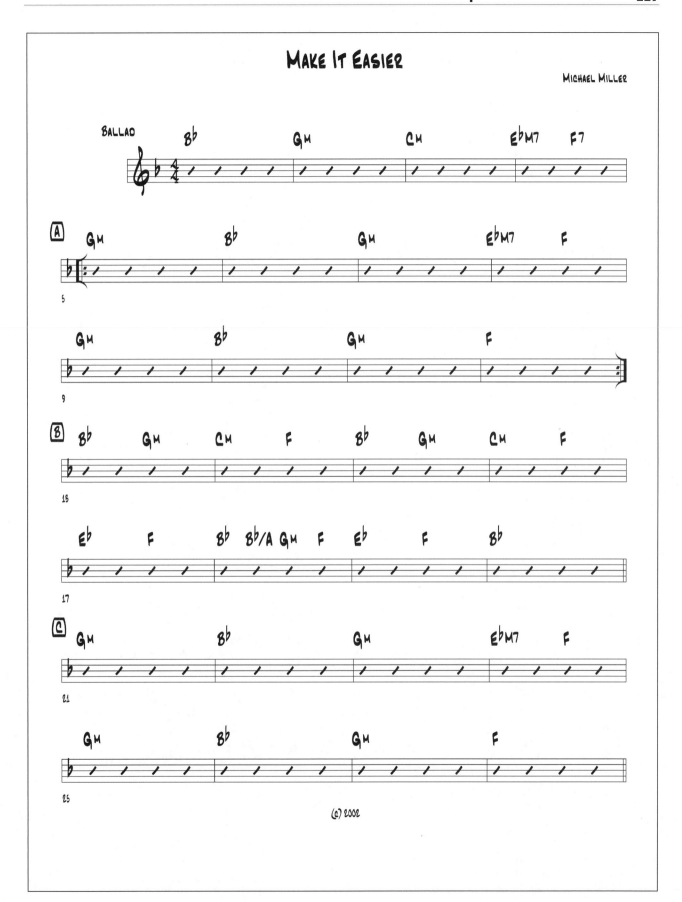

A typical chord sheet.

A song outlined using the Nashville Number System.

A four-part choral arrangement.

Jazz It Up

Another popular ensemble—particularly among high school and college musicians—is the *big band*, or *jazz band*. A typical jazz band includes a lot of instruments, which results in a fairly large piece of music. For example, whereas a choral score might get two groups of staves on a page, a jazz band score typically takes a whole page just to display all the different instruments.

What instruments are we talking about? The typical big band has some or all of the following, listed from top to bottom on the score:

- Flute (sometimes played by a sax player)
- Soprano sax (sometimes played by an alto or tenor sax player)
- One to three alto saxes
- One to three tenor saxes
- One or two baritone saxes
- Three to five trumpets
- Three to five trombones
- Guitar
- Piano
- Bass
- Drums
- Other percussion, such as congas or tambourine

Note
In all band and orchestral scores, like instruments are typically grouped together in *systems*. In a system, the individual staves are joined together, to make it easier to view the instruments as a group.

That's a lot of instruments to put on a single page! But, as you can see in the example on page 232, they all fit.

When you create a big band score, you have a choice of how you deal with transposing instruments. You can create a concert key score, with all instruments written in concert key; if you take this approach, you have to make sure you transpose the individual parts when you create them. Alternately, you can create a transposed score in which each instrument is written in its transposed key; this type of score might be harder for the conductor to read, but it more accurately represents what the musicians see on their individual parts.

Creating parts for the rhythm section is particularly interesting. In most cases you can use slash notation and indicate the chord changes, but you don't have to create fully realized parts. The big exception to this is when you have important rhythms that you want the rhythm section to reinforce; you can note these rhythms using slash notes, as shown in the fifth measure of the example on page 232.

Strike Up the Band

An even bigger band to write for is the *concert band*. Unlike a jazz band, a concert band includes virtually all the brass and woodwind instruments, along with a full percussion section—snare drums, bass drums, timpani, marimba, and so forth. A concert band is almost like an orchestra, but without strings.

Concert bands evolved from traditional marching bands. Not only did the musicians get to sit down, the instrumentation was also augmented from the slightly more Spartan marching ensembles.

When you're writing a concert band score, you include the following groups of instruments, in top-to-bottom order:

- Piccolo
- Flute
- Oboe
- English horn
- Bassoon
- Clarinet
- Alto clarinet
- Bass clarinet
- Alto saxophone
- Tenor saxophone
- Baritone saxophone
- Cornet
- Trumpet
- French horn
- Trombone
- Bass trombone
- Baritone horn
- Tuba
- Timpani
- Percussion (with separate staves for snare drum, bass drum, and so on)

The example on page 233 shows a typical concert band score. As with jazz band scores, concert band scores can be in either concert key or transposed.

A marching band score is similar, but with fewer instruments. A full marching band typically includes the following instruments, in score order:

- Piccolo
- Flute
- Clarinet
- Bass clarinet
- Alto saxophone
- Tenor saxophone
- Baritone saxophone
- Trumpet
- French horn
- Trombone
- Baritone horn
- Mallets (xylophone, marimba)
- Snare drum
- Tom toms
- Bass drum

> **Note**
>
> Marches are typically written in 2/4 time, rather than the more common 4/4.

> **Note**
>
> A popular variation of the traditional marching band is the *drum and bugle corps* (sometimes just called *drum corps*). This is typically a smaller ensemble emphasizing brass and percussion instruments—and precision marching routines

A score for big band.

A score for concert band.

A score for full orchestra.

Make the Big Score

Now we're in the big leagues. Creating a score for full orchestra is a major undertaking, if for no other reason than there are many instruments to deal with. Because of this, most orchestra scores are written on large sheets of paper—11" x 17" or so. Because of the sheer size of the beast, you'll probably get only four to eight measures on each page, which means the typical orchestral score also is fairly long.

As you can see from the preceding example on page 234, instrument families are grouped together in the score in the following order:

◆ Woodwinds

◆ Brass

◆ Percussion

◆ Strings

Note
Keyboards and harp, when used, are typically placed between the percussion and string instruments.

As with big band scores, you can create orchestral scores in either concert key or transposed keys—whichever works better for you.

Because most orchestral pieces are fairly long, it's important to include proper road mapping in your scores. Number each measure, and designate each section with a new letter. This way musicians (and the conductor!) can easily find their places during the starting and stopping of the rehearsal process—or if they happen to fall asleep during a long rest in a live performance!

Tip

You also can create a *condensed score*, in which individual parts are collapsed into single staves. This type of score is easier to read, even though it doesn't contain the part detail necessary for initial rehearsals.

Use the Computer

In the old days, it was a real pain in the rear to create scores for large ensembles. Every part had to be written separately, by hand, and transposed as necessary. That was a lot of writing, and didn't always result in the most readable pieces of music.

Today, thanks to computer technology, a lot of this notation process can be automated. Read on to discover how you can ease the pain of notation—and make composing more fun using computer software.

Tip

You have the option of cutting down the number of staves in the score during long sections of music where fewer instruments are playing.

Music Notation Software

The most useful type of software for composers and arrangers is *music notation software*. These software programs, available for both Windows and Macintosh computers, enable you to create a complete piece of music—including full orchestral scores—from your computer keyboard. The result is a professional-looking piece of music, complete with proper note spacing and notation marks.

All music notation programs let you enter notes on the page with either your mouse or computer keyboard. All you have to do is click a position on the staff, and a note appears.

Many of these programs also let you connect a *MIDI* keyboard and input music directly from the keyboard to your computer. The notation program translates the notes you play on the keyboard into corresponding notes on a staff. You can then fine-tune the music onscreen as necessary.

Entering music with Finale.

There are all different types of music notation programs, although they all perform the same basic functions. Some programs let you include more parts than others, though, and some include more professional notation features. So when you're shopping for a music notation program, here are some things to look for:

> **Definition**
>
> **MIDI** stands for musical instrument digital interface, and is a computer protocol for passing audio information digitally from one electronic device to another.

- The number of individual staves (instrumental and voice) you can create for a piece of music.
- The quality of the printed music. (Look especially for proper note spacing, full extension of note stems, and the automatic avoidance of note collisions, in which a note or marking from one staff overlaps a similar note or marking on another staff.)
- The capability to extract individual parts from a score.
- The capability to automatically transpose parts.
- The capability to include lyrics.

- The capability to include guitar tabs.
- The capability to write in standard percussion notation.
- The inclusion of advanced notation markings and the flexibility to place them wherever you want in the score.
- The capability to create notation based on MIDI keyboard input.

The most popular music notation programs, at the time this book is written, are shown in the following table:

Music Notation Programs

Program	Publisher	Suggested Retail Price
Allegro	Coda Music Technology (www.codamusic.com)	$200
Amadeus Opus Lite	Allegroassai (www.allegroassai.com)	$90
Autoscore Deluxe	Wildcat Canyon (www.wildcat.com)	$120
Autoscore Pro	Wildcat Canyon (www.wildcat.com)	$250
Cubasis Notation	Steinberg (www.steinberg.net)	$60

continues

Music Notation Programs   (continued)

Program	Publisher	Suggested Retail Price
Finale	Coda Music Technology (www.codamusic.com)	$600
Music Master Publisher	Datasonics (www.datasonics.com.au)	$140
Opus	Allegroassai (www.allegroassai.com)	$300
Overture	GenieSoft (www.geniesoft.com)	$350
PhotoScore Professional	Neuratron (www.neuratron.com)	$200
PrintMusic	Coda Music Technology (www.codamusic.com)	$70
Score Writer	GenieSoft (www.geniesoft.com)	$80
Sibelius	Sibelius (www.sibelius.com)	$600
SmartScore Professional Edition	Musitek (www.musitek.com)	$400
Songworks II	Ars Nova (www.ars-nova.com)	$125

Obviously, the higher-priced notation programs have more features—in particular, more professional features—than do the lower-cost programs. The two most popular notation programs today are actually the highest-priced (and most fully featured) of the bunch: Finale and Sibelius. Either of these programs can do just about anything you need them to do, even though they both have fairly steep learning curves.

> ### Note
>
> All prices are approximate U.S. retail prices as suggested by the software publishers; you can probably find lower prices by shopping around. These programs are available at most large music stores, some computer stores, and directly from the software publishers. (If you're a student, you may be able to get an educational discount if you order through your school.) Availability of and pricing for any of these programs will change over time.

Music Sequencing Software

Related to music notation software is the genre of *music sequencing software*. Sequencing programs enable you to create reasonable facsimiles of your scores, using MIDI technology, for your own personal or professional playback. The sequencer acts as kind of a fancy virtual digital recorder, and MIDI helps to recreate the sounds of multiple different instruments. So you can use the sequencer software to play back a complete symphony, sounding more or less like a full orchestra.

Just as with music notation programs, there is a huge price difference between low-end and high-end music sequencing programs. As you might expect, the higher-priced programs include many more professional-level features.

The most popular sequencing software, at the time of writing, is listed in the following table:

> ### Tip
>
> Some high-end sequencing programs (such as Cubase VST Score) also include basic music notation programs—just as some notation programs include built-in MIDI playback. If you're just starting out, stick with a music notation program with MIDI playback, such as Finale or Sibelius; when you go pro, you might discover a need for a more full-featured sequencing program.

Music Sequencing Software

Program	Publisher	Suggested Retail Price
Cakewalk Home Studio	Cakewalk (www.cakewalk.com)	$130
Cubase VST	Steinberg (www.steinberg.net)	$450
Cubase VST Score	Steinberg (www.steinberg.net)	$600
Music Maker Professional	Magix Entertainment (www.magix.com)	$100
PowerTracks Pro Audio	PG Music (www.pgmusic.com)	$30
Sonar	Cakewalk (www.cakewalk.com)	$480

The Least You Need to Know

◆ Lead sheets present melody, chords, and lyrics.

◆ Chord sheets are used to present chords only—and can use standard chord notation, or the simplified Nashville Number System of notation.

◆ Choral scores include individual parts for soprano, alto, tenor, and bass; plus piano accompaniment.

◆ Band and orchestral scores include separate staves for each instrument—and can be written in either concert or transposed keys.

◆ The chore of creating written music can be made easier by computerized music notation programs, such as Finale or Sibelius.

Exercise

Exercise 19-1

Using the following blank score, create a simple four-measure chart for big band. Base your piece on the chord progressions listed in the rhythm parts, and use the transposed keys for each instrument.

Conductor Score

Chapter 20

Performing Your Music

In This Chapter

◆ Preparing the parts for the individual musicians

◆ Ensuring an effective and efficient rehearsal

◆ Learning how to conduct a large ensemble

◆ Choosing the appropriate method to start a song

You've done it. You've learned enough theory to compose your own piece of music, and you've arranged it for a vocal or instrumental ensemble. Now it's time to venture out into the real world, and get that music played.

Scary, isn't it?

Having your music performed can be a nerve-wracking experience. Will all the parts fit together? Did you write in the proper ranges? Did you transpose all the parts properly? How will it sound?

Of course, to hear your music performed, you have to arrange for a group to do the performing. If it's a simple song, that might be as easy as gathering together your local garage band for a quick read-through. If it's a vocal arrangement, you might be able to recruit your school or church choir for the job. If it's a big band piece, your high school or college jazz ensemble probably is the group to ask. And if you've written a symphony or other orchestral work, it's time to call in some favors from your community orchestra.

Once you have the group lined up, the fun really starts—and you get to be a conductor!

Preparing the Parts

As you learned back in Chapter 19, every musician must have his or her own personal copy of the music. That doesn't mean copying the conductor's score a few dozen times; it means writing out the specific part for that individual instrument or voice.

Most commercial music comes with all the individual parts you need for your group. However, if you're playing an original piece, it's your responsibility to create the individual parts for each instrument or voice, and to pass them out to the musicians. Ideally this happens well in advance of the first rehearsal, so they'll have the opportunity to practice their parts on their own.

Remember to transpose the parts to the proper keys, to make the music as readable as possible, and to include proper signposts and road mapping throughout. (That means numbering the measures, lettering individual sections, and including cues of some sort when you're coming off an extended section of rests.)

Rehearsal Routines

You've arranged the music, and arranged for the musicians. The big hand of the clock is almost in the full-up position, and it's time for your first rehearsal.

What do you do?

When you're rehearing a chorus, band, or orchestra, you need to warm up the group before they start playing (or singing) full blast. Then you have to effectively and efficiently rehearse the piece at hand—you have to get the musicians up to speed as quickly as possible. (Time is money!)

Here's a suggested routine you can use when you're working with a large ensemble of any type:

1. **Setup**   If you're dealing with professionals, they'll know to be set up and ready to play at the appointed time. If you're dealing with younger or amateur players, you need to allow them time to get settled in and ready to play.

2. **Tuneup**   You need to take a few minutes to get an instrumental group in tune with itself.

> **CAUTION**
>
> **Warning**
>
> Your rehearsal time will inevitably be limited—and less than what you'd ideally like to have. Plan out your rehearsal routine in advance to take best advantage of the time you have. Don't spend so much time on the beginning of the piece that you never get a chance to rehearse the end!

3. **Warmup**   It's especially important for nonprofessional players—both vocalists and instrumentalists—to "limber up," musically before they tackle the hard stuff. Have them play or sing some scales, or run through a simple and familiar piece of music, to help them stretch their musical muscles, so to speak.

4. **Play-through**   Once everyone is set up, tuned up, warmed up, and ready to go, you can start rehearsing your music. You might want to start by playing the piece all the way through, to give everyone a feel for the piece. Then you can go back and rehearse specific sections, focusing on those parts of the music that are particularly tricky, or that seemed to give the musicians problems on the first play-through. Remember to end the rehearsal with a final play-through of the entire piece.

How to Conduct Yourself

If you've composed or arranged a piece of music, you'll probably be expected to lead the band or orchestra or choir when it's time for that music to be played. That means you need to know a little bit about conducting—at least enough to get everybody started and stopped at the same time!

> **Tip**
>
> You can use a baton (a short wooden or plastic stick) for conducting, but you don't have to. It's perfectly acceptable to conduct using nothing but your bare hands.

At its most basic, conducting is about setting the correct tempo, counting in the musicians, and leading the way through any important changes in tempo or dynamics throughout the music. Professional conductors also shape the flow of the music, and can turn a generic orchestral or choral performance into a personal statement and a moving work of art.

However, when you're first starting out you'll have your hands full just finding the downbeat. Fortunately, better musicians can soldier through, even if you're busy waving your arms around like a broken Dutch windmill.

The thing is, conducting is pretty simple. There are a few set patterns you need to learn, then it all falls into place.

Conducting in Four

Most music is written in 4/4 time, so it's very important to learn the pattern for conducting in four.

You work through this pattern using your right hand—unless you're left-handed, of course. For the four-beat pattern, your hand has to move to four different positions. You don't have to use huge movements, but your hand has to move enough for the musicians to tell what the heck you're doing. Try moving your arm from the elbow, directly in front of your chest.

The four positions of this pattern describe a cross—up, down, left, right, like this:

> **Tip**
>
> The right hand is used to conduct the beat; your left hand is used to add emphasis or point out specific parts. You also can just stick your left hand in your pocket, or mirror your right-hand movement with your left hand.

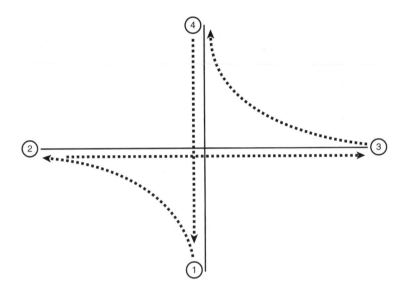

Conducting in four.

You start with the 4 position. This is the upwardmost movement, and actually serves as a kind of preparatory (or "get ready") beat before the downbeat of one. You move your arm up to a point, coinciding with the fourth beat of the measure (or the upbeat before the first measure of the song).

Now you bring your arm down, all the way to the bottommost position, exactly on beat one. This is position 1, and it's the most important movement in your conducting. The musicians have to get a solid "one," and that's where your downbeat comes in.

For the second beat in the measure, move your arm up slightly and to the left, to position 2. Then, for the third beat, move your arm straight across, to the right, to position 3.

Now we're up to the fourth beat of the measure, and your upbeat. Swing your arm back up to position 4 and get ready to start all over again for the next measure.

Practice this movement—(up)-down-left-right-up—again and again, at different tempos. Once you get this mastered, you're conducting!

Conducting in Two

Conducting in 2/4 or 2/2 time is pretty similar to conducting in four. All you have to do is leave out the left and right movements to positions 2 and 3.

That's right: Conducting in two is a simple up-down, up-down movement; up for the preparatory beat, down for one, up for two, down for one … again and again and again.

Here's what the pattern looks like:

Conducting in two.

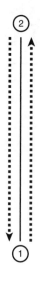

Conducting in Three

Conducting in three is slightly more difficult than conducting in two or four. It's kind of like the four pattern, but without the left, or 2 position. In terms of movement, you start with the preparatory beat (of course), then go down for one, to the right for two, up for three, then back down for one again. Down, right, up—like this:

Conducting in three.

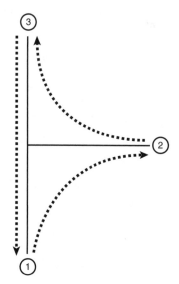

Finding the Beat

As I said earlier, one of the chief duties of the conductor is to set the tempo. There are two ways you can do this:

◆ **Timing the preparatory beat**   This approach, preferred by professionals, gets you right into the music. You don't count anything out in advance, just start by swinging your arm up for the preparatory beat. The time between the preparatory beat and the initial downbeat is the duration of a single beat, and very quickly sets the tempo. (Of course, the drawback to this approach is that it's very difficult to master—and, for that reason, isn't recommended for beginners.)

◆ **Counting the beat**   This approach leaves no ambiguity over the tempo of the song. You simply count out the beat, in tempo, like this: "One, two, three, four," or "One, two, ready, go." You count out one measure (or more), which serves to count the band in—and everybody starts on the same beat at the same tempo.

> **Note**
>
> Setting the tempo with the preparatory beat is the norm in the world of classical music. In the pop and jazz worlds, it's more common to count off the tempo.

You can use whichever method you prefer, although when you're first learning a piece, it's probably better to count off before you start. This way you can set the tempo in your head, and the other musicians won't be guessing about where the one is.

Practicing in the Real World

The best way to practice conducting is to do a little conducting in the privacy of your own home—to your favorite songs and pieces of music. You should practice to a variety of different CDs, to get used to the different beat patterns used in different types of music.

But before you go out and face the world for your first honest-to-goodness conducting session, you need to practice with other people. Gather a few of your friends, and practice with the piece you'll be conducting—even if it's just a few of the parts. Run through the piece a few times, and encourage your friends to tell you what you could do to improve your conducting.

That first downbeat in front of a group of musicians can be daunting. Use your friends to help you get over any shyness or fear, so that you appear confident when you pick up the baton for real. (Remember—musicians, like wild dogs, can smell fear.)

The Least You Need to Know

◆ Before your first rehearsal, make sure that every musician has his or her own personal copy of the music.

◆ Make sure you warm up and tune up the musicians before you start rehearsal.

◆ To conduct a piece of music in 4/4, move your right hand from the up position to the down position for the first beat, to the left for the second beat, to the right for the third, and back to the up position for the fourth beat. (That's down, left, right, up—1, 2, 3, 4.)

◆ Although you can let your preparatory beat establish the music's tempo, it's probably better to count off the first measure ("One, two, ready, go") to help everyone feel the right beat.

Exercises

Exercise 20-1

Put your favorite piece of music in your CD player, pick up a baton, and start conducting!

Coda

Thus ends this book—and your first exposure to basic music theory. I hope you've found the information in these pages helpful, and that I've passed on some of my love and enthusiasm for how music gets created.

The key thing to remember (aside from all the notes and rhythms and such) is that these musical building blocks exist for you to use—however you like. We may say that there are rules and conventions, but when it comes to creating music, all the rules are made to be broken. What ultimately matters is how a piece of music *sounds*—to you, and to your listeners.

Theory is good, but it's just a guideline for what happens out in the real world. If you want to use parallel fifths in your harmony, go ahead. If you want to flat a fifth or resolve a turnaround to the ii chord, do it. Some of the greatest pieces of music have broken all sorts of rules. As long as it sounds good, it's all okay.

Just because you're done with this book, however, doesn't mean that your music education has ended. In fact, if you choose to make music a part of your life, your education *never* ends. Every song you listen to, every piece of music you hear is an opportunity to learn more about the music you love. Keep your ears open and your mind free, and you'll continue to expand your knowledge and skills for the rest of your musical life.

You can also further your music education with more reading. If you're serious about becoming a better musician, I recommend you check out the following books:

◆ *Arranging and Composing for the Small Ensemble* (David Baker; Alfred Publishing; 1970—revised edition 1988)

◆ *Arranging Concepts Complete* (Dick Grove; Alfred Publishing; 1972—second edition 1989)

◆ *The New Harvard Dictionary of Music* (Don Michael Randel, editor; Belknap Press; 1986)

◆ *Hearing and Writing Music: Professional Training for Today's Musician* (Ron Gorow; September Publishing; 2000)

◆ *Total Harmony* (Dorothy Payne, Allan Schindler, Stefan M. Kostka; McGraw-Hill; 1995)

◆ *What to Listen for in Music* (Aaron Copland; Mentor; 1939—softcover revision 1999)

◆ *Tunesmith: Inside the Art of Songwriting* (Jimmy Webb; Hyperion; 1998)

Of course, if you really want to learn about music, you need a good teacher. Whether you study one-on-one with a professional educator, or attend music classes at your favorite school or university, a teacher can provide the individual instruction that's necessary to develop your own unique musical skills.

There are also many music theory resources on the Internet. Some of the most useful include Music Notes (library.thinkquest.org/15413/), Music Theory Web (www.teoria.com), and Musictheory.net (www. musictheory.net).

While you're on the Internet, make sure you check out my personal website (www.molehillgroup.com). There you'll find information about my latest book projects, as well as any updates or corrections to the information in this book.

The Internet is also a good way to get in contact with me; my e-mail address is theory@molehillgroup.com. I encourage and appreciate any comments you might have about this book, or about music theory in general; it's always good to hear from fellow musicians.

If you love music, as I do, you'll want to experience as much of it as possible. The more you play, or sing, or just listen, the more you'll learn about the theory behind the music. So put down this book and put on your favorite CD—or pick up your instrument and start playing. The music is waiting for you!

Appendix A

The Complete Idiot's Music Glossary

a cappella   Vocal music, without instrumental accompaniment.

a tempo   Return to the previous tempo.

accelerando   Gradually speed up. (Abbreviated as *accel.*)

accent   A note played louder or with more emphasis than regular notes.

accidental   A marking used to raise and lower the indicated pitch; sharps raise the note a half step, flats lower the note a half step, and naturals return the note to the original pitch.

adagietto   Tempo marking for a moderately slow tempo, slightly faster than adagio.

adagio   Tempo marking for moderately slow.

adante   Tempo marking for a moderate, walking tempo.

adantino   Tempo marking for a moderate tempo, slightly faster than adante.

Aeolian mode   A church mode starting on the sixth degree of the corresponding major scale, equivalent to the natural minor scale. *See minor and mode.*

allegretto   Tempo marking for a moderately fast tempo, not quite as fast as allegro.

allegro   Tempo marking for a fast, cheerful tempo.

alto clef   A clef, used primarily by the viola, that places middle C on the middle line of the staff.

alto voice   The lowest female voice.

arpeggio   A chord that is broken up and played one note at a time.

articulation   The manner in which notes are struck, sustained, and released. One indicates articulation by the use of markings such as legato, staccato, tenuto, and so on.

atonal   Having no tonal center, and no underlying key.

attack   The beginning part of a sound.

backbeat   In 4/4 time, beats two and four, typically played by the drummer on the snare drum.

bar   *See measure.*

bar line   The vertical line placed on the staff between measures.

baritone voice   A male voice pitched between the bass and tenor voices; not always isolated in choral music.

bass   The lowest pitch of a chord (not necessarily the root).

bass clef   A clef, used by lower-pitched voices and instruments, that places middle C on the first ledger line above the staff.

bass voice   The lowest male voice.

beat   Any pulsing unit of musical time.

block chord   An unbroken chord.

blues progression   A 12-bar sequence of chords common in blues and jazz music, as follows: I-I-I-I-IV-IV-I-I-V7-IV-I-V7.

brass   The family of instruments, typically made of brass, that produce sound by blowing through a mouthpiece. The brass family includes the trumpet, trombone, tuba, and French horn.

cadence   A pause or stopping point, typically a short chord progression inserted at the end of a phrase or piece of music.

chord   Three or more notes played simultaneously.

chord progression   A series of chords over a number of measures.

chord sheet   A sheet of music containing only the chords of a song.

chromatic   Pitches outside the underlying key or scale.

chromatic scale   A scale containing 12 equal divisions of the octave—all the white keys and black keys within an octave.

clef   A graphic symbol placed at the beginning of the staff to indicate the pitch of the notes on the staff.

Coda   Ending section of a piece of music.

common time   The 4/4 time signature.

contrapuntal   *See counterpoint.*

contrary motion   Where one voice moves in the opposite direction to another.

counterpoint   Two or more simultaneous, independent lines or voices.

crescendo   Gradually louder.

cut time   The 2/2 time signature.

D.C. al Coda   Navigation marking meaning to go back to the beginning and play to the Coda sign; then skip to the Coda section.

D.C. al Fine   Navigation marking meaning to go back to the beginning and play through to the end.

D.S. al Coda   Navigation marking meaning to go back to the Segno sign and play to the Coda sign; then skip to the Coda section.

D.S. al Fine   Navigation marking meaning to go back to the Segno sign and play through to the end.

decrescendo   Gradually softer.

diatonic   Notes or chords that are in the underlying key or scale.

diminished chord   A chord with a major third and a diminished fifth (1-♭3-♭5).

division   Fractional parts of a beat.

dominant   The fifth degree of a scale, a perfect fifth above the tonic; also refers to the chord built on this fifth scale degree.

dominant seventh chord   A major chord with a minor seventh added (1-3-5-♭7); typically found on the fifth degree of the scale, and noted as V7.

doppio movimento   Play twice as fast.

Dorian mode   A church mode starting on the second degree of the corresponding major scale. *See mode.*

double bar   Two vertical lines placed on the staff to indicate the end of a section or a composition.

downbeat   The major beats in a measure; in 4/4 time, the downbeats are 1, 2, 3, and 4. (Some theoreticians hold that there is only one downbeat per measure—the very first beat.)

dynamics   Varying degrees of loud and soft.

eleventh chord   A triad with three notes added, a seventh, ninth, and eleventh above the root of the chord.

enharmonic   Different notations of the same sound; for example, F# and G♭ are enharmonic notes.

extended chords   Chords with additional notes (typically in thirds) added above the basic triad. (Some theoreticians consider seventh chords extended chords; others don't.)

fermata   Symbol used to indicate that a note should be held indefinitely; sometimes called a "bird's eye."

flam   A grace note (and subsequent main note) played on a drum.

forte   Loud. (Abbreviated as *f.*)

fortissimo   Very loud. (Abbreviated as *ff.*)

fortississimo   Very, very loud. (Abbreviated as *fff.*)

frequency   A scientific measurement of how fast the molecules of air are vibrating; the faster the vibrations, the higher the *pitch.*

fugue   A contrapuntal form that is built from a single subject.

gig   A musician's job.

glissando   A mechanism for getting from one pitch to another, playing every single pitch between the two notes as smoothly as possible.

grace note   One or more notes, played lightly and quickly, that precede a main note.

grave   Tempo marking for a very slow or solemn pace.

half step   The smallest distance between notes in a chromatic scale.

harmonic interval   Two notes sounded simultaneously.

harmonization   The choice of chords to accompany a melodic line.

harmony   The sound of tones in combination; also used to refer to the accompanying parts behind the main melody.

interval   The distance between two pitches or notes.

inversion   A chord in which the bass note is not the root of the chord.

Ionian mode   A church mode starting on the first degree of the corresponding major scale, equivalent to the major scale. *See mode.*

key   A combination of a tonic and a mode. For example, the key of F Major has F as the tonic and major as the mode.

key signature   The sharps or flats that are placed at the beginning of a staff to indicate the key of the music.

larghetto   Tempo marking for a slow tempo, slightly faster than largo.

largo   Tempo marking for slow and dignified.

leading tone   The note that is a half step below the tonic; thus leads up to the tonic.

lento   Tempo marking for slow.

Locrian mode   A (theoretical) church mode starting on the seventh degree of the corresponding major scale. *See mode.*

Lydian mode   A church mode starting on the fourth degree of the corresponding major scale. *See mode.*

major   The most common mode, consisting of the following intervals: whole-whole-half-whole-whole-whole-half.

major chord   A chord with a major third (1-3-5).

major seventh chord   A major triad with a major seventh added (1-3-5-7).

measure   A group of beats, indicated by the placement of bar lines on the staff.

mediant   The third degree of a scale, or a chord built on that degree (III).

melody   The combination of tone and rhythm in a logical sequence.

meter   The organization of beats and their divisions.

mezzo forte   Medium loud. (Abbreviated as mf.)

mezzo piano   Medium soft. (Abbreviated as mp.)

minor   One of three modes, each with a flatted third of the scale. Natural minor is identical to *Aeolian mode*, with the following intervals: whole-half-whole-whole-half-whole-whole. Harmonic minor contains the following intervals: whole-half-whole-whole-half-whole-half-half. Melodic minor is different ascending and descending; ascending, the intervals are whole-half-whole-whole-whole-whole-half, whereas descending it uses the same intervals as natural minor.

minor chord   A chord with a minor third (1-♭3-5).

minor seventh chord   A minor chord with a minor seventh added (1-♭3-5-♭7).

Mixolydian mode   A church mode starting on the fifth degree of the corresponding major scale. *See mode.*

mode   A series of notes that indicate the structure of a major or minor scale key or piece.

mode   A set of scales, based on centuries-old church music that preceded today's major and minor scales; these include the *Dorian, Phrygian, Lydian, Mixolydian, Ionian, Locrian,* and *Aeolian* modes.

moderato   Tempo marking for a moderate pace.

modulation   A change of key.

molto   Modifier for tempo markings; means "very."

motif (or motive)   A *brief* melodic or rhythmic idea.

music notation software   A computer program that automates the writing of musical notes on paper.

music sequencing software   A computer program that automates the playback of music.

neighboring tone   A tone one diatonic step away from (either above or below) the main tone.

ninth chord   A basic triad with two notes added, a seventh and a ninth above the root of the chord.

notation   The art of writing musical notes on paper.

note   A *symbol* used to indicate the duration and pitch of a sound, as in whole notes, half notes, and quarter notes.

octave   Two pitches, with the same name, located 12 half steps apart.

odd time   Any non-4/4 time signature, such as 3/4, 5/4, or 9/8.

parallel motion   Two or more voices that move in identical steps, simultaneously.

passing tone   A pitch located (scale-wise) directly between two main pitches; passing tones are typically used to connect notes in a melody.

percussion   The family of instruments that produce sound when you hit, beat, crash, shake, roll, scratch, rub, twist, or rattle them. Included in this family are various types of drums and cymbals, as well as mallet instruments (marimba, xylophone, and so forth) and timpani.

perfect pitch   The ability to hear absolute pitches in your head, without any outside assistance.

phrase   A musical statement with a beginning, end, and a clear shape.

phrase   Within a piece of music, a segment that is unified by rhythms, melodies, or harmonies and that comes to some sort of closure; typically composed in groups of 2, 4, 8, 16, or 32 measures.

Phrygian mode   A church mode starting on the third degree of the corresponding major scale. *See mode.*

pianissimo   Very soft. (Abbreviated as *pp.*)

pianississimo   Very, very soft. (Abbreviated as *ppp.*)

piano   Soft. (Abbreviated as *p.*)

pitch   The highness or lowness of a tone. (In scientific terms, a specific frequency.)

prestissimo   Tempo marking for an extremely fast tempo, faster than presto.

presto   Tempo marking for a very fast tempo.

primary chords   The most important chords in a key: I, IV, V.

rallentando   Gradually slow down. (Abbreviated as *rall.*)

relative keys   Keys that share the same key signature, but not the same root. For example, A minor and C Major are relative keys.

rest   A symbol used to denote silence or not playing a particular note.

rhythm   The organization of sound in time; the arrangement of beats and accents in music.

ritardando   Gradually slow down. (Abbreviated as *rit.* or *ritard.*)

ritenuto   Hold back the tempo. (Abbreviated as *riten.*)

root   The fundamental note in a chord.

SATB   Shorthand for soprano, alto, tenor, and bass. (Choral scores are sometimes called SATB scores.)

scale   A sequence of related pitches, arranged in ascending or descending order.

score   The written depiction of all the individual parts played of each of the instruments in an ensemble.

seventh chord   A triad with an added note a seventh above the root of the chord.

shuffle   A rhythmic feel based on triplets or a dotted eighth note/sixteenth note pattern.

similar motion   Two or more voices that move in the same direction, but not with the same intervals.

sixth chord   A triad with an added note a sixth above the root of the chord.

song form   The structure of a short piece of music.

soprano   The highest female voice.

staff   An assemblage of horizontal lines and spaces that represent different pitches.

string   The family of instruments that produces sound by moving a bow across a string. The string family includes the violin, viola, cello, and double bass.

subdominant   The fourth degree of the scale, or the chord built on the fourth degree (IV).

submediant   The sixth degree of a scale, or the chord built on that degree (VI).

subtonic   The seventh degree of a scale, or the chord built on that degree (VII). (In classical theory, the subtonic is the lowered seventh, while the normal seventh is called the *leading tone*.)

supertonic   The second degree of a scale, or the chord built on that degree (II).

suspension   A nonchord note (typically the fourth) used within a chord to create tension; the suspended note typically resolves down to the third.

syncopation   An accent on an unexpected beat—or the lack of an accent on an expected beat.

tempo   The rate of speed at which beats are played in a song.

tempo primo   Return to the tempo designated at the beginning of a piece.

tenor voice   The highest male voice.

theme   A recurring melodic or rhythmic pattern.

third   The interval between the first and third degree of a scale; can be either minor (three half steps) or major (two whole steps).

thirteenth chord   A triad with four notes added, a seventh, ninth, eleventh, and thirteenth above the root of the chord.

tie   A curved line over or under two or more notes that "ties" the two notes together into one.

timbre   Sound quality (as in "That trumpet player has a rich timbre").

time signature   A symbol with two numbers, one on top of the other (like a fraction), that indicates the basic meter of a song. The upper number indicates how many beats are in a measure; the bottom number indicates the type of note that receives one beat.

tone   A sound played or sung at a specific pitch. (The term is also used sometimes to indicate *timbre*, or sound quality.)

tonic   The primary note in a scale or key; the first degree of a scale or a chord built on that degree (I).

transpose   *See transposition.*

transposition   Translating pitch.

treble clef   A clef, used by higher-pitched voices and instruments, that places middle C on the first ledger line below the staff.

triad   Three notes, each a third apart from the previous. Most chords are built on triads.

triplet   A group of three notes performed in the space of two.

tritone   An interval consisting of three whole steps; sometimes called "the Devil's interval."

upbeat   The eighth-note "and" after the downbeat.

vivace   Tempo marking for a lively tempo.

voice   Melodic or harmonic lines.

voice leading   The motion of a single voice.

voicing   The way the notes of a chord are arranged.

whole step   An interval equal to two half steps.

woodwind   The family of instruments that produce sound by vibrating a wooden reed. The woodwind family includes the clarinet, saxophone, oboe, and bassoon. Also included are the flute and the piccolo, which do not use reeds.

The Complete Idiot's Chord Reference

Here it is: everything you've ever wanted to know about creating chords, but didn't know where to ask (or something like that …). In any case, the next few pages present, for each degree of the scale, the notes and guitar tabs for the following types of chords: major, minor, diminished, augmented, major seventh, minor seventh, dominant seventh, major ninth, minor ninth, and dominant ninth. Turn here when you want to write a chord but don't know how!

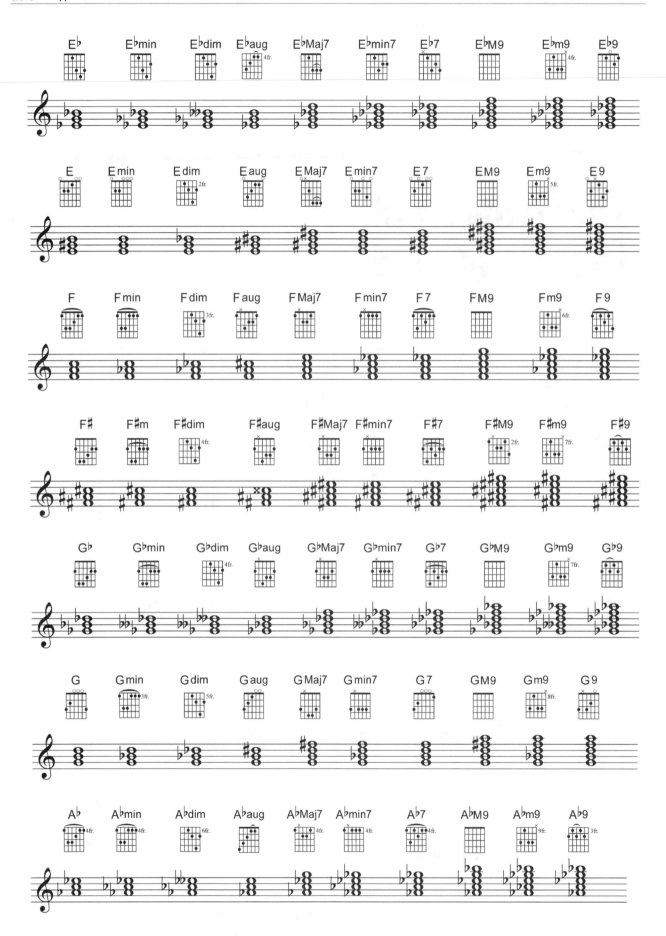

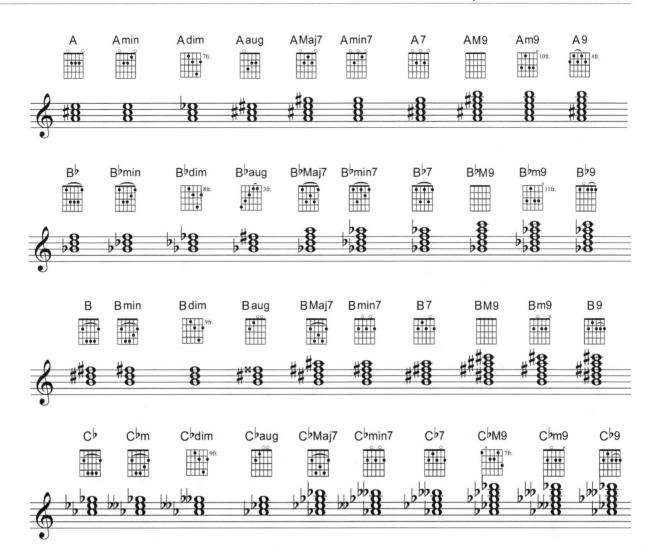

Appendix C

Answers to Chapter Exercises

Here are the answers to those chapter exercises that weren't open-ended in nature. (The open-ended exercises—"write a melody to this chord progression," and the like—don't have a single correct solution.) If you haven't completed the exercises yet, don't cheat—go back and do the exercises before you peek at the answers!

Chapter 1

Exercise 1-1

F   B   A   E   F   D   C   G   G   C

Exercise 1-2

C   A   A   G   D   G   C   B   F   E

Exercise 1-3

A   C   G   F   B   G   D   E   D   B

Exercise 1-4

E   F   D   G   C   A   B   G   A   C

Exercise 1-5

Bass   Treble   Alto   Tenor   Treble (octave above)

Exercise 1-6

G   B   A   D   C   B   D   C   E   F

Exercise 1-7

Exercise 1-8

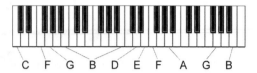

Chapter 2

Exercise 2-1

Exercise 2-2

Exercise 2-3

Exercise 2-4

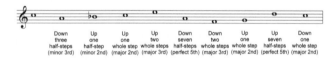

Exercise 2-5

Exercise 2-6

Exercise 2-7

Exercise 2-8

Chapter 3

Exercise 3-1

A Major, D Major, B-flat Major, E-flat Major

Exercise 3-2

D minor, G minor, E minor, F minor

Exercise 3-3

Exercise 3-4

Exercise 3-5

Exercise 3-6

Chapter 4

Exercise 4-1

G Major, A Major, F Major, E-flat Major, E Major, B-flat Major, A-flat Major, D-flat Major, D Major, B Major

Exercise 4-2

A minor, C minor, E minor, D minor, G minor, E-flat minor, B minor, C-sharp minor, F-sharp minor, F minor

Exercise 4-3

Exercise 4-4

Exercise 4-5

Eb   C   Ab   G   D   Eb   Bb   F   Bb   F

Exercise 4-6

Exercise 4-7

Exercise 4-8

C   F   Bb   Eb   Ab   Db

Chapter 5

Exercise 5-1

Whole note, quarter note, sixteenth note, eighth note, half note, sixteenth notes, eighth notes, half rest, quarter rest, sixteenth rest, eighth rest, whole rest

Exercise 5-2

One two three four   One two and three and four   One e and two and ah   Three e and ah four

Exercise 5-3

Exercise 5-4

Exercise 5-5

Exercise 5-6

Exercise 5-7

Exercise 5-8

Chapter 6

Exercise 6-1

3/4   7/8   2/2   5/4   9/8

Exercise 6-2

Exercise 6-3

Exercise 6-4

Exercise 6-5

Exercise 6-6

Exercise 6-7

Chapter 9

Exercise 9-1

G Major, E♭ Major, D Major, B♭ Major, B Major, A♭ Major, F Major, D Major, C Major, G♭ Major

Exercise 9-2

D minor, G minor, C minor, A♭ minor, B♭ minor, E minor, D♭ minor, A minor, E♭ minor, B minor

Exercise 9-3

A   E♭   G   B   D♭   E   F   G♭   D   A♭

Exercise 9-4

Exercise 9-5

Dm7, G7, FM7, B♭M7, CM9, Cm7 (or Cm7/E♭), Gm7, B11, C♯m7, A♭7

Exercise 9-6

Exercise 9-7

Exercise 9-8

Chapter 10

Exercise 10-1

Exercise 10-2

Exercise 10-3

Exercise 10-4

Exercise 10-5

Exercise 10-6

Chapter 12

Exercise 12-5

Exercise 12-6

Chapter 14

Exercise 14-1

Exercise 14-2

Exercise 14-3

Exercise 14-4

Chapter 15

Exercise 15-1

One possible solution is as follows:

Chapter 16

Exercise 16-1

Exercise 16-2

Chapter 17

Exercise 17-1

Exercise 17-2

Exercise 17-3

Exercise 17-4

Exercise 17-5

Exercise 17-7

Tan-ger-ine el-e-phants high in the sky croc-o-dile tears in my beer - - -

Chapter 18

Exercise 18-1

Trumpet

Exercise 18-2

Alto Sax

Exercise 18-3

Fr. Horn

Exercise 18-4

Blank Staff Paper

Just in case you don't have any staff paper sitting around the house, here are a few pages of blank staves that might come in handy. Just run these pages through a photocopy machine, and you'll have an endless supply of blank music paper for your personal use.

Index

N

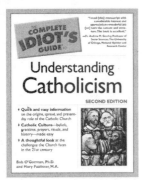

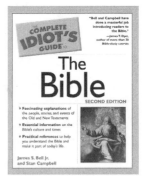

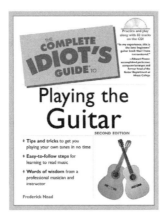

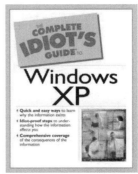